Some Days Chicken,
Some Days Feathers

By

Bob Ferguson

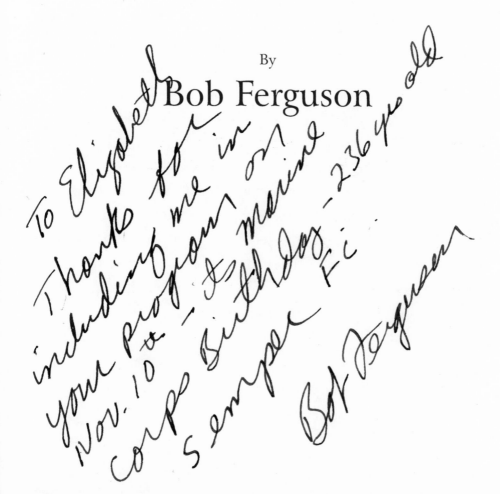

To Elizabeth

Thanks for
including me in
your program march —
Nov. 10 — Birthday 236 yrs old
corps Birthday
Semper Fi

Bob Ferguson

Occasionally I wear a lapel pin. It is a small bar with a purple center and little white stripes on the ends. I am often asked what it represents. I reply "It was given to me when I was awarded the Purple Heart in Vietnam, but I wear it for all those who didn't come home."

Like the wearing of my tiny pin; this book is dedicated to them.

Acknowledgements

Many thanks go to my parents, Mary and Burton Ferguson, for giving me a great childhood.

A big thank you to Ardi, my wife of over forty years for supporting this multi-year project while I attended the numerous writers' critique meetings necessary to procure the skills to get this book into publication.

Thanks to John Daly. In my first critique meeting he said my writing "...is awful." He was right. He suggested three books for me to read. I bought them that night and the adventure began.

A gigantic thanks goes out to Kristen Hall-Geisler for sharing her many additions and corrections over three years of meetings. Her straight-talk critiques and shared insights into the writing process have been invaluable.

A special thanks to you, the reader. I am humbled that you are reading this epistle. I have provided the flavor of the events and characters as they have crossed my stage of life. While they do not always appear in their correct chronological or story order, all of the basic facts are true. It is my fondest hope that you will say to yourself "Hey, I should write my own story." If "God's willin' and the crick don't rise," I will be happy to get you started. Contact me at robefergus@aol.com

Table of Contents

SOME DAYS CHICKEN, SOME DAYS FEATHERS

CHAPTER 1

Earliest Recollections

His trench coat flapped in the wind and he held onto his hat with one hand as he chased me with all his might. The man wouldn't give up. He wanted to catch me—bad. I hid behind the porch steps of the first project house I came to. He wasn't fooled. There were ten small houses lined up on each side of the street with more precision than squares on a checkerboard. They had once been used for military housing—green, functional, with a stoop made of three stairs. Now, workers at the ship yards in Astoria rented them.

The man with evil intent could see me as I ran from one stoop to the next. He was gaining on me. I couldn't let him catch me. Why didn't our neighbors stop him? My chest hurt from running. Fear gripped me. Our house was at the end of the row—a long way for a tad of four to outrun a grown man, but I made it. I bounded up the three steps in one leap, ran into my bedroom, and hid under the double bed I shared with my older brother, Larry. The trench-coated, beady-eyed man knocked on the door. He told my mom the whole story.

My friend Marlin and I had been throwing my baseball over the tops of cars as they drove down our street. We were on opposite sides of the narrow lane and having a lot of fun. The man had stopped his brand-new, shiny turquoise car and warned me not to throw the ball over his gleaming pride and joy. I scuffled my feet, gave him a defiant sneer and turned to walk away like a good little tike—then spun around and threw it anyway. *Thump!* It landed smack-dab on the top of his chromed chariot.

"Bobby Earl, get out here right now!" Mom yelled from the kitchen. "You apologize to this man, and I don't mean maybe." Mom's "Bobby Earl" voice meant I was in serious trouble.

I half-heartedly apologized because my ball was still in his pocket and I could tell he wasn't going to give it back.

"Just wait until your father gets home. He'll spank you good," Mom said. The standard procedure in our home was to say "I'm sorry," followed by a good hard spanking. Punishment was swift, sure, and always administered after Dad got home from work. I learned to obey adults at an early age.

My shipyard-working parents didn't have time to apply reverse psychology or use time-outs or any other now-popular child-rearing techniques. This was the way discipline was meted out across the country. Parents knew from experience that a paddle on the derriere worked quickly and left no emotional scars. They had the discipline to discipline their kids, the integrity to work for a living, and the grit to stand up to the world's bullies. Maybe that's why, after hundreds of interviews with people like Mom and Dad, Tom Brokaw dubbed his book about folks of that era *The Greatest Generation*.

Soon after the chase scene, Dad landed a job in Bend, Oregon as a lineman for the Pacific Bell Telephone Company. He spent the rest of his working life with this single employer. We packed up the Astoria household and made the first of about ten moves we would make before I graduated from high school.

Dad's work was hard, but "Ma Bell" offered outstanding benefits and the best job security someone with the psychology of the Great Depression could ever hope for. Mom always said, "We may not have much, but we'll always have Dad's job." He repaired phone lines between Bend and the California border— right down the middle of Oregon. In the winter, bad weather regularly downed the phone lines, so he worked lots of overtime.

Many times I watched him lace up his boots in the middle of the night to venture out to work in weather not fit for man or beast. Mom would fix him a lunch and thermos of coffee as he collected his gear to climb telephone poles. I can remember days filled with rain, sleet or snow when Mom would say, "We didn't get our mail today, but our telephones are working." My dad made that happen. He set the example for hard work that the rest of us were expected to follow.

When I was about five years old my first job was carrying empty gunnysacks on a potato farm. Mom filled them with the potatoes she plucked out of the loose dirt that had been turned by a digging machine. She had a sack hooked to the middle of her belt as she straddled a furrow and bent over to pick up the spuds out of the cold, fall ground and throw them into the sack. When it became too full to lug, she would set it in the middle of the row for the weigh master to record the poundage of the sack. As she stretched her aching back, I would hand her a new sack.

I have a snapshot focused in my mind of my six-foot-tall, big-boned mother wearing coveralls and three layers of plaid flannel shirts. She wore a red bandana tied around her head like a do-rag, with two knots in the front like Aunt Jemima, the syrup queen. We ate lunch out of her black lunch box shaped like a barn, with a thermos of milk in the lid. When she opened it, the smell of peanut butter and jelly sandwiches wafted through the air. After we devoured lunch, she would fill the lunch box with potatoes. Free spuds were a small perk provided by the grower, but to us, it was a mother lode feast. We ate potatoes cooked every imaginable way: mashed, hashed, fried, stewed, in salads, but never baked—they took too long.

I don't remember any other children, but I could not have been the only kid in the field, because all of the workers were women. If they could have afforded a baby-sitter, they wouldn't have been out in the chilly weather, stooping over to pick up spuds until their backs hurt.

The brain squeezes out the harsh memories of life and replaces them with softer, kinder recollections of times gone by. I have never relived the chill of those cold days on the potato farm, or the cold blasts of arctic air on those nights when the door flew open as Dad disappeared into swirling snow. But I do get warm fuzzies when I eat mashed spuds with country gravy or home fries laced with onions for breakfast. I can smell that old lunch box every time I fix myself a peanut-butter-and-jelly sandwich, and I remember falling asleep on Mom's big, soft shoulder during the lunch break. For a child, life was good. I thought we were living high on the hog. But I don't kid myself by thinking that those were "the good ol' days." Life was hard for Mom and Dad, but they managed to get three kids through college—and that is a long way from the spud fields.

CHAPTER 2

Elementary School

"Mush, you Husky!" The dog pulled at his reins and my sled lurched forward. My red coat clearly identified me as a Royal Canadian Mounted Policeman. "Let's get 'em, Yukon King."

Bad Buster Billy got the drop on me, but the bullet he fired from his Colt .45 finger-barrel only grazed my head, so I came up swinging. As always, I captured Bad Buster without firing a shot. I didn't even have to sic my dog on him. I was bigger and stronger and could easily tie up that robber, claim jumper, and all-around dastardly fellow. He was, after all, only five, and I was already five and a half. Besides, Snuffy, our little mutt (part cocker, part neighbor's dog), would go into a tail-wagging frenzy whenever I said "sic 'em."

Billy Kitner's mom called him in for dinner so the fun came to an end. He didn't complain; he didn't much like being tied up anyway. We hailed some hearty goodbyes. Tomorrow, he would get to wear my brother's old red coat and be Sergeant Preston, and I would be Bull Dog Bobby.

Every Saturday morning we stayed in our pajamas, ate cereal and toast, and listened to "Sergeant Preston of the Yukon." We heard it through the static on our old, wooden, Philco radio, which was shaped like the arched doorway of a Catholic church. We then bundled up and met in the alley to reenact the scenes. We didn't simply play the parts of that radio show; we *lived* them. Billy and I acted out grand sagas packed with enough adventure to make a screen writer envious.

Somewhere in the race to grow up, the rickety sled, the red coat, and the epic dramas were put away forever. With all of the usual adult responsibilities—kids, work, etc.—I have sometimes forgotten to "mush the husky."

At age sixty, I decided to start living with the same sense of fun I had as a kid. All of the financials were lined up. My checkbook isn't anything stunning, but my bed is always warm and I don't have to work for a living, just like when I was a kid. When I sing "Your Cheatin' Heart" at a karaoke bar, I *am* Hank Williams (sorry about the singing, Hank). I once pretended to be a big-time author and led a memoir workshop at a small book store. I'm working on a stand-up routine for an open mic night at the local comedy club, and I attended a World Laughter Tour workshop and earned a degree as a Certified Laugh Leader (it is a real title). Putting my CLL to work, I took a chance and led a chorus of laughter at Aunt Midge's funeral service. The pastor didn't know quite what to think, but the eldest folks on the cusp of being the next such honorees enjoyed it the most.

By now you are probably thinking, "Fergy's ready for the funny farm." But here's what I think: Most of us occasionally plunk down our eight bucks, binge on buttered popcorn, put our imaginations on hold, and watch actors have all the fun. Why not *be* the actor? Why not *live* the adventure? Your imagination lets you do that, and nobody is the wiser.

To be honest, writing these silly stories helps me relive some great times. I want to be a kid again. I'm keeping an old red coat in the garage. My grandson has a sled and a good dog. Now I'm just waiting for a little snow.

I had been looking forward to that day for a full year. At the family reunion, I had bragged to all of my aunts and uncles about it. I could hardly wait. The coat of blue house paint I had slapped on my bike was still fresh, but it was already flaking off faster than crumbs on a stale biscuit. Larry said it wouldn't stick to the metal bike. Who cares? The paint and brush were handy, it wouldn't get painted unless I did it myself, and I wanted it to look good in the bike rack for this once-in-a-lifetime event.

The anticipation of new adventures woke me up earlier than usual. Larry and I madly peddled the four blocks to a huge structure hewn out of gigantic stone slabs. It was a fortress. My first day at Kenwood Elementary School might not be the fun and games like I had thought it would be.

Larry dashed into the fourth-grade room while we first-graders were cheerfully greeted by Mrs. Otto. She styled her grayish-red hair in a bun and wore a dark dress that covered a large, matronly frame. Her big arms strained the short sleeve cuffs of the dress. Her makeup was minimal. Her upper lip had a slight red mustache, and she smelled like mothballs. She looked stern but proved to be nice—although she was loud and mean to those who didn't pay attention during the lessons.

That first afternoon recess is still vivid in my mind. There were lots of kids to play with, and I showed off by pumping the swing to the top of its arc and bailing out. My foreboding thoughts were gone and school was even more fun than I thought it would be. After rest period, a lady from the PTA gave us each a Dixie Cup ice cream to eat with a small wooden spoon. She said it was "a special treat to welcome you to Kenwood Elementary."

Lyle, a kid who wore his brother's hand-me-down britches that were too big for him and shoes with no socks asked, "Do we get ice cream every day?" The class giggled. Realizing his question was silly, he turned beet red.

Lyle needed everything to be repeated. It took him longer to learn the rules of playground games. He never caught on that the morning inspection of clean faces, brushed teeth, and washed hands meant he should come to school clean. If I didn't wash up for class, my mom would scrub me until my skin practically came off. I wondered why his mom didn't do the same to him. I had no way of knowing that some parents consider their kids to be a horrendous mistake.

We were always making fun of Lyle. When he had spaghetti on his shirt, we mocked him for wearing last night's dinner. But it was probably the only thing he could find to eat for breakfast. Lyle had the symptoms of a rough life, and like kids do, we made it rougher by teasing him. He got no help at home and only grief at school.

After several weeks of school, things completely unraveled for Lyle during music time. Mrs. Otto was playing the piano while we held hands in a circle and were skipping around the room singing, "Here we go lupe-de-lu, here we go lupe-de-li. Every time I passed the piano, it smelled like a plugged toilet. I sang, "Here we go lupe-de … sniff, sniff … here we go lupe-de … sniff, sniff." Everybody in the circle began snickering and looking for the guilty party. As I skipped toward the piano, I saw it. It was a whopper! It was a giant brown log of poo! I burst out laughing.

The music stopped. Mrs. Otto pushed the bench back and in one angry motion bounded up from the piano to examine the evidence at close range. Her face was so apoplectically red it covered up her slight mustache. She blustered, "Who did this?" Lyle slowly raised his hand and hung his head. "Well, for heaven's sake, go to the bathroom and get something to clean it up with!"

Tears streamed down Lyles face as he left the room. We

stopped laughing. It wasn't funny anymore. After she had cleaned up the mess, in an extra mean voice Mrs. Otto said, "Go to the office and call your mother to take you home." Lyle was sobbing when he left the room. A dark cloud of collective embarrassment shrouded the room. We were all sorry we had laughed at him, but glad it wasn't one of us.

After the teasing he took for the ice cream question that first day of school, I think he was afraid to raise his hand for anything—even to go to the bathroom. Our laughing and Mrs. Otto's yelling devastated him. Maybe he was too humiliated or maybe his mom decided to hold him back for a year, but for whatever reason, Lyle never came back to our class.

When I was sixty-one, I went back to school and got a master's degree in teaching. The certification allows me to teach kindergarten through eighth grades. As a substitute in first-grade classes, I see kids who are dead-ringers for Lyle. The symptoms of a rough life haven't changed. I cannot undo the hurt that I caused Lyle, but I can give these kids some of the attention that I know is lacking at home. Every once in a while, I see that the extra effort makes the day go a little easier for a Lyle—it's a small atonement for me and maybe a little help at the right time to a kid who had spaghetti for breakfast.

The next year, I was the Lyle of the class. Dad got transferred to Eugene, and we moved to the outskirts of town on Meyers Lane. I started the second grade at Willakenzie Grammar School under the watchful eye of Mrs. Applegar. Over the summer, I had grown a set of big buck teeth and my ears stuck out like the doors on a taxi cab. The kids' favorite taunts were, "Hey Bugs Bunny, you must like carrots," or "Can you fly with those ears, Dumbo?" I was skinny, always chosen last for teams, and

I frequently incurred the wrath of Mrs. Applegar for things that were out of my control, like the scraping sound my chair made when I squirmed in it, which seemed natural to me.

I was noticing that the leaves were all gone from the big oak tree at the bus stop when an older boy pushed me from behind. I fell face first, hitting my two front teeth on the pavement and ran home bawling at the top of my lungs. Mom and Dad had already left for work, so I stayed home by myself, turned on the radio, and listened to "Queen for a Day." The program was about a hard-luck housewife who was hoodwinked into coming down to the show's studio. Like a surprise birthday party, they announced, "Yes, Mrs. Hardluck, you are Queen for a Day!" She would answer some easy questions and win a Kelvinator washer and dryer or a Mix-Master blender.

Arthur Godfrey was on next. It seemed like a miracle that I could hear him in Eugene while he was in Miami, Florida. Mr. Godfrey played the ukulele and sang fun little ditties in a voice that sounded like he was suffering from a bad head cold. He spoke as though he could see me through the radio speaker and his interview style made his show guests look important. Those programs made me feel good, so why go to school and feel bad? There was plenty of cereal for lunch and several snacks.

When Mom came home I got the "what for" because there was no cereal left for breakfast the next day. I was eager to go back to school.

My buck teeth made me shy and self-conscious, but Mrs. Applegar—sometimes known as Mrs. Applesauce—made it worse. For instance, when I had my tonsils removed and missed a week of school I got to stay home and eat a lot of ice cream, but during that time, the class learned subtraction. To get me caught up after I returned, she put me in a corner by myself during an indoor recess. While the other kids had fun playing games, she began my horrific subtraction lesson.

"If I have seven acorns and subtract four, how many do I have left?"

"I don't know. I'm not sure what subtract means."

"Look, subtraction is the opposite of addition, so if I subtract four acorns, how many will be left if I started with seven?"

Using the word "subtraction" in her definition she left me even more confused.

"I don't know," I squeaked.

She created a kerfuffle (not quite a hullabaloo) as she stomped over to her desk and grabbed a jar of acorns. Everyone was watching her growing fulmination. She slammed down seven acorns into the little groove for holding pencils on the top of my desk. All eyes were on me.

"Here are seven acorns and I take away four." She scooped up four of the nuts with her bony, witch-like hand. "Now, how many do I have?"

"Don't you have four?" I whispered.

She was livid. She shouted louder than when Mrs. Otto had yelled at Lyle. "How dumb are you, anyway?"

Those five words were seared into my brain like a brand on a steer. I knew exactly how Lyle felt. The other kids stopped their games and stared at me. I put my head down on my arms so the other kids couldn't see me cry.

I saw myself as a dumb, ugly kid—but Mrs. Applesauce wasn't through pulverizing my impressionable psyche. Further evidence of being the last link in the food chain came on a spring day when we were choosing instruments for the rhythm band. The instruments the school had were minimal: a tambourine, colorful sticks that looked like broom handles, a zither, and little bird whistles that tweeted when they were filled with a bit of water. What held my attention were the newly purchased shiny triangle and a brand new drum set.

When Mrs. Applegar asked who wanted to play the drums,

my right hand shot up, supported by my other hand, and on tiptoes I cried, "Me, oh, me Mrs. Applegar, oooh, oooh, me, please pick me!"

"The person who plays the drums has to be very responsible," she cautioned.

"Me, oh me, please me, me, I can be responsible, I know I can."

She looked right at me. She was going to pick me! My squealing and hand wiggling increased. I created my own kerfuffle.

"Jack Darr, I think you could be a good drummer for us," she said.

My heart sank to my stomach. "I knew it! He's teacher's pet," I grumbled.

The next instrument was the new triangle. I knew I could play it. I increased my hand wiggling, begging, and squirming in my chair because she must not have seen me waving for the drums. Bobby Graham was selected for the triangle.

I raised my hand for every instrument, even the dumb old sticks, which I didn't want to play anyway. I was the only person who didn't get an instrument. I was near tears—again.

She called me up to her desk. "Robert, what are we going to do with you?" She asked the question like I was some sort of inoperable wart. "Maybe you can get some sticks at home, or buy a bird whistle."

"Only the girls are playing the bird whistles, and I don't like the sticks."

"Then maybe you can play a nail or something that sounds like a triangle. I saw that you raised your hand to play it. Why don't you see if you can come up with an instrument at home?"

Mom, as usual, could tell I was down in the dumps and asked, "What's wrong Bobby?"

"Call me Robert, Mom; Bobby sounds like I'm a baby." I didn't want to tell her, but I finally said, "Mrs. Applegar wants me to find a nail to play for my band instrument."

"A nail—what kind of nail?"

"One that sounds like a triangle I guess, but I would rather not play anything than have to play a stupid nail. We don't have one anyway."

The next day, Dad brought home a giant, shiny, steel spike from his job with the telephone company. He may have gotten a sheepish smile out of me. I was going to get to be part of the band. When I hung it on some twine (also retrieved from Dad's work) and struck it with a smaller nail, I thought it rang prettier and louder than the real triangle. I would show the teacher and the whole class what a good band member I could be.

After the concert, I felt good. Everyone talked about how they could really hear my triangle. Indeed, one parent remarked that I played "very enthusiastically." I knew that word meant something good, and my chest swelled. It was the happiest day of the whole school year.

I had to search to find Mom in the crowd. She was off by herself. The strong, spud-picking woman knelt down and gave me a gentle hug, but she had become afflicted with a rare disease. She was laughing and crying at the same time.

The late spring sun had dried up the mud puddles on Meyers Lane. It was a small road that served four houses and ended right at our garage. School was almost out, somehow I had learned to subtract, the band concert had been fun, and I began to like myself again.

It was Saturday and I was wearing my cowboy outfit, complete with an orange-handled Gene Autry cap gun. I was ready to capture a bunch of bad guys in black hats. I rode down to the start of the lane to see my buddy Earl. His first name was the same as my middle name, so that made us blood-brothers.

We got hold of some rope and each made a lasso. We practiced on his little sister—until she ran into the house crying. We actually got pretty good, so when people came driving down the lane, the stanchions on their bumpers began to look like the horns on a bull. I picked a car that was going slow, like a real cow. It almost mooed. The temptation was too much.

Like I had seen Gene do in the movies, I twirled the lasso over my head and caught the bumper. Gravel spit everywhere as the neighbor skidded to a halt. He jumped out and gave me a good spanking for "scaring him to death." He thought my lasso was hooked to my belt. Because a neighbor had to spank me, I got another licking when Dad got home. They said I scared them too, and they loved me. But if they loved me and I wasn't hurt, why spank me?

That wasn't the only time I got swatted that summer. I was walking on a log that had fallen across Blue River. We often camped in the park about two hours east of Eugene. We had been warned to stay off of it, but I was an incurable show-off and fell in. After Dad fished me out of the river, I got lots of hugs followed by lots of spankings—because, of course, they loved me. Sometimes I wished they hadn't loved me so much.

For centuries, kids have met under hot summer suns and azure skies at the old swimming hole where they dared each other to dive off of the highest point into the deepest part of the pool. Each person remembers their oasis a little differently, but they all have some things in common: the sun glints off of the water like it was sprinkled with a bazillion tiny diamonds, there is a happy din of squealing kids, and eventually, everyone does jump off the high dive. It's more of a state of mind than a location. It's a gathering of children who have the unquenchable belief that the world is good, people are kind, and it is okay to take chances because life will have a happy ending. That's exactly how I remember the Jefferson Street swimming pool.

Larry was a fish when it came to swimming. He stayed in the water all day, but I loved to jump in and out of the shallow end and lay on the hot concrete apron to get a tan. We raced to see who was the fastest swimmer, dipped under water to see who could hold their breath the longest, and swam between each other's legs. The challenges of diving deep for a stone were part of growing up. We stayed in until our lips turned blue, our fingers wrinkled, and we would absolutely die if we didn't get to go every day.

It was only a few miles from our home, but for two kids, ten and seven years old; it might as well have been in the next county. If we took the bus, we would miss half of the four-hour swimming session, and the country road was too narrow for our trusty bikes. We devised a plan that put our complete trust in our fellow human beings.

Mom gave each of us bus fare and a dime to get into the pool. After she left for work, we walked down to the main road, stuck out our thumbs, and hitchhiked into town. We used the bus money for snacks. (My personal favorite was the Sugar Daddy because it lasted so long.) We must have resembled a couple of cast members from "Our Gang." Larry looked like Spanky, and I was as skinny as Alfalfa. Maybe that's why we always got a ride.

We ran the bus scam almost all summer long. The jig was up one day when we didn't get a ride home from the pool, and on her way home from work, Mom caught us hitchhiking. She didn't rant and rave. She wasn't even alarmed that her two kids were thumbing rides into town. She was mad about the money! She stopped giving us bus fare and sent us off with only an extra nickel for a phone call if we couldn't get a ride home. We still went swimming every day and got our snacks by finding returnable bottles along the way.

Thumbing a ride into town came naturally to us. We had heard the stories about how Dad left North Dakota and hitchhiked all the way out to Oregon and got a job with the Civilian Conservation Corps. He had been working with them for over a year when a state policeman came up to him and asked, "Are you Burton Ferguson?"

"That's me," he answered, "but you can't be looking for me because I haven't done anything wrong."

"That's not why I'm here. Your mother wants to hear from you. She says she hasn't heard from you since you left. I'm taking you to headquarters so you can call your neighbor, who will tell your mom you're okay."

Hitchhiking was not uncommon, but in his case it was extraordinary; he was only thirteen when he had left home with his thumb in the air.

As I write this, gas prices are headed north of four dollars a gallon. Therefore, I have formed the National Hitchhiking Committee to reinstitute riding your thumb as a mode of dependable transportation. Think of it! It would save us money, help the environment, and thumbing a ride seems to be about as safe as riding a commuter train.

It's simple. After a background check, drivers could put something like a pizza sign on top of their auto identifying them as a "safe car." Hitchhikers could wear a blinking strobe light tagging them as "safe riders." This would create a community of trust where all kids could once again safely thumb a ride to their favorite old swimming hole. My motives are purely to save the world from itself. But if you send a non-tax deductible, hundred dollar check to Bob Ferguson you can become the second member of the NHC.

Day and night, big trucks hauling gigantic logs rattled our house on Sixth Street. Their headlights shined through my bedroom window, creating a kaleidoscope of dancing squares on the wall. They grew taller and picked up speed until they reached the far corner, where they jumped off as fast as a lightning bolt. I had wedged a Popsicle stick between the sill and the window frame to keep it from clattering when the trucks hit the manhole cover out front.

When Dad got an offer on the Meyers Lane property, he found this drafty, dilapidated Victorian house on a busy thoroughfare through Eugene. He was sure it had commercial property potential because there was a small store and motel right next door. Like all of his real estate deals, he "got it for a song," as he liked to say.

Sixth wasn't really a street; it was a main corridor to 99W, which passed the saw mills as it wound itself all the way to Portland. This unique location and Larry's love of fishing put us into a business that made us money beyond our wildest dreams.

The Long Tom River, our favorite local fishing hole, was just off the highway. We rode our bikes there and the crappies were plentiful. We packed sandwiches, bought worms for thirty-five cents a dozen from a nearby tackle shop, and spent many Saturdays watching for the tap-tap on our bobbers that signaled a fish bite.

One Friday, Larry decided we could get our own worms. We heavily watered the lawn that night, and by about ten o'clock, the worms glistened in the rays of our flashlights. Hundreds of fat, fish-tempting night crawlers had climbed about an inch out of their holes making it easy to grab their head, pull them gently out of the ground, and toss them into a coffee can. We had over fifteen dozen of the slimy critters. Far more worms than we could use.

Early the next morning, Larry put a small, cardboard sign in front of the house advertising "NIGHT CRAWLWERS—25cents a Dz." The fishermen on their way to the river knew our price was a bargain and we sold ten dozen worms. We watered again that night and asked our neighbors to do the same. We caught another bumper crop of worms. The quarters were pouring in as people began to buy a couple dozen at a time.

After a hard rain, we would be out with our big flashlights (recruited from Dad's work), picking up scads of worms from all over the neighborhood. We reasoned "Worms belonged to nobody, no matter whose lawn they were on." No worm was safe with the Fergusons on the prowl. It was a family effort. Dad made a box to keep them in, Mom found out what they ate, Larry and I caught the worms and made the sales. It was as much fun as fishing.

One day we hit it big. The man from the tackle shop stopped by and offered to buy fifty dozen worms a week for twenty cents a dozen. He would provide bedding material and the little Chinese food boxes to put them in. We made ten bucks a week guaranteed—we were rich! We never missed delivering the worms all summer long. We kept our own thriving business on the side and made an even higher profit. We had a good laugh when some of our customers told us our worms were far better than those at the tackle shop.

Dad, an inventor as well as a real estate magnate, rigged up a lamp cord attached to a quarter-inch, three-foot metal rod inserted into an insulating wooden handle. When it was plugged in and stuck into the ground, any worms within a two-foot radius would eventually wriggle to the surface. It worked, but it took a long time for them to climb out of the ground. It never replaced well-watered lawns or a good, hard rain.

Dad was right about the fantastic commercial value of the Sixth Street property—it was the best location in all of Eugene for selling worms.

Dennis Van Sant was a boy my age who lived directly across Sixth, and we became best pals. We played all over the neighborhood that summer, and I discovered that I could run faster, swing higher, and splash the biggest cannon balls of anyone my age at the Jefferson Street pool. I gained confidence and I looked forward to getting a fresh start at Lincoln Elementary and walking to school with Denny.

Miss Tillie Doerfler was a thin, grandmotherly-looking teacher. She used the Bible almost as a third-grade curriculum manual. She had a Bible Club that met once a week after school in her classroom. I joined and became an ardent believer, and began going to Sunday school. She told us about a revival week that would take place at the Evangelical Church on Eighth and Van Buren.

I went every night by myself. The meetings always reached a feverish pitch and lasted until about nine. I was afraid of the dark, so I ran the entire three blocks back home, carrying a handful of bulletins advertising the great preachers of the Cavalcade of Blessings. I became a religious fanatic.

A pastor of the same magnitude as Billy Graham preached the last night of the revival. At the altar call I went up front to make my public confession of sins. Miss Doerfler knelt next to me and put her arm around my shoulders. She actually did care about all of her students.

At the next Bible Club meeting, her cheeks turned rosy, and

she beamed as she told everyone about me going up front during the altar call. She gave me a New Testament Bible, which became my prized possession. My religious piety didn't transfer to any favors in the classroom, however.

Despite regaining my confidence over the summer I was still scared to death of math. The class was divided into two groups for reading and arithmetic. Miss Doerfler designated them group A and B, which was only slightly better than calling us "flowers" and "weeds." It was obvious that I was in the dummy group. Kids notice those things, but I fancied myself as being the smartest dummy. I stayed in that group all year for arithmetic, but moved up to the A group for reading and spelling.

During the first week of school, we heard about Cub Scouts. Denny and I raced home and told his mom, who became our den mother, and Mom signed up as her assistant. I loved Cubbies. We played "Steal the Bacon" or "King of the Hill," and the crafts were fun. I took pride in my main project: a square, plywood wastebasket with a wood-burned picture of a dog on each side. I laced the sides together with a leather thong and then topped it all off with a thick coat of varnish. Denny and I worked on a lot of extra projects found in the handbook and our uniforms began to get covered with badges of gold and silver arrows.

During Cub Scout Week, we wore our Cubby shirts and gold kerchiefs to school everyday. At noon recess, we played cavalry and galloped all over the playground chasing the Indians—all of the boys who weren't Cubbies.

Nancy Dinsmore was the only girl we allowed in the game. She loved horses, and every day she galloped around the playground—she was way ahead of any of the boys in the galloping department and was the hardest Indian to catch. Playing cavalry during the entire Cub Scout week became a highlight of school for the next three years.

The mixture of having a best friend, being a Cub Scout,

finding the church, starting the worm business, and having a good teacher was the exact tonic I needed to cure my bad case of Mrs. Applegar.

Out of the blue, someone made an offer to Dad on the old Victorian house. The price was high enough that Dad made his usual "fortune." Just before school started, we moved to a new home on Almaden Street, a block from the equipment barn where Dad checked out his pickup truck every day. Shortly after we moved, an apartment building was built on the space of our old house and the little store.

My fourth grade teacher, Mrs. Glouser, smelled good, wore lipstick, and was a lot younger than my other teachers. Reading was no longer a problem, but I stayed in the dummy group for math.

Denny wasn't in my class, so I chummed around with Jim Fossen, one of the smartest kids in school. He finished his work way ahead of everyone, which left plenty of time for him to think up ways to get into trouble. One day he put a red thumbtack on the teacher's chair. She promptly sat on it but didn't say a word. When she stood up and turned around to write on the blackboard, there it was: a red thumbtack stuck to her bright yellow dress. It was stuck in her thick girdle between her cheeks, and she didn't feel it at all. We snickered; she turned and glared. She turned back to the board—more snickering. "Robert and James, you better be copying this down," she said without turning around.

The tack worked itself out of the girdle's death grip, and she never noticed it. Fossen had scored a colossal victory, and at recess we celebrated with unrestrained laughter. But I liked Mrs.

Glouser and was glad she didn't get stuck. It would have been a better joke on Mrs. Applegar.

The next year, James went to a school for gifted students. We didn't meet up again until high school. By then, we each had different friends and never again ran around together. He was off the charts academically, but he became a little weird socially. In college, he took up acting at one of the California schools, but in his sophomore year, he died of a drug overdose.

If intelligence does not pass through the focused lens of common sense, it often gets distorted into arrogant foolishness.

In the fifth grade, I must have taken a sabbatical. I can't begin to remember who my teacher was, and my grades got lost in one of our moves, but I know sports became my passion. Cub Scouts and school work were pushed into the background. We moved, again, to a smaller house on Twelfth Street. It was a tiny, two-story Cape Cod with two bedrooms up stairs. Larry and Danny shared the big room, and I had a small room all to myself.

Danny had been born when we lived in Bend, but it's on Twelfth Street, when he was five, that I begin to remember him as a pesky little brother. He would leave his marbles out, and our cat would bat them all over the hardwood floors, sounding like a bowling ball hitting the gutter. I would pick up all of his marbles before I went to bed, but that cat would invariably find the one I missed. Before the birds chirped the next morning, I would be on my hands and knees trying to outsmart that cat and grab the marble. It was the cat's game. I eventually gave up and fixed myself a bowl of Corn Flakes, which I would spill trying to strangle the cat. Mom would get mad at me for the cereal mess, but I could never make her understand how it was really all Danny's fault.

Our small, yellow house with white trim was only two blocks west of Lincoln Elementary. On weekends, the school yard became my personal playground. A lot of us began to hang out there, so it was natural that we began to choose up sides for sports. In baseball, the gloves ranged from new to antique, and a few kids had a bat and ball. We scrounged rags or pieces of cardboard for bases. We guessed at the rules, added a few of our own, and when we didn't have enough players for each base, we played cross-out. (The batter is out if you throw the ball between him and any base he is running toward, thereby gaining a cross-out.) I used Dad's ancient glove, which had a huge wrinkle right in the middle of the pocket. It didn't matter; I could always borrow a mitt from a batter. Captains chose their players, first at-bats were decided by who got to the field first, and arguments were a part of the game—but nobody, and I mean nobody, ever took their ball and went home.

I was quick and fast, but had no idea how to play the games. I was okay in baseball and basketball, but in football, speed and agility were more important than hand-eye coordination. On the playground I felt like a gazelle. I even won the one-hundred, two-hundred, and four-hundred yard dashes at a city-wide track meet sponsored by the Eugene Boys Athletic Association.

Even though I don't have an ounce of memory about the school year, I remember knowing exactly what job I would have as an adult—I would be the first, two-sport professional athlete to play for the New York Yankees and the San Francisco Forty-Niners.

Organized sports began to dominate my life. I was a forward on the Golden Ball League sixth-grade Hot Shots basketball team. We passed the ball to our center, Bo Black, who towered over everyone else, and he would score about twenty points a game. The rest of us combined to score about six or less, and we went undefeated two years in a row.

Dad put up a backboard and hoop on the street, and it became our playground. I would practice foul shots, hooks, and two-handed set shots for hours—sometimes before school. It became the gathering spot for all of our games. The small, grassy parkway between the street and sidewalk became a sea of mud during the winter. The four-by-six post was home base for hide-and-seek, kick the can, and the safety zone for tag. Kids came from all over to play the shooting games of "Horse" or "Three Away." Everyone developed a trick shot to put the others out of the game. Those shots became game shots and improved everybody's basketball skills.

The basket was next to the curb and faced the street making it illegal. A few neighbors complained to Mom, but she made the case that the street wasn't busy, and at least she knew where we were. (Years later I made that same case—many times. I knew the kids weren't into mischief if I could see them playing in front of our house.)

That spring, a bunch of us tried out for the neighborhood baseball team. I used Dad's wrinkled mitt, which made fielding impossible. It didn't matter. The coach had pretty much pre-selected his team. We were given token tryouts and then cut, but we wanted to play baseball. We decided to form our own team, but we needed a coach.

Morris Henninsgard, a kid I had met at school, was small, as devilish as a raccoon, and he couldn't remember ever having a father. Don McNeil's dad was a farmer and didn't know anything about baseball. Because of his job, my dad never had time to participate in anything, but he was our last hope. We burst into the small house with our best sorrowful faces.

"Aww, come on Dad, puleeeez? We won't get to play unless you coach," I pleaded.

"Yeah, c'mon, Mr. Ferguson. We need a coach bad," Moe said in his innocent voice that could charm the mukluks off an Eskimo.

"Sure he'll do it," Mom said.

Nobody was more surprised than me when Dad said, "Why not. Maybe I can show those other coaches a thing or two."

Dad got Robertson Auto Sales to sponsor our team. His job of installing telephones took him all over town, and being the outgoing guy that he was, he asked everybody he met to sponsor us.

We didn't have enough players, so Moe and I recruited other kids who hadn't tried out for the other team. We ended up with the two best pitchers in the league and some good hitters. Mom cut inch-high block letters out of red felt and had the other mothers sew them onto the backs of white T-shirts. The name R-O-B-E-R-T-S-O-N arched over A-U-T-O. The sponsor bought us red hats with a white R on the front giving us a red and white uniform scheme. After the first washing, the shirts became bright pink.

The team that cut us beat us in a laugher, and we heard them chuckle about our pink uniforms. They were on their way to another championship. They couldn't be stopped.

Dad relished coaching; we had some good athletes, and were getting better with every game. Mom kept score, and even my brother Larry helped us win a game in a way I haven't ever seen. It was the classic, bottom-of-the-last-inning type of play. The other team was ahead by one run, and we had two outs with men on second and third in an important game. Our batter hit a rainmaker of a pop-up right on the third baseline. The third baseman drew a bead on it for an easy out. From the bleachers, Larry yelled, "Look out for the bicycle!" The player stopped dead in his tracks. The ball hit the chalk line and squirted into the outfield. Our runners were off at the crack of the bat, scoring two runs to win the game.

Our cleats clicked-clacked as we clamored up the wooden bleachers to pat Larry on the back for his game-winning genius. The other coached groused about an unfair play. The rule book clearly stated that players cannot make distracting noises, but said nothing about a fan.

For the league championship, Robertson's Auto would face the team that had cut all of us. They were flashy in their full uniforms, but we had won a lot of games in our pink T-shirts and old jeans. Their early season thumping intimidated us. "No way could we beat them," was our collective thought. To make matters worse, Dad was called out to work that Saturday and would have to miss our final game.

When Dad came home from work that evening, the first thing he saw was a sign on the lawn declaring "Robertson's 3, Eagles 0." Behind it were a bunch of rag-tag players who, to my knowledge, made up the only boy's team anywhere in the galaxy to ever wear pink T-shirts as an official uniform. He wiped his eyes a little bit before he got out of the truck.

"No doubt in my mind that we'd beat 'em, just a matter of how much," he crowed.

Dad had left the line-up with Mr. Adams, the father of our left-handed catcher. The starting pitcher would be Don McNeil. They had no chance against his left-handed heater. Their coach had to be wondering how he missed such an enormous talent at the tryouts. He had missed Don because the boy had never pitched before Dad gave him the chance. After our first prac-tice, Dad said we needed a pitcher. Don went home and began throwing baseballs at an old mattress nailed to the barn. He was a natural.

A local sporting goods store asked Dad if they could sponsor his team the next season. He was pleased as punch. We got to wear real uniforms with Hendershott's on the back. We won a few more championships, but for me, nothing could touch that first year.

The baseball years were easily our best times together as a family. Danny was old enough to play on the swings at the ball parks, and Larry's bicycle trick helped us win the league title. Mom was getting good tips as a waitress at Foo's Chinese Restaurant, where she worked the evening shift so she could keep score at our games.

The family made friends for a lifetime. Dad became respected by parents from the professions, players who went on to college careers, and coaches who thought he knew nothing about the game.

In 2005, I was traveling to a golf outing with Mike Hodges, a former Herndershott's player. I was shocked when he said, "Your dad was one of the best coaches I ever had. He had a knack of putting players where they were needed, like our left-handed catcher. He had to have that special glove made because there are never any lefty catchers, now that's flat out coaching."

His words stunned me. Mike went on to have a great career in track at the University of Oregon under the legendary Bill Bowerman. After a long successful coaching career of his own, Mike is enshrined in the Oregon Sports Hall of Fame. The man knows about coaching, and he said, "Burt Ferguson was one of the best."

The sixth grade was my year to shine. I made the top math group, and I was doing great in sports, but it was also the year of one of my great regrets.

For two years, Loren Thompson had lived two blocks from

me in a massive Victorian house with his grandmother. He had some sort of skin disease and always wore long-sleeved, corduroy shirts. He was an odd duck. He was sickly and never rode his bike in the neighborhood; after school he went straight home. When he knocked on his front door, it opened just wide enough for him to slip inside a house that Hollywood could have used as a set for horror films. He never came back outside except to attend school, not even on weekends or during the summer.

On Halloween, we wouldn't dare venture up those inhospitable stairs. The shades were drawn so tight that no light ever escaped the house's inner sanctum. During the Christmas holidays, there was no sign of any decorations; it was devoid of any good will toward men. In the summer, the house looked like it was still shrouded in the cold fog of winter. It was a tiny island of lifelessness; there was no warmth or joy, just existence.

"Look who's coming," Bo Black said one day as we stood sipping Cokes on the steps of the little store down the street from the school.

It was Loren walking with Patty Ballard. She was the type of girl who would hang by her knees upside down on the monkey bars while wearing a dress. Even in the sixth grade she got noticed, but she could not have cared less. Patty ignored us whenever we chanted, "I see London, I see France, I see somebody's underpants." She was pretty, wore lipstick, a trace of rouge, and was fiercely independent.

She and Loren were smiling and laughing as they neared. It was a rare moment of pleasure for them both. As they reached the store, I sang out, "Two little love birds sittin' in a tree, k-i-s-s-i-n-g."

Loren dropped his books and hit me upside the head. Throwing my pop aside, I responded with a right to his mouth. His braces cut his lips. Blood spattered across his books. He kicked me in the shin, and I hit him in the mouth again. He was bleeding like a stuck pig. It was no contest, but he kept coming. Patty screamed at me to stop. Mercifully, the store owner came out and ended the set-to.

Only trouble could come from beating up someone as defenseless as Loren, and the punishment flooded over me in torrents. The store owner told me never to come back. At home, I was given extra chores and got spanked with a belt when Dad got home. At school, I had to apologize to Loren and sit in the office during lunch recess for the entire Cub Scout Week. I missed my final year of galloping around the playground.

I don't know why I mouthed off, but I knew I had hurt Loren—not so much his face, but his ego. I had embarrassed him in front of the only person he cared about. I have regretted those fisticuffs ever since. He and Patty were more than friends. They clung together like tiny, hairless mice warming each other on a chilly night. It's hard to think that sixth-graders could be drowning in such deep loneliness, but it drew them together. Alone they suffered "The slings and arrow of outrageous— children," but together they stood against the world.

We moved a few more times, and I only saw Loren in high school when we exchanged awkward greetings in the halls. In 1971, at our ten year high school reunion, I looked forward to seeing Loren and getting the whole matter off of my chest by apologizing. He was a no-show. The twentieth came and went, but no Loren. Ditto the thirtieth. At the fortieth reunion, I looked for him in the class obituaries. It was a good guess because he had been a sickly kid, and he had missed the previous reunions, and right there in those pages—no dead Loren.

At our forty-fifth, it was deja-vu. He was wearing a long-sleeved, corduroy shirt in August and held the reunion binder up to his chest like he and the girls used to do in the lunch room, with both arms wrapped around it. Loren was exactly where you would expect to find him, on the edge of the hotel ball room, by himself. I was half afraid to talk to him, but after four decades of remembering those bloody lips, I had to say something. I was compelled to apologize.

My feet walked across the room with a will of their own. This could have an unpleasant result. I tentatively approached him thinking, *I'm probably the last person he wants to see.*

"Hello Loren, it's nice to see you," I lied. I should have said, "Hello, Loren, this is very awkward, and I hope to high heavens you haven't stayed away for forty years because of me."

"Hi Bob, how have you been?" Loren's voice was as squeaky as I remembered it. He hadn't changed. In the sixth grade, he had looked like a little old man—now he was one.

"What have you been doing all these years?" I asked.

"I'm a photographer. Would you like to see some of my work?"

He whipped out a portfolio of photographs before I could respond. I wanted to unload my burden and get out of there. But for the next several minutes I oohed and aahed, feigning interest in his photographic postcards featuring landscapes, seascapes, and sunsets.

Shut up Loren! I need to bare my soul! I screamed inside. He finally took a breath. "Loren, do you remember back when we were kids? I could be a bit of a jerk sometimes, and I want to apologize for some of my stupid stuff." I beat around the bush. I couldn't bring myself to talk about how I had battered his lips and embarrassed him in front of his only friend.

"You know, I always wanted to go out and play with you guys, but my grandmother never let me out of the house," he said.

He hadn't heard me at all, *I'll have to humiliate myself again,* I groaned inside.

"She was always afraid I would get hurt or sick. In the winter it was too cold, and during the summer it was my allergies, so I never got to ride bikes, or do any of the playground stuff at school. She wouldn't even let me be a Cub Scout," he continued with a blank stare.

He was looking at me, but I think he was visualizing scenes from his past. To make sure he understood me, I was about to explain my lament in greater detail when he said, "I always had to just sit and read. I never got to gallop all over the playground like you kids did, but you probably never knew why."

I had always thought that he had a disease that specifically prevented galloping. We joked that it was leprosy and his leg might fall right off in mid-gallop.

"My parents were killed in a car wreck when I was just a baby. I was my grandmother's only living relative, and she became mentally unbalanced. She said we only had each other, so I needed to be extra careful. I didn't realize what I had missed until my childhood was gone and there was nothing I could do to change it."

He looked down at one of his sunset photos like it was a chapter in his life. "I really missed out on what being a kid was all about, and I certainly don't remember anything at all you would ever need to apologize for."

I wanted to jump back in time, grab Loren by the arm and say, "Come on, Loren, get off the steps, and let's gallop on over there and see if we can corral Nancy Dinsmore."

Loren had never married, and he asked everybody he saw about Patty Ballard. I began to ask about her myself. It would be incredible for them to reconnect.

I began to thumb through his portfolio again. They were no longer ordinary postcards. These were photographs of the unfettered distances and beauty he never saw as a child. They were a witness to his release from an affection so stifling it left no room for a childhood. They were proof that human resiliency allows us to forgive and forget. I hope he captures another burnished sunset just like the one he showed me, but with one small addition—he and Patty Ballard are in the foreground.

CHAPTER 3

Junior High

We hated picking beans, but it was part of the middle-class culture in Eugene (okay, lower-middle-class). It was always too hot, wet, or cold to pick the four to six-inch string beans. They hung on vines that climbed up seven-foot wooden stakes and were shaded by large green leaves that made you itch. The stakes were driven into the ground three feet apart, fastened to a taut, thick-gauged wire that ran over the top of them, and set in rows of about a hundred yards in length. From a distance, the fields were picturesque. The luscious, green rows would have been a perfect subject for Van Gogh to paint, with his exaggerated colors and shapes. Those of us who actually worked inside this bucolic picture would have opined that it was more worthy of a child labor scene from Dickens' *Oliver Twist.*

Every summer since my fourth grade year, Larry and I joined hundreds of kids in catching the bean trucks at seven every morning at the Francis Willard school yard. The trucks were rigged with benches for our half-hour trip north of town, which ran right by our old house on Meyers Lane, ending at the Walls Bean Farm. Later, the trucks were reconfigured to haul sacks of beans to the cannery. Our bean-picking money was normally used to buy our school clothes, but this summer I would need to earn enough to also buy a bicycle. As a seventh grader, I wanted cool, stylish clothes, not the cheapest things from J.C. Penney. And I was going to try out for the basketball and baseball teams at Wilson Junior High, so I would need a bike to ride home after practices and games.

In previous seasons, I fooled around too much to be a good picker, but that summer I knuckled down and worked hard. Bean picking was no longer forced labor; it became a money-making opportunity, but to the Mexicans who worked alongside us, it was their living. They drove to the field in crowded, beat-up sedans and were already picking beans by the time we arrived on the trucks. Their group usually produced the picker with the most pounds for the day. I began a friendly competition with them, and on a few days, I was the top picker, but on average, I didn't come close to their steady work habits. They knew the gringo kid was a flash-in-the-pan.

The Mexicans stayed to themselves, took siestas on the hour-long lunch breaks, seldom spoke English, and worked all day—hard. After Eugene's bean season, they moved on to Hood River for the apple season. The lives of their children truly rivaled anything Dickens could conjure up. At the end of the day I went home to a nice shower—they went to their camp down by the Willamette River.

Larry was a big kid and always had good jobs because he was a hard worker. He landed an hourly paying job as the bean-weigher. We emptied our five-gallon buckets into gunny-sacks; when they were full, he would hoist them up and snag them on the hook of a scale that hung down from a tripod. He made good money hefting the sacks, which weighed about fifty pounds each, and he weighed several hundred sacks a day.

It seemed like the grueling bean season lasted forever, but just as it ended, Dad got an offer on the Twelfth Street house from some Californians. Dad had a unique negotiating technique. He would let people think they were taking advantage of him. With a tear in his eye, he would say, "Well, I hate to move the family because it's such a nice neighborhood …" The offer would increase in direct proportion to the tears in his eyes. When the offer reached more money than he and Mom could both earn in two years, he would seal the deal, get them to sign on the dotted line, dry his eyes, and laugh all the way to the bank.

The Schwinn Corvette gleamed under the lights of the showroom. It was a beauty, with red hand grips and a chrome headlight mounted in the middle of the handlebars. The whitewall tires were skinnier than regular bike tires because they were built for speed. I had been hooked on it since my first test ride. I had drooled over it all summer long, and it motivated me to pick enough beans to be able to plunk down the required sixty-six dollars and still have enough money for a wardrobe befitting a cool seventh grader.

We didn't take bike rides for fun. Our bikes were for transportation to school, jobs, fishing, and wooing our best girl. I rode my gleaming steed to school on practice and game days. It stood out among the other bikes in the rack, and I was proud of it because I had paid every cent myself.

Lila was my woman. Sometimes she would wait for me after school. I would push my bike as we romanced while walking home. I'd get home about seven, which didn't leave much time for studies. That was okay; I never did homework anyway.

On Sundays, I used the bike to help Larry deliver the early morning edition of the Eugene *Register-Guard.* After delivering the papers, we rode to the American Legion Hall, where they waged heavy drinking parties every Saturday night. We scavenged through their garbage and filled our canvas newspaper bags with rescued beer and pop bottles. Quart-size pop bottles were worth a nickel, regular ones brought two cents, and we got a penny for beer bottles. For delivering the papers, Larry paid me his "little brother price" of hardly anything, but on the bottles, I demanded half the take. We always found enough to get us into the afternoon movie with money left over for popcorn, a Coke, and a Sugar Daddy that lasted the entire movie. But on New Year's Day we took a couple of extra gunny-sacks to the legion hall and made as much money as we would have in a full day of picking beans.

Bikes were an essential part of our youth. We fixed our own flat tires and oiled the chains. Eventually every bike wound up having its fenders taken off. Now, as gas prices soar, people are rediscovering that bicycles are one of the most functional machines ever invented. And the trusty five-speed I ride is now worth twice the seventy dollars that I paid for it in 1973.

On Twelfth Street, Larry's large collection of model airplanes hung from his bedroom ceiling. A few days before we were to move, our imaginations caught fire. We doused most of the war planes with Dad's lighter fluid and lit them with Dad's Zippo lighter that he carried through WWII. When they were burning spectacularly, we threw them out the second story window, with only minor damage to the curtains.

A few planes escaped the inferno because we immediately stopped when a police car rolled into the driveway. They informed us that what we were doing was extremely dangerous. So be it. But for an exceptionally deep bonding experience, I recommend that all brothers do exactly what we did: come very close to burning your house down.

We had moving down to a science. Borrow a pick-up, get a few friends to help, and it's done in no time. Within a few hours of leaving Twelfth Street, Larry and I were comfortably settled into the detached double-car garage/bedroom of the salmon-colored house on Ninth Street, just off Chambers. The garage was big, and its pervasive smell of mildew and wet cement plus the echo off the high, raftered ceiling reminded me of visiting the Oregon Caves.

Living in a dark and dank cave was perfect for a couple of teens. Larry and I saw the advantages right away: sneaking out at night would be a snap, Mom wouldn't be bugging us all the time about keeping the place clean, and it was so cavernous we each had our own, essential teenage space.

Our twin beds were separated by our chest of drawers in the middle of the room, which also represented the kid-mandatory, my-side-your-side imaginary line. On the floor was an old maroon carpet, and a space heater sat in the corner on part of the concrete not covered by the rug, but there was a small drawback—no bathroom. We had to traipse all the way into the house to use the lavatory. Convenience overtook us, but it didn't last long. Mom figured out right away what was killing the daisies planted next to the side door of the garage.

Despite the ever-present musty aromas, drafty walls, and lack of sunlight in the room, we were happier than fruit bats in a deep cavern. Moe's house was now only a few blocks away, and he said it best: "Hey man, this is a cool pad. Just like your own apartment. Now you won't have your ol' lady bugging ya to keep it clean, and how're they even gonna know you're here at night?" He was preaching to the choir.

A block away from our cave there was a small park where scads of kids gathered to play, trade secrets, and occasionally one of the older kids would let us peek at a scandalous picture or magazine. The four Pruitt kids, five Azalins, and other regulars were about the same ages as my brother and me so we became constant visitors in each other's homes.

Mrs. Azalin was the first divorced person I ever met. She always looked like she was just getting out of bed no matter what time of day it was. In one hand, she held a glass filled with something that was probably not the ice water she told us it was; in the other was her ever-present cigarette. There were brand-new cars parked at their house on a regular basis.

Gene Azalin brought an extra special picture to the park one day just for the boys to look at. He got it from his older brother who bought it in Tijuana just before he came home on leave from Navy boot camp. It was not a medical picture of the female anatomy, but it was part of our "park education."

The Azalins lived on the north side of West Eleventh, across the street from "shanty town" where the "colored folks" lived. None of the Negro kids, like Irv Wilson or Moisha Potts, ever came to the park. I can't remember any true prejudice in our household, but it must have run deep in the town, because every Negro in Eugene lived on West Eleventh. Our house was a good stone's throw away from Irv's, but the difference was light years apart. I was blissfully naïve about racism.

Another meeting place was the school bus stop at the corner of Eleventh and Chambers. Every school day, a diverse group of kids waited in the parking lot of a small diner. The black kids, our ragtag lot and a few kids with a little money all had one thing in common: everyone was afraid of the Broder brothers.

Andy and Alex Broder were malcontents trying to fight the world for reasons known only to themselves, and one day I became their target. Andy was the worst of the two. When he was in his sick humor he would stick his leg out in the aisle of the bus. When the girls stepped over his leg, he would try to lift up their skirts. Lila, my woman, didn't put up with it. She was the product of a beer-swilling, mill-working father and a chain-smoking, teeth-missing, trash-talking, bartending mother. When Andy tried to lift her skirt up, she slapped him. He stood up to slap her back, and I grabbed his arm. He was a tough-as-nails ninth grader. He grabbed my jacket at the chest and slugged me in the face. Before I knew what happened, I was knocked out and woke up on the bus floor.

"Gonna be a big hero," he taunted.

On wobbly legs like a KO'd boxer, I sheepishly got up and went to the back of the bus. I knew when I was licked, and none of my friends thought the less of me. I had never heard the phrase, "Discretion is the better part of valor," but I learned its meaning that day.

The bus driver must have reported Andy to the school. I was called into the office to give my side of the story. Alex had only laughed at his brother's antics, but they both were banned from riding the bus. They had not finished with me yet. They thought I ratted them out.

They weren't on the bus the next morning, but they caught me in the hall. Andy tried to slap my notebook out of my hand. I put it behind my back, and Alex pushed me against the locker. My little finger got caught between my books and the latch on a locker door, mangling the tip and just missing the bone. Blood spurted like a fountain. I took off running for the office. Smashed fingers hurt, but there's no crying if you want to be cool. Crying is for sixth graders.

Mom was steamed because she had to take time off from work to take me to get stitched up. She must have laid it on the school pretty good because the Broders never bothered me again.

The Broders were never in Cub Scouts, never played sports, never picked beans, but they always seemed to have time to be in trouble. In their mid-twenties, they beat a man to death. It was predictable, but I'm not sure with these two if it was preventable. Some people are just violent.

Locker room talk at Wilson Junior High revolved around sports, rock 'n' roll, who wore the coolest clothes, and girls. The sex topics were always led by Cordy Larsen. He knew so much about sex, he could have taught our eighth-grade health class. In fact, he did—in the locker room where he regularly regaled us with his unabashed "sexploits."

He was always teasing us about our obvious shortcomings. Cordy was a man-child while a lot of us still looked like third-graders. He laughed at our sexual awkwardness, and we sought revenge.

We threw him out of the locker room buck naked with only a small shower towel for cover. We knew if he got caught in the raw, it would be no big deal to him and he would never squeal on us. Instead of using the towel as a wrap and trying get back in the locker room door, he threw it over his shoulder and ran up the stairs to a seldom-used side entrance to the school. We leaned out the top of the frosted windows and watched him run into his girlfriend, Betty Hoffman. To our surprise and laughter, he nonchalantly walked passed her and back into the locker room like he was wearing a coat and tie.

"It's no big deal to her," he said. "She's seen it all before."

Cordy had money, wore only the coolest clothes, and was one of those guys who drew a crowd when he did "the Bop" at school dances. Every school has a Cordy. He was the catcher on our baseball team and owned his own catcher's mitt. He was the first to wear a genuine rock 'n' roll jacket with the solid-color, high, knitted collar that wrapped around the neck and ended in the lapels. His was easily distinguished from my J.C. Penney's rock and roll jacket, which had a stripped collar. Mom said, "Nobody will even notice." After I was laughed at for wearing an imitation, I never wore it to school again. Cold? Yes, but cool—in every sense of the word.

Mom was right. The quality was just as good, it kept me warm, and it looked nice. It is the same advice I gave my kids during their middle-school angst. Their closets were filled with Nike shoes, Ocean Pacific shirts, and accessorized by Esprit, et al. The passion for fashion dominates every generation.

"It's my dream house. We'll never have to move again," Mom said of our next house as Larry and I sadly packed up to leave the cave. It must have been our form of *Rebel Without a Cause,* because we climbed up on top of the garage, lit the rest of Larry's planes on fire, and sent them sailing off to a proper demise. It was anticlimactic. No police showed up. We had done it all before, and that was when I learned that glorious events of any kind can never be repeated to the same level of thrill, so live in the moment!

It was the spring of my eighth-grade year when we moved into the double-garage, four-bedroom/one bathroom rambler-style house on Eighteenth near the corner of Polk Street. I think it was a combination of a fireplace made of Roman brick and the black, brown, and white, "never shows dirt" wall-to-wall carpet that made it Mom's dream house. At fourteen hundred square feet, it seemed ginormous.

The house was close to a brand new school, Thomas Jefferson Junior High, where I would start in the fall and be in the first graduating class of ninth-graders.

Lila now lived a lot further away. While finishing out the year at Wilson, it was impossible to walk her home and then ride back to Eighteenth Street. Besides, by this time only dorks were riding bikes to school. They became passé now that we ogled cars.

During the summer, she discovered a guy with a hot rod while I was hauling hay every day. Our true love melted faster than ice cream at a picnic. She would become pregnant and drop out of high school within two years.

At Jefferson, school sports became paramount. I began to recognize that I could probably play high school sports. We played all the other junior highs in town, and like young ponies, we began to establish a pecking order. We had played games with Roosevelt and Wilson, which would be the two other feeder schools to South Eugene High. I liked my chances. School was fun, a few more girls began to notice me, and I had a solid C average in every class without working too hard.

Our PE teacher, Mr. Erickson, started a program that kept the gym open every Saturday and nearly every weekday during the Christmas vacation. Moe and I went every day it was open. Mr. Erickson became my role model. He was short, muscular, dedicated to the kids, and enjoyed his job. It seemed a lot easier than climbing telephone poles like Dad did.

In the spring, we had a unit topic about careers. Our assignment was to investigate one occupation in depth. We first took the Kuderle Personality Inventory Test, which was an analysis of personality traits which told us what jobs we might enjoy. My test results definitely ruled out putting clocks together or filling out forms from eight to five, but I did have the personality to be a teacher. The next step was to make a notebook of our findings, including an interview with someone in your chosen field.

The professions chosen spanned a spectrum of life. The smart ones were going to be doctors or lawyers, Blain Charnelton was going to take over his dad's service station, and Gary Penny was sure he would end up being a professional pitcher in the big leagues.

It was a natural for me to investigate becoming a physical education teacher. I interviewed Mr. Erickson. Everything about the job was perfect except, ugh, four more years of school after high school. That was a long way off. No need to get serious about school yet, so I didn't. My focus was on sports and running around with Moe. School existed for my entertainment.

Nobody was more shocked than me when I was elected King of the Valentine dance. I guess my head had grown into my ears, my teeth had straightened out, and the winning margin was probably razor thin. It was a nice honor, and I danced with Queen Margaret to "Moon River," even though my heavy date for the gala was my woman, Bonnie Miller, whom I had met at a Sea Scout Dance.

Ronnie Zingle got me interested in Sea Scouts. It was about boats, and they had lots of dances and moonlight cruises. We pretty much left the merit-badge stuff to the real scouts, and we showed up for the fun. Bonnie was pretty and at four feet, eight inches tall, she was a bit of a living doll. I was smitten. My two dancing speeds were slow and stop, so we did a lot of serious cheek to cheek at that first Sea Scout dance. She went to Roosevelt Junior High, so it was a long distance affair, which added to the teenage pain. It's funny how all of the songs that get played on the radio are about your romance when you're a teen: "Puppy Love," "Sixteen Candles," and "Don't be Cruel" were all songs that described every teenage crush.

We only had to last out the rest of the school year; then we would both go to South Eugene. I would somehow get a car and we would be together—forever.

Amid rumors that their mortgage payments couldn't be met, Foo's restaurant burned down and Mom lost her job. She went to work as an aide in a nursing home, which had to be a humongous downer. She had to buy a white nurse's uniform, including a cap with no stripe on it, and rotate between the graveyard, swing, and day shifts while getting paid the same hourly wage as at Foo's, but without the tips. Emptying bedpans and giving enemas with constant moaning was a far cry from delivering fried rice and fortune cookies amidst pleasant conversation. She took it in stride. She had compassion for the residents, whose highlight of their day was a "Gussy bath." Gertrude, a.k.a. Gussy, demanded a sponge bath every day and soon the other residents also demanded a Gussy bath. Mom obliged without complaint.

One of her temporary charges at the home was a young boy recuperating from corrective surgery. His legs had been ravaged by polio, and his parents were too old to take care of him at their home, so he ended up with the old folks. His parents noticed Mom's abilities and recommended that she apply for a job at the Children's Hospital School, where the boy attended. She did and landed the best job she would ever have, as an aide. It was a school operated by the Easter Seal Society for physically handicapped kids.

At CHS, she did the same thing she did at the nursing home, changing diapers and cleaning up messes, but it was with kids instead of adults. She was smart, and despite only having a high school education; she quickly worked her way up to become the volunteer coordinator. She recruited others to do the stuff she had been doing and soon became an integral part of the highly educated school staff. She talked for hours on the phone with her colleagues, and many came over to the house for coffee. One day, she asked me if I would like to volunteer at their summer program, Camp Easter Seal. It sounded good, but it meant leaving Bonnie for the entire summer; I had to think it over.

Tab Hunter captured teenage angst perfectly when he sang about "Young Love" being "… filled with deep emo-o-o-tion." Bonnie and I were like Romeo and Juliet—nothing could keep us from spending every spare minute together. We talked for hours on the phone every day, revealing our deepest secrets and desires. We snuck under the fence at the drive-in theater, turned on the back row speakers, and sat on a blanket up on a small hill at the back. "The Blob" was engulfing the world, the giant silver screen was reflecting off the tops of a sea of cars below us, and we were romancing under a full moon. I would have to be crazy to leave an entire summer of such bliss.

In contrast to this pleasurable affair, the summer was also shaping up to become one of miserably hard labor: hauling hay, driving the stakes into the ground that the beans climbed up, and whatever else I could wrangle. There would be tons of hot, sweaty work before anymore romancing would ever take place.

The fates intervened. During phys ed, I tore the cartilage in my right knee. I had to be in a wheelchair for a few days, so I tagged along with Mom to CHS. I met a lot of the kids that would be going to the summer camp and thought, "This could be a lot of fun." I was halfway to camp, but I needed a lot of money to buy some fine threads for my high school debut.

The Fate of Good Fortunes smiled on me when Dr. Marian Wood, a physician at CHS, asked Mom if we could take care of her fifteen-year-old dog until it died. None of her family wanted to see it suffer, nor did they want to put it to sleep. She would pay twenty dollars a month, plus provide all of the dog's food. Since it was only May, I would clear almost $100 for clothes and fun before school started. If the dog lived through the winter, I would have plenty of spending money. Like most teenagers, I ate about $900 worth of groceries per month, the folks considered it a bargain to take care of the dog while I was gone for the summer and let me keep the twenty bucks. My thinking went, "Fun and games at camp or sweltering, dusty work, and romance?" The scales of indecision were tipping.

The Fate of Extreme Irateness—that would be Mom—delivered the clincher. She got up a full head of wrath when my grades arrived in the mail. I had flunked Metal Shop and Drama.

"Blaming Mrs. Applegar for these grades won't work this time," Mom bellowed in a rage. She was apoplectic with fury. She would be insufferable all summer; I played my "get out of town card" and went to camp.

Mom found it hard to believe I could flunk shop and drama, but I had it down to an art form: if you goof off the entire class period for a full term, Fs are quite easy to get.

The director of Camp Easter Seal was a great big, red-headed, life-loving twenty-five-year-old named Lee Zumwalt. At the camp, he and his wife, Mim, lived in an old farmhouse with Bruce and Janny Whittaker. Bruce was quiet and worked behind the scenes; as the assistant director, he was the perfect complement for the effervescent Lee. Janny was a senior counselor, and Mim was the camp secretary. Being fifteen, I was called a junior counselor, which was a euphemism for cleaning toilets, mowing the lawn, and emptying the camp garbage, along with caring for and feeding of campers.

Other staff included two cooks, a nurse, and Karla, a twenty-two-year-old senior counselor. She was drop-dead gorgeous. Her brunette, shoulder-length hair framed an oval, movie-star-beautiful face. She was petite, shapely, and had a Coppertone tan. She was a traffic stopper in a sweatshirt, but in her fluorescent pink swimsuit, she was as hot as the Chicago fire. Bonnie was my woman, but Karla was a *woman!* I developed an impossible crush on her. It must have showed, because Janny and Mim regularly teased me about it. It was a fantasy for sure, but I found myself acting like an adult trying to impress her. Tab Hunter's song about "deep emotion" no longer had the same meaning. That was kid's stuff. It was obvious; Karla could marry me, I would mow the lawn at our little house and she could drive me to my school and football practice.

The camp sat on the top of a high-rising isthmus that sloped sharply into the north end of Ten Mile Lake, near Reedsport, Oregon. The only practical way to reach it was by boat. The camp naval fleet consisted of an old, donated Chris Craft cruiser and another thirty-five-horse runabout. The cruiser could carry four wheelchairs and five other people. The runabout could only hold two wheelchairs and three people, but it was three times as fast.

The finger-like piece of land was an ideal setting for a camp, but pushing kids up and down hills, loading them on and off boats, making beds, and wiping fannies required a lot of physical effort. I relished the hard work because I was getting into shape for my first year of organized football. I tried to be one of the men, like Lee and Bruce. The harder I worked, the more they relied upon me, and I was soon trusted enough to drive the small boat.

There were lots of camp pranks, short-sheeting the beds and campfire skits that poked fun at everyone. Singing around a campfire is the best part of any camp and regardless of your singing skills. You were expected to vociferously blend your voice with those of kids who could barely sing at all. Together we made a "joyful noise," as the Good Book says. The camper disabilities ran the gamut: cerebral palsy, polio, birth defects, muscular dystrophy, and assorted car accidents were the norm.

The total care and feeding of campers was a tremendous

responsibility for a teenager, and I was determined to rise to the occasion. By working with the kids, I grew beyond being a superficial caregiver and learned to recognize the personalities trapped inside contorted bodies.

It was the perfect place to be myself. I forgot about being cool and loved it. My obligation was only for a ten-day stint, but I stayed the entire summer. I wouldn't trade all of the coolness in Eugene for one rousing chorus of "This Land is Your Land."

As camp came to a close, I had forgotten about being a PE teacher. I knew for certain that one day I would return as the camp director. Lee was my Dali Lama and Camp Easter Seal was my Shangri-La.

There were two weeks left of summer after camp ended. I imme-diately forgot about my altruistic experience at camp and relapsed back into my cool-seeking self. Moe and I went to see the movie *Rebel Without a Cause,* which we adopted as our guide for cool-ness. I combed my hair in a duck-tail with a little spit curl like James Dean's. Moe was even weirder. The character played by Sal Mineo could not stand being touched for some reason not fully explained by the movie. Moe, of course, became untouch-able. He would get miffed if your elbow touched his while he was riding next to you in a car.

Blue Levis pegged tight at the ankles, a clean white T-shirt with the sleeves rolled up, along with my leather jacket with an upturned collar was often my uniform of the day. Moe and Scott Ross, a friend he had met while I was at camp, wore navy blue tanker jackets with little pockets for pens on the left sleeve. They had purchased them at the local G.I. Surplus Store. They repeated my white T-shirt motif, but Moe wore blue suede shoes, and Scott opted for desert boots. I preferred heavy brogues with turned-up toes and taps on the heels that clicked when I walked. Scott had long, red hair, but Moe never gave up his individuality of sporting an old-fashioned, Mr. Erickson-style, PE crew cut.

The socialites of South Eugene High School leaned more toward clothes that favored Pat Boone's style. They wore saddle shoes, sun-tan pants, V-neck sweaters, and plaid shirts—like the clean-cut Kingston Trio. We were greaser wannabes who called the socialites "squares" or "soshes."

Life began to imitate art—but without the stunt men. Moe and Scott started carrying switchblade knives in the remote case of a "rumble," like the one we saw in *Black Board Jungle.* Living on the edge was exciting, but it came with some consequences. I wanted to be a part-time greaser, a part-time athlete, and a part time camp do-gooder. When high school started, I would have to make some hard choices.

CHAPTER 4

High School

It was just a small line that had been drawn down the middle of Sixth Street by the Eugene School District, but for Moe it was a barrier higher than the Berlin Wall. He lived on the north side of the line, which forced him to go to the new high school, North Eugene, while all of his friends went to South. Moe was our leader, but at North Eugene, he got lost in the shuffle and began skipping school and getting into trouble. A fight in his metal shop class was the last straw. A greaser wound up to slug Moe, but Moe held up a piece of thin iron and the kid's fist hit it, slicing his hand between the middle and ring fingers nearly to the wrist. In that fight, Moe was James Dean, the coolest. He became an instant legend at both schools. He showed us that two-foot piece of metal like it was a war trophy. He was small, but as tough as a snake-killing mongoose.

Moe said he had not started the fight, but he still caught the full anger of the school administration and was going to be suspended. I persuaded Mom to take up Moe's case. She had hired his mother, Beulah, to clean the floors at CHS. Beulah was older than any other parent I knew. She was probably younger than I thought, but raising Moe and his older sister, Velma, by herself must have aged her greatly. Velma had dropped out of high school and did nothing that I ever saw to support herself.

Beulah was a good old soul, but she was no match for school principals, but Mom, on the other hand, was. She persuaded the district to let Moe go to South. She argued that all of his friends were at South, and he had never been in any trouble before. It had been their mistake in the first place when they ignored his request to go to South. It made perfect sense.

By the time Moe transferred to South, I had finished the tough daily-double football practices and played in a few junior varsity games, which forged a lot of new friendships with other sophomores. After the third JV game, a varsity player got hurt and I began starting on the varsity as a defensive halfback. The only time I could see Moe was on weekends. After school each day, he and Scott began to drift in their own direction.

One Saturday, the three of us were hanging out down town eating big plates of pancakes at Seymour's restaurant. We all had money, but I let them talk me into the dine-and-dash routine. They said they had done it a lot of times and had never been caught. After stuffing ourselves, we bolted, but Seymour was ready for us. He grabbed Moe and me by the collar just as we got outside the door. Moe broke free and dodged traffic as he ran across Willamette Street against a red light. By the scruff of my neck, Seymour marched me over to the counter, where I shamefully paid for all three of us.

"Okay, you guys each owe me half a buck," I said when I caught up to them.

"No way Ferguson, you were stupid to go back. You could have run like us," Moe said.

"The owner remembered you guys and he was laying for us. He was going to call the cops if I didn't pay for you guys too."

"So what? He doesn't know where we live," Scott said.

"I can't afford to get mixed up with the cops; I'd get kicked off the team."

"Hey, Ferguson, you're the one who turned chicken, so we don't owe you nothing," Moe said with a hint of distance in his voice. "Have a cigarette and cool off." He flicked his wrist and popped a fag to the top of his Lucky Strike package and held it out for me to take it.

"I can't man, if the coach saw me smoking, I'd be dropped from the team."

"Let's go play some pool at Max's, the coaches will never see you smoking in there," Moe said.

"Na-a-ah, man, that pool hall is too smoky, even if it is the cheapest place to play. Let's go to the Spud-Nut-Hut and get some of those potato doughnuts."

"Ferguson, you're always thinking of your gut," Scott said. "Come on Moe, let's split for Max's."

I saw trouble ahead for the rest of that day, so I said, "I'm going over to Bonnie's pad; her old man's working today. I'll see ya later, gator."

Our relationship changed that day. That was the first time Moe had sided against me. He and Scott were now best friends. I was the odd man out. Now whenever we got together, there was an element of delinquency attached. Like the time we threw rocks at the water tanks next to Moe's house. The cops showed up and asked us if we had slingshots or were throwing rocks. "No sir, officer," we lied.

Another time we went over to the nearby lumber company. Moe and Scott figured out how to hotwire a forklift and started driving it around the lumber yard. We heard the sirens. "It's the fuzz man! Let's split," Moe said. I was out of there. I wasn't going to get caught in that mess. We stopped running after a few blocks figuring we had ditched the cops and laughed at our cleverness.

It wasn't so hilarious when a cop car cruised by and stopped just ahead of us. We tried to be casual as we walked by.

"Hold on fellas, where're you going?" called the cop.

"To his house," I said, pointing to Moe. "It's in the next block."

"You boys have ID?"

"I do," I said, fumbling to get my student ID from my moneyless wallet.

"What do you boys know about some kids over at the mill driving a forklift?"

"We walked by the mill and saw some older guys running the other way," Moe said.

With a crew-cut, blue eyes and a baby face, Moe looked clean-cut. He gave no hint that behind his cherubic looks was a liar of exceptional skill. The cop didn't see Scott and I glance at each other, or he would have known it was us.

"Okay, you boys get home so you don't get into trouble for this thing, because we have another unit on the way."

Moe and Scott went back the next night. "Fergy, you shoulda' been there. Scott got one of the forks stuck in a big floor plank and almost tipped the Jitney over," Moe said over the phone.

"Did the cops come again?"

"Na-ah, we weren't there that long. We're going back Sunday night. Wanna come along?"

It was out of control. It was now a game of "how can we top ourselves?" "No man," I said into the phone. "I'm starting on the varsity next Friday, and I don't want to do anything to screw that up."

"Starting varsity? How'd that happen?"

"Stuart got hurt just before the end of the game. I filled in for him the last four plays and knocked down a pass."

"Hey man, that's cool you getting in. Was it like knockin' one down in the old park?"

"Yeah, kinda like that. I guess he dislocated his shoulder and is out for the season, so I've gotta practice hard and stay out of trouble."

"Hey man, all you gotta do is to keep a look-out for the fuzz and you can split at the first sight of a cop."

"I can't, man. My ol' lady's getting wise to us doing stuff and the coach is always preaching about staying out of trouble," I whispered into the phone.

At the first whispered word, Mom glanced over the top of the *Register Guard* she was reading.

We had been involved in lots of shenanigans—stealing hubcaps, pilfering the clear light bulbs from car lots and throwing them just to hear them explode. One time, we set off a CO2 cartridge aimed at the fifth floor window of an apartment building. We couldn't believe it—it actually went straight and broke a window and smashed a large, ornamental lamp. Our antics were getting dangerous, but we still thought they were funny.

"You're turnin' chicken on us, Ferg."

Moe and I had been best friends all through junior high right up until high school sports. We had discovered girls together, double dated, played ball at the park, and won baseball championships, with him at second base and me at third. Those memories went through my mind. I paused to let him think about what he had said. It was like staring at a red couch that had sat too long in a sunny window; I realized our friendship had slowly faded.

"Hey man, you know I'm not chicken, but this isn't like firing off a gas cartridge at a window and then running. Besides, the cops have already stopped us once."

"Man, don't be a chicken and come with us." His tone said that he missed his old friend. I had always gone along with Moe no matter what the prank was.

"Man, you guys are gettin' carried away with this. If something gets wrecked, that's not just a dine-and-dash rap, it's serious." I knew my words were useless. There was no way he would lose face with Scott by not following through with the stunt.

"Ya, but we're first offenders. You know they don't do anything to ya for that."

His words chilled me. He had decided to stay on a reckless path until he was caught. I wanted no part of it. "Not if you wreck that forklift. Even if the coach didn't kick me off the team, my old man would make me quit football to work it off. I can't do it. I'll catch your act later. And don't call me a chicken."

Mom got a phone call from Beulah late Sunday night. She needed a ride to go down to the juvenile center to pick up Moe. They were caught on mill property before they got the rig started and were charged with trespassing before being released to their parents.

The judge hoped they would learn something from their arrest, but they didn't. They went on a small crime spree. Darrin Wilson had replaced me in the triumvirate. He was smooth and smart enough to always let Moe and Scott take the rap for anything that went wrong.

They were fast becoming losers. Moe had started getting into trouble at South, so he was sent back to North High. That ended our many years of hanging out together. I was relieved of a huge pressure, but I saw Moe as a drowning person I couldn't pull back into my boat.

Moe and Scott both dropped out of high school and joined the Navy. I heard that Scott had committed suicide and Moe got heavy into drugs. I met Darrin on an airplane when I was in my early forties. He was a professional table-shuffleboard player and had just won the national tournament. I didn't even know there was a league. At least he wasn't in jail or on drugs, so for him, that was a success.

There were rewards for being a "chicken." I was the only

sophomore to earn a letter in football. I saw a possible future beyond high school, and running for yardage was a lot more fun than running from the police.

I was becoming a young adult. Family arguments erupted as I asserted my independence. The opinions of my peers were more important than those of my parents. Every teenager takes the plunge into those black, churning waters by themselves—without a life jacket.

I couldn't entirely give up the tough, greaser image and I started getting razzed for the way I dressed. I wanted to be cool, but I also wanted to blend in. I switched from the clicking brogues to desert boots and cut the duck-tail shorter so my hair was combed only slightly back on the sides.

Fashion was only part of the angst, hormones were another and "going steady" was part of the teen culture. It meant "engaged to be engaged," so I followed Elvis's lead and asked Bonnie, "Won't you wear my ring around your neck?" A psychologist of that day pontificated that teenagers who went steady felt unloved at home. Mom asked, "Don't you think your Mom and Dad love you?" Of course I felt loved, but I always gave a sarcastic answer like, "Yeah, isn't that why you used to spank me so much?"

Toward the end of the year, Bonnie and I grew in different directions and we broke up. I always thought we might get back together down the road and I kept my agate ring for years—just in case.

The folks had a rule: if you're not out for sports, you have to get a job. It was an easy decision—basketball would be fun and work was, well, work. I had the grace of a gorilla on the maples, but I was good enough to make the JV team. I usually got into foul trouble and scored very few points, but even if I had to ride the pines—work was a four letter word.

It was a Saturday night, and I was home alone with no prospects for fun. Moe, Scott, and Darrin were getting into trouble somewhere and my agate ring was in my junk drawer. I found myself without a best buddy or a steady woman, and I had an innate need for both. In only a few weeks the kitchen phone went from ringing off the hook to dead silence. I was desperate. Watching the "grunt and groaners," as Dad called the wrestling matches, was not teen entertainment.

I took out one of my most treasured possessions, my ninth-grade yearbook with everybody's picture and phone number in it. Staring back at me from the page was John Dirlam: crew cut, white adhesive tape on the side piece of his glasses, and a slight smile. His picture advertised that he was the type of kid every mother wanted her son to run around with. He was studious, thin, polite, religious, and smart, but not a condescending egghead. He wore clothes more suited for adults, right down to Hush Puppies shoes and cardigan sweaters. With the D-F alphabetical connection in our names we had stood next to each other in ninth-grade PE, exercise line. He was just the type of friend I needed to help me stay out of trouble.

"Hi John, this is Bob Ferguson from ninth-grade PE class," I said into the phone. "How about if we go to a movie tonight? My mom says she'll take us." She would do anything to keep me from running around with Moe.

"Hey Bob, that would be great. My sister Diana and I were going anyway. We can ride with her."

The newspaper ad read, "'Pillow Talk' is a charming romantic comedy starring Doris Day as a prim and proper interior designer who shares a phone party line with a womanizing musician, Rock Hudson. Hudson disguises his voice and poses as a wealthy Texas businessman to win her affections." It was the first movie I'd seen in a long time that didn't have guys running from cops, a radioactive amoeba gobbling up the entire earth, or a gigantic Tyrannosaurus Rex stomping on Japan. Along with the audience, we laughed loud and often.

John had been friends with John Blair, who we called J.B., and Babe Edman since they had been in grade school. They all went to Grace Lutheran Church. My third-grade religious fervor had waned then became extinct when I started running around with Moe in the sixth grade. Eventually, they roped me into going to church. Grace Lutheran became the center of our activities—not all of them religious.

In high school, it was natural to discuss religion, miracles, and what heaven is going to look like. We talked without any particular knowledge other than what we learned in Sunday school. One day, we got into an argument. Babe and I often skipped church and went to an ice cream parlor where I spent my offering dime on an ice cream cone. I never had any guilt about it, and the ice cream tasted so good it was a religious experience, but J.B. took the fun out of it.

"You clowns spent your offering money on ice cream, didn't you," J.B. said.

"Hey man, it's my own money and I can spend it anyway I want. My folks don't give me any offering money. Besides, the church has plenty of money," I said.

"Well, if the Ruskies, drop the bomb and you're at the ice cream parlor instead of in church, you'll be sorry."

"You mean you go to church because you're afraid the Russians are going to drop the A-bomb?" I asked.

"They've got the bomb, they hate capitalists, and it could happen anytime. That's why most people go to church." Blairman had just defined the undercurrent of cold-war fear that was imbedded in our national and religious consciousness. "Do good, just in case the bomb is dropped."

John Blair became a lay leader in his church. He always had a way of teaching things like card games in a calm, logical manner. It is only natural that he has led large men's Bible studies for years. I admire his rock-solid faith and a family life that revolves around the church. I might eventually come around, but right now—I'm still sneaking out to get some ice cream.

"Can you possibly imagine my embarrassment, Robert Earl? Huh? can you?" Mom said in exasperation, waving my orange text book in front of me. "Your geometry teacher showed us this book, and he said he hoped we were all familiar with it. I turned four shades of red because I've never, ever seen this book!" She slammed it on the table as her volume increased. "And he said you never hand in any homework!"

"Mom, you know I can't do math, and if I get a D, I still pass. The counselor said it's the last math class I have to take in high school. I'll get an A in PE and still be eligible for sports."

"Robert Earl, you've been saying you can't do math since the second grade, but last year you were in an advanced algebra class and got a C while flunking drama and shop. Now, you're not going to tell me you got those Fs because you played the nail in the band, or another phony excuse about your second grade teacher are you? Huh? Are you? You better start bringing this book home here mister because you should be getting a C in this class!" She was fulminating. She needed to take a breath—but hadn't. "I had to beg that skinny little man to let you turn your homework in late, and I'm never going to do that again. Mr. Heuka told me you're failing and you can kiss sports goodbye, because if you don't pass this class, you won't be eligible for anything!"

She had my attention. I thought I had the eligibility requirement worked out, but I had not considered a failing grade. I was scared. I began to sweat. I took the book, got out some paper, slunk off to my room, and made up some of the homework that night.

I found out from a careers counselor that the admission requirement for a state college was only a 2.00 GPA. I knew I could do that. Average became my goal—get by, stay eligible, and don't miss any fun. It was a delicate balance, but I aimed for mediocrity.

It drove Mom crazy that I played it right on the edge. She was the poster mother for that bumper sticker, "Insanity is contagious: You get it from your kids." I was a major carrier.

"Get out there and run! And when you're tired, run some more!" The bear-like voice belonged to Coach Barnhart as he exhorted his sprinters to scurry out onto the track and start their workouts. Along with a few running techniques, those were pretty much his entire instructions to the sprinters on the track team. Track was a great sport. The spring weather was only going to get better, you got to know your competitors between your events, and all I had to do was run straight down the track.

I tried lots of events, but the 100-yard and 220-yard dashes were my forte. I was quick out of the blocks, and in my first race as a sophomore, I ran the 100 in 10.3 seconds. I ran that time in any weather, on any track, but in three years I never got any faster, although I did manage to place in enough meets to get a varsity letter. It was fun, but it was really a diversion until football season rolled around.

While I was enjoying school, Larry was attending classes at the University of Oregon. He lived at home and really didn't have much of a chance of making it in college. The folks still wanted him to keep the same hours he did in high school; they didn't understand that college is a time to be on your own. They were irate about his underage drinking, and battle royal arguments became the norm.

One day, Larry came home and abruptly announced "I've done what Dad did, I've joined the US Navy." He would be shipping out to San Diego for boot camp in a few days. Being nineteen, he asserted, "I'm a full-fledged man, and I'll be going to Tijuana the first chance I get." I secretly made him promise to bring home some of those pictures like Gene Azalin had brought to the park.

The family went to the Greyhound bus station to see him off. The goodbyes were tearful, but for the first time, he and I shook hands like men. He said he would write and come home on leave after he finished boot camp. As he boarded the bus, Mom stunned us as she yelled, "We'll be waiting for you to come home, but don't you bring any of those Tijuana pictures to the house." How did she know??

Camp was still the nirvana I remembered. I stepped out of my own aura of coolness and into the uninhibited personality of Counselor Bob. Along with camper care and other work, Lee let me lead some campfire sessions. In an environment filled with acceptance and encouragement to take the lead, I began to grow into a person I liked. The corny camp songs were easy to sing. My off-key warbling blended with the noise rising from mouths that struggled with words. Together we twisted tunes into something that resembled a campfire song.

In 1959, I stayed at camp the entire summer, even during the three-day session breaks. I mowed the lawn and helped the caretaker with whatever needed to be done. I was hooked on the camp lifestyle, and was certain this would be my career path.

The minute school started, I slipped right back into trying to be cool. The two Johns, Babe, and I remained on the perimeter of social cliques. We were content with our own group, but being cool was still cool.

Our school's athletic teams were better and were now vying for state championships. We lost three games in football, with a team made up predominately of juniors, and ended up second in our league.

In basketball, I was the only player that stayed on the JV for two years, and I got ribbed for it quite a bit. I was pulled up for the state tournament, but Barry Rubenstein, a senior, after he had played the entire regular season was cut to make room for me on the tournament roster. If I had had any sand at all, I would have told Hank Kuchera, even if he was a coaching legend, to let Barry stay on the team.

In our last tournament game, we were playing for third place and getting beat pretty badly by Saint Helens, so the coach put me in for the last minute and a half. I was so excited I fouled four times in less than a minute. If such statistics were kept, I'm sure that would still be a state record. To make the experience worse, I missed an easy lay-up in the closing seconds. I was so pathetic, even a few of my friends booed me.

At the traditional post season basketball banquet, Kuchera said, "Fergy isn't too delicate on the basketball court, but he's a heckuva football player. If you don't believe me, just ask those

St. Helens players." It was a great laugh for everyone, but I didn't think it was so funny. I laughed—but it hurt.

The weather warmed and a new track season was a welcome relief from the ridicule I had taken on the basketball court. Track was a team sport only insofar as you added the scores together for an overall result. If you were the fastest in an event, you were put in that race. I was still the second-fastest on our team in the dashes. We had our fastest guy and they had theirs, so the race for third was usually between me and their second-fastest guy. Every once in a while I would sneak into second place.

To put sprints into perspective, I consistently ran the 100-yard dash in 10.5 seconds. The Oregon high school record was 9.9 seconds, and the world record was 9.4 seconds. The most rigorous training translated into an improvement of only tenths of a second. To knock a few tenths of a second off of my time I would have to be a lot more dedicated than I was willing to be. I worked hard, but not as avidly as I did for football, where I wanted to be the very best I could be.

Melvin Busch was a camper with cerebral palsy who needed feeding, dressing, bath-rooming, and tucking into bed every night. It was an all-consuming job done every day by his parents. John Dirlam came to camp to be Mel's attendant during that summer before our senior year.

Mr. and Mrs. Busch were worn to the bone when we picked up Mel at the dock for the teen-age session at Camp Easter Seal. As his parents aged and got weaker, Mel grew older and heavier, which would eventually necessitate him moving to the Fairview State Hospital. The Busches breathed a sigh of relief when we put him on the boat. For ten days they would get a well-earned respite. I developed a tremendous respect for the commitment such parents make to their disabled kids.

That same session, three girls came to camp as kitchen aides. They helped the cook, washed dishes, and worked hard. Alice Jorgenson had a peaches-and-cream complexion, and was drop-dead beautiful and sweet as a drop of honey. Shirley Ferris was full of personality with a plumpish body. Marge Davidson was classy-attractive, but religious to the point that you knew there would never be any hanky-panky.

"Did you see those kitchen aides? They're gorgeous!" John blurted out within hearing distance of Hank, the caretaker.

"This session is going to be the best ever!" I blurted back.

"Hey fellas," Hank whispered. "You gotta keep your mind on your jobs and you don't wanna be talkin' too loud or their parents will put them back on the boat. Then you'll be doin' the dishes, because I sure ain't."

Vernon Hankins (Hank to campers and counselors) and his wife Ruthy, both in their early forties, had checked out of the rat race to become year-around camp caretakers. Hank had a way of indirectly getting a well-made point across. John and I went back to pushing wheelchairs up the large hill from the boat house, toting luggage into cabins, and keeping our mouths shut while still ogling the girls.

John fell hopelessly in love with the beautiful Alice who became a Rose Festival Princess. She was a year younger, lived in Portland and had a boyfriend. John's first true love was unrequited, but Sally, Marge, John, and I carried our friendships into adulthood.

In the beat of a humming bird's wings the summer was gone. As we rounded the point, camp faded from view. But I knew I would return someday as the camp director. There were no other career options to be considered.

It wasn't medicine, the law, or an occupation parents brag

about in their Christmas letters. But it was a job where I knew I would make a needed difference if only for a few days, in the lives of kids and parents, like the Busches. Camp was always mentioned as the yearly highlight in their Christmas letters.

We held the Black Tornados for three downs on their first possession. "We've got these guys," someone said in the defensive huddle. I was sure of it, but Medford surprised me when they decided not to punt with fourth down and four yards to go. They had to pass, because we had stuffed their running game. Their quarterback, Dick Ragsdale, dropped back to pass then ran a quarterback draw up the middle for a forty-yard touchdown run. After that, they turned us every which way but loose. The Medford Black Tornado, coached by the legendary Fred Spiegelberg, handily dispatched us. Our best player, Dave Tobey described the Tornado perfectly at the year-end banquet when he said, "We thought we were a pretty good team until we played the University of Medford." (Tobey went on to a distinguished career at the University of Oregon and in the NFL.)

My goal of making the all-state football team fell like an elevator with a snapped cable. A few early season injuries kept me out of four games, and I failed to garner any all-league honors as either a fullback or defensive halfback. My hopes of getting noticed at the college level took a further bashing in the first half of the Medford game when I dislocated my left shoulder. My football days were over. Three years of football were not enough, but it was over.

Basketball was a non- issue. The shoulder would need four weeks to heal, so I tossed in the towel. If Kuchera kept true to form, I would be cut from the tournament team anyway, and my ego couldn't take that. I didn't have the character Barry

Rubenstein did. It was the first time in six years that I wasn't playing a school sport.

My parents were true to their word. "Get a job," Mom said. I got a job delivering prescriptions for a local pharmacist. It paid well, and the little car used for deliveries was a five-speed Triumph sedan that was fun to drive. It took only a few hours after school to complete my duties, so there was plenty of time for fun. The two Johns and I became rabid basketball fans and went to every game. I didn't miss playing the sport as much as I thought I would.

Spring rolled around and a sophomore, Gordon Payne, became our number-one speedster on the track team. Luckily, I was still fast enough to keep my number two spot. No shame in this—Payne went on to match the state record of 9.9 seconds in the hundred. He ran right into a distinguished career at the University of Oregon.

I was teamed up with three fast, talented sophomores on the 880-yard relay. We won our district championship, which put us into the state finals. With the football season ending in disaster and no basketball season for me, it felt good to be part of a team where I could give an all-out commitment.

In the state finals I ran the anchor leg. I was on the outside lane with a staggered start on the curve. It seemed like a huge lead, but after the hand off, I heard the feet chomping up the track behind me. As we hit the straightaway, I was caught and passed by three other runners, one being Mel Renfro of Dallas Cowboys fame. A fraction of a second translates into several yards at the finish line, but we scored enough points at the Oregon State Championships to take fourth as a team. I had worked hard and ran a personal best. It was a good finish, not top dog, but better than most. I had left everything on the track; I was satisfied.

She had been voted the prettiest girl in school as a junior at Albany

High, and there was no denying that Toni Carroll was a beauty. Unfortunately, her personality was somewhere between "I totally love myself" and "You're lucky I let you spend your money on me."

She had transferred to South for her senior year, and I have no idea how Toni and I ever hooked up. She smoked, swore like a truck driver, and was far from the sweet and innocent type of girls that I liked. Our brief affair came to an ugly, scene-making end on prom night when she purposely humiliated me by winking and flirting with the lead singer of the band, Dave Ellerson.

"Ohhh, gooo Dave," she swooned. "Don't you think he's just the most Bob?"

"Uh, sure, yeah, Dave's a good guy. We played football together." I was mortified.

"Dave, I'll be at Kelly's party after the dance," Toni said as she winked at him.

"Uh, Toni, don't ya think ya ought to let the guy sing?" She had purposely embarrassed me in front of everybody.

Kelly's party was held at her mega-house, complete with swimming pool and a downstairs billiards room. Toni took off the expensive corsage I bought her and avoided me at the party. She was waiting for Dave to show up. I was downstairs in the billiards room with several guys while she was upstairs making me look like chopped liver.

"Hey Fergy, aren't you with Toni?"

"Hey Fergy, you gonna learn to sing like Dave?" I was disgraced, the taunts were unbearable, and my shame was turning into vengeance.

"Well, if you guys want to see a show, why don't one of you go up and tell her I'm leaving and if she wants a ride home, she needs to get down here—now."

She blew into the room like she was the belle of the ball.

"Bob, oh Bob, what's wrong?" Toni whined in a high, cat-like voice.

"You wench, you know what's wrong, but at least your disgusting cigarette breath won't be smellin' up my car any more because it's over between us."

"Goooo Fergy!" was mixed with cat calls, whistles, and clapping hands from the peanut gallery urging me to go on. A crowd gathered, with me at center stage—I liked it.

"Well, you're the wench. You knew it was over at the prom, so you can't drop me because I already dropped you," Toni said.

"Toni, you're a superficial gold digger and I've only been taking you out for one reason."

"Oh, and what's that?" She inhaled deeply from a cigarette someone handed her.

"Come on Toni, you know—it wasn't just to lock lips, because kissing you is like licking an ashtray." *That was good, but she deserves more,* I thought. "I dated you for the same reason all the other guys took you out."

"Well, you didn't get very much, did you!"

"Oh, didn't I?" My Humphrey Bogart tone insisted that we were in a steamy relationship, and my fan club filled the room. They were cheering me on, so I was obligated to be crueler. "Dave Ellerson didn't even notice you. He's classy and you're trashy."

"Well, you're the trashy one, with that stupid little car you think is so cool." She wiped at her eyes as she started to cry.

"Come on, Toni. Don't give us the fake tears. Snakes can't cry." Wow! That zinger felt great. "Go Fergy, go Fergy," the crowd chanted—so I did. "Toni, you might think my little car is stupid, but your ash tray breath won't stink it up anymore." Her tear-smeared mascara didn't faze me. "Carlin and Trudy broke up, and I'm going to the beach with her. Maybe you can ride home with him."

"You're an egotistical jerk!" She said between sobs as she ran back up stairs.

"Oh, Toni, you've deeply wounded me." I grabbed my heart

like I had been shot with an arrow. The laughter was music to my ears.

The statute of limitations has run out, so I can tell all of those at Kelly's party that I was a bit creative with the truth. The fact is; I implied we had a torrid affair, but Toni and I had hardly held hands. However, since several other guys did get their windows steamed up with her, I do not apologize.

Even as I write this episode nearly half a century later, I regret only one thing: I wish I could have told her four husbands what she was really like before they married her.

I joined the Future Teacher's Association to pad my college resume and to show the folks that I was serious about doing something beyond high school. I convinced my parents that I needed a car to drive to the little grade school where I would be doing something similar to student teaching.

I had made enough money during the basketball season to pay two hundred dollars for a 1958 Renault. Toni was right; I did think my little car was cool, but I knew it wasn't much. (On the eve of 2000, when lists were made about the best and worst of everything, one of my classmates sent me an email showing that the '58 Renault had been voted the worst car of the millennium.) But it was unique. It was the only one in Eugene and so ugly it was cute, and it was mine. It was green the exact color of pea soup so it was dubbed the "Green Pea." With my thirty cents of lunch money, I could buy two gallons of gas and cruise around town for an entire night. Toni, wherever you are, that's what made it cool.

The smell of Spanish rice, spilled milk, and years of floor polish wafted on the lunch room air as Doug Marsh titillated us with a story of sex and intrigue. His coolness mesmerized us. I wanted to be like him—no, I wanted to be him. I would settle just to be in his crowd, which was now gathered around him like disciples listening to a guru. I ached to be cool and had tried most everything from being the class clown to playing three sports to stealing a few hubcaps. None of them ever got me invited to Marsh's wild parties when his folks were out of town. In a few weeks, "Pomp and Circumstance" would play, and my years at South Eugene High would be over. Time was running out for me to be cool. I had to act. I was desperate for all of my classmates to remember me at the reunions as doing something super cool. I jumped into the middle of the group, taking the lead from Marsh.

"It couldn't be, not right here in Eugene, that's too much," I said.

"Naaaaaaaaaah, too weird," another chimed in.

"No kiddin' man?" I said.

"For real?" "No bull?" "Are you serious?" Others asked in rapid-fire disbelief.

"Who told ya?" I asked. I was unconvinced, but hoped it was true.

"Larry Stevens," was Marsh's matter-of-fact reply.

"And how would he know?" I said.

"He's seen it. Well, actually he knows someone who's seen it, but it's for real." Marsh's story had five or six of us babbling like dolts.

"Okay, give it to us one more time, and no jivin' us," I said.

"It's just like I told you guys. It's a whorehouse where white women hook up with Negro men, and that's no jive. It's right at the foot of Pearl Street, 535 is the house number."

"There's only a handful of Negroes in all of Eugene, so why isn't it out on West Eleventh, where they live?" someone asked with perfect logic.

"How should I know?" Marsh said with some irritation. "Maybe they come down from Portland, but the question is—what should we do about it?"

Marsh was the student body vice-president at South Eugene, and Larry Stevens was his counterpart at North. Stevens told Marsh about the house of ill repute while they were rooming together at the Boy's State Leadership Convention.

"Well, I know Stevens from picking beans back in junior high. He's a cool head, and I run into him once in a while, but he's a Jesus Jumper. How could he know about a deal like this?" I expected my question to end Marsh's charade.

"He says he heard it from someone who has really seen it for sure. Do you know Ron Brown?"

"Sure, but he's a greaser. I wouldn't believe anything he says." I felt like kicking myself for saying that. I liked Ron, and I was half-greaser myself. Brown worked a few days a week after school at the bottling plant within eyesight of the 535 Pearl Street house. He had to work to help support his family. I admired him for doing that.

"He was taking a smoke break on the loading dock of the bottling plant one night, and he saw it all take place across the street." Marsh then added the clincher. "He told Stevens, and if he says it, you know it's true."

Brilliance struck me! I saw a sure-fire way to be cool and get into the in crowd. "Okay, tell you what. Tell Stevens to get ten guys from North. and we'll get ten guys from South, and we'll all raid the place for the good of the community. You can count it as one of those nicey-nice Boy's State projects you guys are always doing to clean up the city. It'll be a lot more fun than you playing Tom Sawyer and telling us how much fun we'd have painting those benches at the city bus stops," I said.

"Smooth! Cool! Swift! Neat!" Approval came from every direction. My coolness was ascending.

"Okay, Bob and I will check it out and organize a panty raid on Friday night, just like the frat guys do to sororities," John Dirlam said.

Where did he get the pluck to say that? He was an honor roll student who was never tardy, went to church every week, was never even shushed by a teacher. Now he's suggesting a panty raid on a whorehouse? There must have been something extra in the Spanish rice that day.

"A panty raid is nothin' let's take all of their clothes and then see what happens. It's a whorehouse—they can't call the cops," I blurted out to regain the center of attention.

"Nice talk." "I love it." "Outta sight." "It'll be an all-timer." Gushing approval in guttural tones issued from a group of teens who had just lost their minds.

A sudden glimpse of being handcuffed flashed across my mind. This was way out of our league. It was time for a gut-check. The door to coolness had been flung wide open, but was it worth the risk of committing a minor crime? Absolutely!

"Okay, you guys, don't tell anybody else. Let's get the right people for this. Marsh, you set it up with Stevens."

The lunch bell rang. We were all excited. The candle was lit. The warmth of coolness swept over me.

The Green Pea would be providing a week of stake-out duty at 535 Pearl Street. That night, John and I headed for what my parents thought was the library. I had not been in any trouble since we had become as thick as thieves in my junior year. My grades had improved because we did—occasionally—go to the city library and get some homework done, so I could always go with John—but no library this night. Two hormonally charged teens would be on stake out.

We parked across the street, with the bottling plant to our left and the small wooden-frame home directly in front of us. It must have been built in the thirties. So much of the white paint had peeled off it looked gray. The green composition roof shingles were covered with moss, but their scalloped edges revealed a bygone era of pride in ownership. A front porch ran the full length of the house, with a white dowelled railing open in the middle for the steps. In a large front window dusty, white lace side curtains were draped and tied at the sides. They were left in an unkempt position and puddled on the sill. The pull shade was yellowed by the sun and fully drawn, so there was no way to get a peek inside. John and I wondered if this dilapidated dump could really be a house of lust.

Marsh had told us that the ladies would arrive by taxi and get out at the corner of Fifth and Pearl, then walk the quarter of a block to the house. We had been waiting about half an hour when, at about 7:30, tally ho! We saw her! Out of a taxi stepped a doll dressed in a short, black skirt, leopard print blouse unbuttoned for maximum effect, ruby red lipstick, hair piled high in a bee-hive hair-do, and spiked heels that accentuated long legs covered in black fish-net stockings. Her fake mink stole screamed tramp, and we immediately fell in lust with her. We were laughing, leering, and salivating like Pavlov's dogs. We watched the object of our affections walk up the stairs to the house and rhythmically knock three times: rap ... rap .... rap. A tall Negro man answered the door and let the young lady in. He looked around outside, then closed and locked the door. A few minutes later, a Negro man arrived in a taxi right in front of the house. Rap ... rap .... rap, the door opened and he entered. The tall Negro looked around, then closed and locked the door. This was too good to be true.

A few more white women and several more Negro men arrived. All gave the coded knock and entered. There were more men than women. This caused our youthfully perverted minds to speculate about all of the combinations that must be taking place at the raging party going on inside the little house. On school nights we had to be in by ten, so we had no idea how long this strange parade lasted, but we fantasized that it was all night.

The lunch hour buzzed with excitement as we exaggerated our lurid sightings in explicit details to guys with gaping jaws. We were now the center of attention; Marsh was just a gaper.

"I think Gumby and I'll go down there tonight and take a look-see for ourselves," Jim Beckley said.

I took a big drink from the waxed, half-pint milk carton and swallowed hard. Beckley and Gumby were two of the most popular guys in school. His '54 Ford had sweet-sounding pipes, it was lowered, painted a beautiful baby blue color, and had just been featured as car of the month in the *Axman,* the school newspaper. They would easily take over our act and cut John and I out altogether.

"Listen, you dorks! You go tooling down there and start cruising around and rapping your pipes, you'll make them suspicious and blow the whole thing," I said.

"Let Fergy and Dirlam check it out," said one of the cats.

Another said, "That Green Pea is so ugly nobody will pay any attention to it." I interpreted this as my having attained coolness and my funny looking car getting respect.

"That felt sooo good to call those guys dorks," I whispered to John as we left the lunchroom.

It was set. Stevens had ten guys, we had ten guys. We'd meet at Barger's Drive-In south of town and cruise on down to 535 en masse at exactly eight o'clock. Military precision would be required to get the right bodies in the right places. Jim Tynan would lead us through the front door. He was built like a bull on steroids and as hyper as spit on a griddle. The excitement of a whorehouse raid would make him charge with reckless abandon—which is why he was the most important person in the group.

As Friday night drew closer, some guys chickened out with lame excuses. Charley Cohen claimed he was grounded, and Fred

Dudley fished out saying he had to be at work too early the next morning. Stevens had a few guys drop out, too. It didn't matter; together we still had about ten guys, and Tiny. He was worth twenty good men, and we felt comfortable following him through the door which would splinter on contact.

The genius of our plan lay in its simplicity: Tiny knocks with the code, rap ... rap .... rap. When the Negro opens the door just a crack—boom! We all push the door open and start grabbing panties, stockings, bras, whatever we could find, and run out the back. Then we watch to see what the naked people inside do to solve their predicament. They couldn't call the police, so we'd have them in a pickle. It was a foolproof scheme.

Friday's agenda called for me to pick up John at his pad after track practice. Next, we'd tool on out to Barger's Drive-in, meet up with the cats, and head on down to 535 Pearl.

The Green Pea nimbly climbed the hill to John's house. She was running good, and the thrill of the raid made me giddy. Like a good horse sniffing out danger, the Pea sensed the excitement in the air and was giving me all she had. Man and machine became one. The Pea raced around the corners with an extra dose of derring-do. No longer was the Pea a get-by mode of the cheapest transportation available; it was now a low-slung Indy car. Danger lurked—all the better. Full throttle ahead! The Pea responded. As I backed off the gas, the tailpipe spit out a back-fire that sounded like a Vespa scooter with a bad spark plug. No matter. The Pea was on a mission of extreme importance: to carry me into coolness.

I pulled into Neslo Lane and tapped the horn button on the end of the turn signal. The Pea responded "meep, meep," just like the cartoon Roadrunner. They knew it was me. Only one car in Eugene "meeped."

John was wearing the uniform we had discussed, a dark jacket and pants to provide night camouflage, black, low-cut, Chuck

Taylor Converse tennis shoes for speed, and a strap to keep his thick glasses on. If those babies popped off, he'd be blind. I had missed one small detail in telling him how to dress for a dangerous night operation. At ninety feet away, the white tape holding the earpiece of his Coke-bottle glasses beamed like a bike reflector. It was so much a part of his bookworm personality that I couldn't mention it. *No sweat. Our plan can't miss,* I thought. When he slammed the door shut it sounded like an empty beer can being dropped on a patio. The Pea was not an advertisement for quality.

"Let's hit it," he said, which was about as much slang as John ever used.

The "William Tell Overture" played in my mind as we sped off to Barger's. *Hiyo, Silver, awaaaaay,* I fantasized. We were the Lone Ranger and Tonto. Adrenalin rushed through our veins and mindless were our brains. The car had a quarter of a tank of gas, which would easily carry us through the night's escapade.

Our friendship had no hierarchy. John helped me academically, and I helped him socially, but it was more than a symbiotic relationship. We were two halves of the same heart pounding a rhythm in our arteries as vibrantly as a salsa beat. We were connected at the hip like two people in a three legged race—but we ran faster tied together. We formed a third personality that dared us to taste life's gourmet banquet, from frog legs to the crème de le crème, which would be the raid on 535 Pearl Street.

We were on Willamette Street in no time. Coming over the first rise, we were greeted by a long, red snake of taillights that went all the way to Barger's. Hundreds of cars snarled traffic. Dragging the gut from downtown Willamette Street out to Barger's was the norm on Friday nights, but this was huge. The cars clogged the large entry into the adjacent drive-in theater which was nick-named, "The Passion Pit," and worried all self-respecting parents.

"This scene is bigger than prom or graduation nights. Must be something else going on, but what?" I asked John, not expecting an answer.

Every greaser in town was there with his hot rod. Most of them had graduated a few years earlier, but they were still trying get into the *in crowd* by getting their primer-covered heaps looking cherry. The problem was, the in crowd had moved on to college while these guys were stuck in a high school time warp.

Wally Thurman was leaning against the hood of his red and white '56 Chevy. He had been in Larry's class of 1958. His blond hair was combed back into a full-blown duck tail, and a package of Lucky Strikes was visible through the rolled up sleeve of his white T-shirt. He looked exactly the same as he did three years ago when he had stopped by the house a few times.

"Hey Wally, what's this scene about?" I asked.

"Haven't you heard little Fergy? We're raiding a whorehouse, ya know?" For all his dark foibles, Wally had a white-toothed grin that radiated sunshine and now lit up his rather handsome face. "It's all over town. All of us Pharaohs are meeting here."

The Pharaohs was the hippest car club in town. They had the best cars, wore their leather jackets with the collar turned up, and were borderline hoodlums.

"What do the Pharaohs plan to do?" I asked.

Wally, dumfounded by the question, answered, "Ya know, cruise on down to the place and, ya know, sorta raid it, I guess. Ya know?" He snapped his chewing gum as he talked.

I didn't know, and asked myself, *Is it possible there are two whorehouses right here in Eugene? Naaah, couldn't be.* "Where is it Wally?" I finally asked.

"I dunno. I'm just gonna follow the crowd, ya know?" For Wally, following was a good thing. He needed direction. He had mentally jumped off the chronological age chart the day he graduated from South. His maturity level stayed the same, but now he could grow a mustache and legally drink beer.

"We have to find Marsh and Stevens—fast," I muttered to John.

"Do you think those guys have this thing organized?" John asked.

"I don't have a clue what they're up to. Hey—scope out the flames and that pin-striping on this '40 Ford. That has to be that little guy Verle Bebee's work. He charges a lot, but they say he's the best. Those guys spend a fortune on their cars," I said.

"Well, if a good job at the mill is your future instead of college, I guess you can afford it," John said, expressing his responsible, adult, and no fun, view.

"Check that out," I said, pointing to a metal plaque standing up on the rear window shelf of a '49 Ford that was deeply lacquered candy apple red; it belonged to another of Larry's friends, Adam Kriek. In capital letters "PHARAOHS" was arched over the name of the car, "Adam's Delight."

"Jeez, the Pharaohs must have thirty to forty cars here. Why would Stevens get the Pharaohs involved?" I muttered.

Our crew was standing under the little porch that went around Barger's. It was a small, square building with a roof that slanted to the back like a lean-to. It was about seven thirty, but we weren't going to make our move until eight. The horde grew larger.

I parked the Pea in a safe place. John and I waded through the crowd, looking at the best car show I'd ever seen. I breathed a sigh of relief when I spotted Tiny with the group. "What's with the Pharaohs cutting in on our act with a couple hundred people? You do this, Stevens?" I asked.

"Man, I've got no idea what they're doing here. How are we going to organize this bunch?" Stevens said.

Was it possible to out cool the coolest guys in town and get everyone to follow us? *This is my big chance,* I thought. My Levis were pegged tight at the ankles. My U.S. surplus blue tanker flight jacket ended at the waist and had little pockets for pens on the left sleeve. I had slicked back my hair into the best duck tail I could manage. I looked like a junior Pharaoh, so maybe I could pull it off. The other guys were all dressed like Ivy League high-schoolers; they couldn't begin to harness this mob.

"Look, we don't know what the Pharaohs are doing, so you and your five guys from North get in one of your cars and our four guys from South will get in Tiny's rod. That's all we need to pull this off." I tried to sound like a man in charge. "I'll try to get the Pharaohs to follow us."

The multitude failed to notice that I was in charge. A Pharaoh resembling Marlon Brando in *The Wild Ones* stood on the running board of his chopped, dropped, channeled, black '51 Mercury with yellow and orange flames engulfing the hood yelled, "Let's go!" Doors slammed, pipes rapped, tires squealed, and the smell of rubber was in the air. The throng was on the move, and the Pharaohs were leading our parade.

John, Marsh, and I jumped into Tiny's gray-primered '48 Dodge, which had been parked for a quick get-away. Not a pretty car, but perfect for our purposes. The Pharaohs were always on the police watch list; their cars were too low or too loud to be street legal, or for just carrying suspicious-looking characters. One by one, they got pulled over for petty offenses.

"With the Pharaohs out of the way, we can do this raid ourselves." Tiny stated.

"There're still a jillion cars behind us, and we don't know any of them. And they're looking for trouble," John said.

I gave him an unconcerned response. "All those guys are like Wally. They won't do anything without being told what to do, and they haven't a clue to what's going on."

With bravado supplied from a gulp of his second beer, Tiny added, "Look, you sissies, when we get down there, we'll just push to the front of the crowd and deal with anybody that thinks they're gonna horn in our raid." He used the "church key" on his key ring to open another Oly and took a large swig. He let out a belch that any sailor would be proud of and asked someone to pull his finger. Marsh obliged. Vvriiipppp. We all rolled down the windows, cursing Marsh. Tiny ripped off another one and continued laughing.

"Someday, you're gonna crap your pants," Marsh said.

"I already have," Tiny said, laughing with the rest of us. Laughing was fun.

We parked in the lot of the bottling company and joined the gathering crowd on the large lawn of a big house surrounded by shrubs just across the street from 535 Pearl. It was a perfect staging area.

A lot of guys were drinking beer. Tiny was on his fourth and declared himself drunk enough to tackle the raid by himself. He was primed for action. The throng consisted mostly of dropouts and losers, so it was easy for us to get to the front of the crowd.

"Don't do anything until I give the word," Marsh said. "Is everybody set?" Marsh shouted to the back of the crowd. Tiny leaned forward like a long distance runner waiting for the starting gun. The tension mounted. Marsh raised his hand. This was it. Here we go!

The door on 535 flew open and a big Negro filled the entire entrance. He waved a fireplace poker like a medieval mace. He looked a lot bigger than on our stake-out nights. There was an understandable pause in the action.

The crowd muttered its ignorant displeasure. "What're you gonna do, you big nigger? You can't get us all," slurred a voice from the back of the crowd.

We were dumbstruck. We northwest white kids had never heard a Negro called a "nigger" to his face. Our brilliant, foolproof plan did not include anyone getting hurt. Racism was confined to the South. This was ugly. The menacing wave of the fire poker held us at bay. The ignoramus was right; this guy couldn't get us all, but who wants to go first? I grabbed a beer from someone and gave it to Tiny for more courage. He took a big gulp, belched, and said, "Okay, I'm ready. I can handle this guy."

"What are you waitin' for up front? Ya chicken? Bawwk, bawwk, bawk," the crowd taunted.

"Shut up, you morons," Marsh shouted. "And wait for me to give the word, or you can come up here and we'll use your bird-sized brain for a battering ram,"

The big Negro closed the door. The surprise of the coded knock was gone. The plan had changed to rushing the door and busting it in. John and I were a few guys behind Tiny.

Did this still make sense? If I twisted an ankle, I would be off the relay team, which had already qualified for the state meet. John could lose his glasses and get hurt. Was it worth risking this much to be cool? Absofreakinglutely!

"Let's go!" Marsh said. The fat was in the fire. I couldn't back out now. I had to see it through to the end or be disgraced.

We started across the street at a slow trot. The front window exploded. Someone had thrown a beer bottle through it. There was no stopping us; we were as ugly as the peasants attacking the hunchback, Quasimodo as he swung on the bells in the tower of Notre Dame.

Deafening sirens, blinding lights, and cop cars instantly surrounded 535 Pearl Street. Where had they come from? We hadn't spotted one cop! The fuzz were everywhere; it was every man for himself. I ran back and jumped into the large bushes of the staging house. I rolled up into a ball so tight it would make a sow bug envious. I cowered in fear. The owner was on the porch with a shotgun and flash light. The cops yelling "Halt!" stopped nobody. Beer bottles crashed as they were dropped by the mindless crowd that ran away like a herd of stampeding buffalos. Mob rule—ruled. Unkind gestures and epitaphs were hurled at the cops as cars burned rubber in all directions.

Spotlights from police cruisers across the street were lighting me up. I was close to a biological evacuation. *They've got me. They'll go easier on me if I give up,* I reasoned. I got to my knees, ready to face decades in jail, and parted the bushes to surrender.

The lights clicked off and the homeowner went back inside. What luck! They hadn't seen me! I lapsed back into my sow bug position. Just as suddenly as they had appeared, the cops evaporated. I relaxed into a worm position, lying flat on my belly.

Things were quiet. I waited for an eternity, then a car I recognized cruised slowly by to check out the happening. I dashed from the bushes bent over in case any cops were still at 535. I tapped on the side of the door, it opened, and I hopped in.

"Fergy, where'd you come from?" Dirk Wicks asked in a surprised voice.

I told him the whole story—how the Pharaohs took over, and the fuzz broke things up, and I ended up hiding in the bushes.

"How come you didn't tell me about it? After all, I'm practically your neighbor," Wicks said. "We were headed to "The Passion Pit" without any chicks and heard about it at Barger's so we decided to drive by to check it out."

"I didn't tell you about it because you're only a junior and this was just for the seniors. But somehow the whole town found out about it. Even the cops knew," I said.

We were looking cool in the '52 Chevrolet fastback sedan. We dragged the gut and headed back to Barger's. I had my swagger back because I had an escape story to tell. There would never be a need to tell anyone that I imitated a sow bug, almost gave myself up, and was so scared I almost peed my pants—so I won't. I was extraordinarily, double cool throughout the entire escapade.

Barger's was still crowded. All of our guys had made it back. I was the only one who'd been trapped, and they thought I'd been caught by the cops. Our stories grew as we talked. Even though it hadn't turned out as planned, it had been a grand adventure.

"Those cops don't know who they're dealing with. Let's do it again," yelled a wannabe leader in the crowd.

The voice sounded like the guy that yelled "nigger" at 535 Pearl. He was a greaser driving a heap that had no cool. His bravado was fueled by alcohol. We wanted no part of the guys that were now jumping into their cars. We hadn't pulled it off with great planning. What were they going to do with no planning?

The cops re-materialized. They knew exactly who they were dealing with: village idiots. They wrote tickets faster than doctors writing prescriptions. We cheered for the fuzz as we witnessed brazen stupidity. There was not one of those cherry Pharaoh cars in sight. They were not only cool; they were smart enough to know that the police had things well in hand.

For thirty-five cents we all had a Barger's "Gut Bomb" with cheese, fries, and a Coke. We lied to each other about what we would have done if the cops hadn't shown up. We laughed loud and hard at ourselves because we knew that our foolproof plan turned out to be the proof of fools.

John and I slept in my big, double bed and recounted every sordid detail from start to finish. We paid special attention to the lovelies that we had seen on our "library" nights.

"What did that lady really say to you that night when you went up to her and asked her if she would meet us in the Pea? I saw her say something." John said.

He was referring to the night I got up the nerve to ask one of the ladies to give us a whirl. I had told John she just walked by, ignoring me.

"She said, 'Go back to kiddygarten, sonny boy, and grow up,'" I said chuckling. "I didn't tell you because I didn't want you blabbing it at lunch."

"I wouldn't tell those guys, they're dorks" he said.

"Yes you would, because it's too funny not to tell," I said as we laughed

"Do you think someone will snitch that we organized the raid?" John asked.

"Naaah, we all got away, and the Pharaohs took the lead from us. Besides, Marsh actually started it, and his dad's an attorney. I've heard his dad's gotten him out of a few jams, so I don't think there's much to worry about." I hoped.

We slept in and Mom fixed us a fantastic breakfast. She always fixed a good breakfast when John stayed over. She then began the inevitable questions.

"What'd you boys do last night?" Mom asked.

"Nothin' much," I said, doing all I could do to keep from snickering, but when I burst out laughing, John almost snorted milk out of his nose.

"So you *were* involved in that fracas last night," she accused. How did Mom know? That is a question every teenager eventually asks himself.

"What do you mean?" I said with a telltale nervous laugh.

She handed me the *Register Guard*. There it was, in black and white. "A melee at 535 Pearl Street erupted at about 7:30 pm. The police questioned participants about the incident and handed out 134 driving citations on Willamette Street, but are still uncertain of what caused the near riot. It was the largest number of traffic warnings and citations ever written by the Eugene Police Department in a single night."

We had outdone ourselves. The local scandal sheet had given our exploit some nice headlines, and it was right there in black and white for us to brag about.

Our, "who, us?" looks gave us away to Mom. "I hope you didn't get one of those tickets. You don't have any money to pay for it," she said.

"When we got to Barger's, there was a big crowd. We just hopped in Tiny's car and followed along. When the cops came, we scattered. I didn't even take my car," I said.

"You're not telling me everything," her lilting voice said. "I'll eventually find out. You know you can't lie to me, Robert Earl."

There was a kernel of truth in my story, and we really hadn't done anything wrong, so it passed as barely believable. But I felt a twinge of guilt when she put a heaping pile of scrambled eggs and country sausage on our plates. "Don't be a follower—like Wally," she said.

John and I glanced at each other. She was a mind reader. How could she possibly have known about Wally?

"And I know you haven't been going to the library all those nights. You didn't even take your books one night. If I find out you got in some sort of trouble, you're going to be grounded the rest of the year. You might be able to fool your dad, but you're not fooling me. I had seven brothers, so you better remember that."

Dad probably wasn't fooled. He just didn't care that we were boys being boys.

I could hardly wait until Monday. We had to be the coolest cats in school, which meant an automatic invitation to Marsh's wild parties.

Monday came and I had the article, but we only got grief for letting the Pharaohs take over our raid. Even those who didn't show up ragged on us. "We told ya, you couldn't pull it off. Ya wimped out when the cops showed up. We heard you hid the whole time, Ferguson." They were like jackals eating carrion and I was the road kill.

"Hey, dorks, we made the papers. They called it a melee, and we didn't get caught. What'd you do, Cohen? Get in another heavy petting session with that fat cow you call a girlfriend?"

His woman, Shirley Todd, was a little chubby, but she was nice. I had no reason to insult her. This was about Cohen, but after that prom night with Toni, I found I could deliver comebacks twice as sarcastic as most people. I could see he was hurt after a lot of guys laughed. I felt good.

"Ooooh, Fergy's hittin' below the belt," said Dudley, another guy that had begged off the raid.

"You're no better, Dudley. Your momma wouldn't even let you out of the house. She's got you tied to her apron strings so tight you can't even bend over to tie your own shoes."

The one time I had met his mother, she had worn a low-cut dress, bright red lipstick, and heavy makeup to some kind of school function. She looked like a tart, and we had all ogled her. She embarrassed him; that's why I mentioned her.

"You're a $%&# Ferguson."

"Thanks, Dudley. I'll tell your momma about your kind words."

I guess you have to be born into cool. The moment the bell rang, we all went back to our classes and our own little cliques. Coolness eluded me. I was never invited to one of Marsh's parties, but for all those that were in on it, 535 Pearl was a high school highlight. In fact, at the forty-fifth reunion, I heard Dudley talking about it as though he had been one of the leaders. I didn't remind him he hadn't even shown up, nor did I ask him about his mother. I had grown too cool for that.

The hard rain and charcoal skies matched my mood. The Green Pea coasted into the driveway just before it died. Even my car had turned against me on this dreary Friday.

It had been announced at the awards assembly that afternoon that four of my high school team mates had been selected to play in the state all-star football game. They also received full-ride football scholarships to the University of Oregon. Outwardly, I smiled and congratulated them like a good sport. Inside, I was insanely jealous. Things couldn't get worse—but they did.

Right after school Trudy announced, "We'll always be friends, but ..." She dumped me to date one of the four scholarship boys.

My angst played out on my transistor radio as Elvis sang about the love he had lost to his best friend giving him a heartache. The King had a way of singing a song like he knew exactly how you were feeling. I felt lower than whale manure in the Mariana Trench. I had no best girl for the summer, no prospect of playing football at the next level, and if things weren't bad enough, I had a zit that looked like a lighthouse beacon right in the middle of my forehead that would surely leave a pock mark at least two inches deep.

Weeks earlier, I had sent letters to every small college where I thought I might be able to play football. After a month of no responses, I still opened the mail box as a matter of habit. There was no longer the excited anticipation like the first few weeks when I was sure someone would immediately respond.

There was one, solitary number-ten envelope inside the box that Friday. We never got mail in business envelopes. Could it be? I yanked it out. The return address said "Linfield College" in purple lettering. There was a cardinal, and purple cartoon face of a wildcat with a purple beanie slanted jauntily on his head.

The envelope was thin, too thin to be good news. It wasn't padded like the ones I had seen my friends get from their chosen schools. John Dirlam's had lots of postage and was filled with pages of forms and instructions from Pacific Lutheran. I had applied there, but they hadn't written back. I even had a letter of reference from Pastor Anderson, but maybe he told them about me sneaking off for ice cream cones.

I took a deep breath and then tore it open. The letter had seven lines. I was afraid to read it all at once. I looked for those key words like "Congratulations," or "It is my pleasure," both sure signs you were in. There were none. I read it with sweaty palms. It was my last chance.

Dear Robert,

Thank you for thinking of Linfield as a choice for your college. If you wish to arrange a visit to the campus please call our office.

Sincerely,

Paul Durham
Head Football Coach

It was a form letter, but the coach had taken the time to write in my name and personally sign it. He must be answering hundreds of letters from marginal players like me. His personal signature could mean only one thing: "He wants me!" I wondered if I would get a full ride like my teammates. What position did he want me to play, fullback or defensive halfback? Who cares? He wants me—bad!

"To heck with you Trudy and scholarship boy, I'm going to Linfield," I exulted in the lifting rain. A few breaks in the clouds refreshed the day as my mood became sunnier. It's funny how your emotions can actually change the weather. The stars had realigned.

I rushed into the house to call coach Durham. My cheap, little radio began to play "Kansas City," but I sang, "I'm going to, Linfield City, Linfield City here I come. They got some crazy little women there, and I'm gonna, get me one ..."

When he graduated from South in 1960, he was a skinny, homely, acne-scarred kid obsessed with the game of football. We called him Freddy Football in high school, because he knew everything there was to know about the pro and college teams. Despite his fanaticism for the game, I gave him zero chance of making any college football team at any level.

The Fred Von Appen that greeted me at Linfield was different. He was wearing his crimson red letterman's jacket with purple and white striping around the cuffs and collar. A large purple L covered most of the left chest. I thought it was an ugly jacket because of the odd color combination, but it attested to his varsity participation in the football program.

"Fred, I hardly recognized you. What happened to you?" I asked, shaking his burly hand.

"I knew I couldn't make the team unless I got some strength, so I bought my own weight set. I've been working out on my own, and I've gained over sixty pounds. I drink brewer's yeast and wheat germ blended with orange juice." It sounded disgusting, but he was living proof of the results. "As you can tell," he said, referring to his large, barrel-chested body, "I'm built for strength, not definition like those pretty-boy body builders."

He had shaved his head bald to show his total devotion to football. He had nothing but disdain for other worldly pleasures, like girls and beer. They interfered with his quest to become a college football player. Through sheer determination, he had willed himself onto the Linfield team. (Fred turned that obsession into two Super Bowl rings as a coach with the Forty-Niners under Bill Walsh.)

He showed me around the campus and introduced me to football players with names like Yosh, Bubbles, Blob, Cactus, and Bull Dog. The majesty of the oak-shaded campus and friendliness of the characters I had met made me want to make the small campus home for the next four years.

"Fergy, the equipment and facilities here aren't as good as we had at South. There are no scholarships, but it's for guys like us." Fred must have known I was hooked. "As far as the studies go, professors are just like Mr. Dedman. Did you have him for English?"

"Yeah, I did, but I got a D. Trudy was in the same class, and I didn't do much studying."

"Well, I know you've had a lot of jobs, and college is just like a job. If you work at your studies eight hours a day, you'll do okay. Have you been accepted yet?"

"Nope. I just got this letter last week and thought I would check it out. I'm not sure I can even afford to come here with a cost of fifteen hundred a year."

"Nobody else here has any money, either, and you don't need a car. It's not like high school, where you've gotta have a car or money. There is no coolness here." I liked what Fred was saying. "People in college like you for who you are and your own abilities, not what your parents give you."

"I'm gonna like that," I said, feeling instant relief from always striving to be cool.

"On this campus, even the jocks aren't anything special. They are at schools like Oregon, but athletes come here because they really want to play a sport. Some high school all-staters come here and think they're going to be God's gift to our football team, but those hot dogs get shaped up pretty fast," Fred said.

That sounded perfect. I liked the way Fred's English had improved since high school. He was more ... "collegiate" would be the word. "That sounds just like what I'm looking for, Fred. What exactly do I need to do at this late date to get accepted and get a football tryout?"

"First, you've got to apply right away. When you talk to coach

Durham, just tell him you don't have any money. Everybody that tries out makes the team. Nobody gets cut, and we all suit up for home games. If you don't make the varsity, you can play in the four or five JV games we have. We had a few guys last year who were seniors who played JV because they were going to be coaches and they wanted the experience. I guarantee you—you'll get your shot if you come here."

I was being reborn! My heart raced faster and I was getting cold chills. I had poured cold water on my dream of ever playing football again to prevent more crushing disappointment. Everything Fred had said created a picture of football redemption. I would get another chance to play. The fire in the belly was back to a roaring flame.

Coach Durham made it clear that all students with financial need can get enough campus jobs to pay for college. "If you are willing to work hard, you'll find enough money to pay for school. You'll appreciate it more if you pay for it yourself," he said

I remembered how much better care I took of the bicycle I had paid for myself. This tall, lanky man with a crew cut made perfect sense.

"After you get accepted, all you have to do is bring your shoes and try out," he said. He must have noticed the look on my face. "You do have shoes, don't you?"

"Well, I used the same pair for three years. They fell apart after the season, but I'll have the summer to earn enough for another pair."

"If you get accepted and you're serious about trying out for football, you'll need a pair to train in over the summer. I'll have the equipment manager get you a pair of shoes. What size do you wear, and when do you think you could pick them up?"

"Our baseball team is playing for the state championship next week, and I'm going up to Portland to see that game. I can come by that Saturday. I wear a size nine and a half."

"Go over and get an application from the registrar's office, get it filled out, and send it back right away. How are your grades?"

"Good enough to get into the state schools, but Fred has set me straight about studying harder."

"Just getting into the state schools isn't saying much. Our average freshman has at least a 3.50 GPA. We tell young people that you should do what is best for you. Do you think you can improve your study habits to succeed at Linfield?"

The interview was no longer fun. What happened to football? "Yes, sir, I know I can. I won't disappoint you in the grade department."

"If you say you'll do it, we consider it done. That's how we work around here. Now go get that application, and I won't forget about the shoes."

It was a far cry from a full-ride, but the exhilaration of getting a "shoe-colarship" engulfed me in a euphoric fog on the way home. On cue, my transistor radio started playing that song again, and I sang along, "I'm going to Linfield City, Linfield City here I come ..."

"Bob, you need to stay after class and talk to me," Señora Anderson said. She was a thin, pretty lady with a deep, raspy voice like Lauren Bacall's. I was glad Spanish was my last class; I wouldn't have time to worry all day about what she wanted. I knew it was about my grades, but how bad could they be?

She got right to the point. "Bob, I've heard that you are thinking about going to college."

"Si, Señora," I said trying for a little levity.

"Well, I checked on your grades. Unless you get a C in my class, you won't even graduate. You won't have a two-point

GPA. Right now, you're getting an F in my class, with no hope of improvement in sight," she said tersely.

Señora Anderson minced no words. She had pureed my future until it looked like a bad liver pâté under a bright light. It was hard to swallow.

"Frankly, I expected you to be failing all of your classes. You've never taken any subject seriously. You don't understand Spanish because you never learned English. You've goofed off your entire life." She wasn't holding back. "But since you are so close to graduating, I'll tell you what I'll do—if you get a C on the final, I'll give you a C for the class, but you're never going to get it without some hard work." It was classic Bacall scolding Bogart about his many faults. "I will work with you every Saturday morning from nine to noon for the next four weeks, but if you're ever late, it's over. Do you think you can do that for once in your life?"

The promise I made to coach Durham about grades was in the back of my mind. "Yes, I'll do it. I just visited Linfield last weekend, and I want to go there, but I didn't know I'd dug myself such a deep hole."

"How could you possibly not know? You've done no work at all in my class. Here's my address," she said, handing me a slip of paper. "My husband is in Spain and a friend will take care of my kids, so there are no excuses for not getting the work done."

She managed to crack a little smile, but ended the conversation by walking behind her desk, leaning forward on both arms, and saying, "Entiendo, Señor Ferguson?"

"Si Señora Anderson. Muchas gracias." I understood her perfectly.

Come Saturday, she had the assignments laid out in a battle plan that could get me a C on the final. In addition to the Saturday work, I would have to turn in all the daily work I had skipped for an entire semester. Nights at the library were now actually nights at the library.

It should not have been such a surprise, but the more I studied, the easier I learned Spanish. I got a C on the final. True to her word, she gave me a C in the class.

John Dirlam and I marched together to "Pomp and Circumstance." I won no awards by graduating 473rd out of 481 students, but I held my head high as I walked across the stage to grab my diploma that was nearly out of reach. Every June when I hear the graduation march, I think of a Spanish angel disguised as an extraordinary teacher and occasionally shout "God bless you, Señora Anderson, wherever you are!"

"It's not what you know, but who you know," Mom liked to say, and for once it worked for me. Uncle Carl Reams, Mom's brother, was president of the local 701 Operator's and Oiler's Union, and he got me in under a summer student program. Operators ran heavy construction equipment and oilers kept the Caterpillars, cranes, and big rock drills gassed, greased, and running. He finagled me a job working on Cougar Dam, up on Blue River. I had to be at work at 5:30 the very next morning after graduation, and it took an hour and a half drive to get there, so I skipped the graduation party. (I mostly regret things I haven't done, and not going to that party is one of them. At our reunions, everyone talks about what a great night that was.)

My job on the dam was to keep a giant rock crusher operating by greasing fittings while the machine was still running. The pay was great: $3.70 an hour base pay, time-and-a-half for anything over an eight-hour shift, and double time for working over a forty-hour week plus $24 a day per diem. We worked fourteen hour days, so from the last couple of hours on Wednesday all the way through Saturday, I was on double time—an amazing $7.40 an hour. At that rate, I was making nearly $500 per week. I would have college paid for in a month!

A rock crusher is the heart of an earthen-dam project. It sits at the bottom of the river between two hills that are being carved away to form the reservoir. Three or four Caterpillars were terraced on the side of the hills. The top Cat pushed its part of the hill down to the next level, where another Cat pushed it down to the next, until the entire hillside ended up in the hopper of the rock crusher. Big rocks went off onto one conveyor belt, small rocks to another and sand was sifted onto still another. The crusher used huge, rubber conveyor belts to carry the rocks and sand to the dump trucks waiting below each belt. The trucks hauled the material to the gaping jaws of the dam, which waited to be filled with the tons of earth, creating a massive berm of dirt. The trucks moved in a continuous stream from daylight to dark, six and sometimes seven days a week. It reminded me of thousands of ants building their hill one grain of dirt at a time.

My job was to grease the joints of this gigantic stone-crushing organ; without grease, the trucks would stop dumping into the fill, the five or six Cats would be idle, and hundreds of men would be stopped if my machine was out of operation. I was woefully under-qualified for such a job, but the pay was terrific! The only mechanical experience I had was fixing bicycles and changing the oil in my car. When I applied for my union license, they asked me if I knew anything about machinery. I recited exactly what Uncle Carl had told me to say: "Yeah, I've done a lot of work on some pretty big farm machinery." That and thirty dollars for dues got me in.

The first day on the job, the operator showed me how to keep it greased. It only needed attention once in the morning and again at noon. The actual work part of the job took very little time. To fight the boredom, I kept busy by shoveling away rocks that had spilled off of the conveyor belts and threw them back onto the machine to get sorted and hauled away. I liked the hard work.

The mountain air was icy cold when I started up the rig in predawn light. By the afternoon, it was hot, dry and dusty. On one of those afternoons, as a driver jumped down from his dump truck, his size-thirteen, hard-toed, calf-high boots raised a cloud of dust around the legs of his badly faded Levis that were held up by wide, red suspenders.

"How do you like your job?" he asked.

"I love it, and it pays well. I need the money for college, so it's perfect."

"Do you want to keep it—college boy?"

Two large, sun-tanned arms jutted out of a sleeveless, sweat stained, white T-shirt. They were attached to a body that was shaped like an oak pickle-barrel and just as stout.

"I'm not in college yet, but I'm working as hard as I can to keep the crusher running."

"We all need money, college boy, so why you keep on doin' all that shovelin'?"

Steel gray eyes with deep crows' feet at the corners peered out from the shadow created by his shiny hard hat. Three days of gray-flecked stubble covered a square jaw that held a lump of something the size of a baseball inside of his right cheek.

"It's my job to keep the rig running, and the rocks keep piling up, so I've got to shovel them away."

"Are you in the Oiler's Union or the Laborer's Union?"

"I'm in the Oiler's Union. Maybe you've heard of my uncle, Carl Reams? He's the president of 701." I thought mentioning my uncle's name might cool his heels a little bit.

"Everybody knows your uncle, and if you don't quite using that shovel, I'll most likely be calling him."

"He told me to work hard and I am, so why would you call him?"

"Because you're an oiler, and you ain't supposed to be shoveling rocks. That's a laborer's job."

"But I don't mind. It makes the day go faster. After we start to work, I only oil the rig at noon and in the evening."

"That ain't the point. If this machine needs a laborer, and you're doing the laborer's job, then you're taking somebody else's job—college boy. Don't let me see you on the end of that idiot stick shovelin' them there rocks. If 'n I do, us Teamsters won't let ya load our rigs."

The brown stream he accurately spat on the ground between my feet told me the bump in his cheek was a chaw of tobacco the size of which only a manly man—which he was—would dare chew.

After lunch, the operator gave me the come-hither sign with his index finger. I climbed the stairs to his perch that overlooked the hopper, conveyor belts, and the entire dam site.

"How come you stopped shovelin' them rocks?" he asked.

"I got chewed out by that truck driver you saw jawin' at me. He said I ain't supposed to be shovelin' them there rocks because it's a laborer's job." I was adopting the local language to shake the college boy image.

"He don't have no authority to tell you what to do, only I do. And I say you keep them there rocks clear because I'm telling you that's part of your job."

This seemed logical to me. I could only hope that the trucker didn't see me "shovelin' them there rocks" again.

The trucks would zip under the conveyor belts to get their loads then rumble off to dump the rocks and sand. They formed a fast-paced, unending line. Then I saw a trucker leaving a gap between him and the loading truck. It was a big gap. The next truck left an even larger space, and every trucker glared at me. I got the message. I quit shoveling and the line went back to normal, but I would soon have to shovel again. I wondered how long the operator and the truckers would play this game with me in the middle.

Late on a Friday, everybody on site was earning double-time. The union safety rules said that the operator must stop the crusher so I could get it greased and oiled. The operator ignored the rules and kept it running while I timidly greased the rollers, belts, and massive steel augers. The last gear I had to grease was back in a tunnel under the hopper, where a cam shaft created a scissor-like action for a gigantic piston that pushed the crushed rocks onto the conveyor belt. I put the grease gun on the fitting and gave the handle a hard squeeze. The tungsten steel nozzle on the end of the rubber pressure hose of the gun flipped up and got caught in between the scissoring arms. With an ear splitting screech the machine came to an instant stop. I ran out of the tunnel, scampered up the stairs, and told the operator what had happened.

"Look at the size of those rocks, boy. You think a little ol' grease gun is going to stop this rig?" I breathed a sigh of relief. It was a coincidence. I thought it was me who had brought the entire dam to a stand-still. It looked like a hundred trucks sitting idle. All over the dam, the Cats stopped shoving dirt because our machine had stopped. The cost per idle minute was in the thousands of dollars. I was glad it couldn't be my fault.

Mechanics climbed all over the rig trying to get it started. Every time they started it up, it screeched with an unearthly noise.

"What did you tell the operator about a grease gun?" the lead mechanic finally asked me after nearly an hour.

"It's not a very big gun; I'll show you where it got stuck." We crawled into the tunnel.

He eyed the problem. "This shouldn't take too long," he said as he placed a big chisel on the wedged nozzle and pounded it with a large maul. "Man, that's tough. I'm not sure I'm man enough to knock it out of there."

"Here, let me give it a try," said another mechanic. This went on until every mechanic had a shot at dislodging the small piece of metal that had pierced the Achilles' heel of the enormous boulder-eater.

A welder finally showed up, and after a fair amount of time amidst smoke and sparks, he emerged from the tunnel with the same cigarette in his mouth that he had used to light his welding torch.

"You melt that gun head out of there, Clem?" asked the project foreman.

"Nope. Wouldn't melt. Had to melt the steel around it and let it drop out."

That fixed the machine, but now there was a noticeably loud "galumph," like rough-edged metal crunching together right where the nozzle had been stuck.

The next day, a field officer from the union came to the site. I was "laid off," which is Unionese for being fired. A phone call from Uncle Carl was the first time I was made aware that I was blessed with extraordinarily good luck.

"Mary, this is Carl and I can't tell you how sorry I am I put Bobby Earl up on that rock crusher," a tearful voice said.

"That's okay, Carl. You shouldn't feel bad about it."

"I can't help it. I feel so responsible for the whole thing," his choked voice said.

"It's really okay. He came back to the union hall right away and they made him the picket captain. He's taking the signs out to the guys on the picket line right now."

"Uh ... er ... What? You mean he wasn't up on that crusher yesterday?"

"Nope. Your union guy brought another oiler to the job and

laid Bobby off before he even started work yesterday. Didn't you send the guy who laid him off?"

"No, I didn't. Why'd he get laid off?" Carl asked with a clearer voice.

Mom told him about the grease gun and how I thought it was dangerous because the operator never shut the machine down when it was time to oil it. There was a long pause on the phone while Uncle Carl absorbed what Mom was saying. "What's wrong, Carl?"

"I thought it was Bobby Earl, but it must have been the kid who took his place that it happened to. I'm going to have that operator's head on a platter, I'll tell you that!"

"What was it that happened?"

"The kid got caught in a conveyor belt and it pretty well sliced him in half and he died right there. He was so new nobody knew his name, but the description sounded just like our Bobby Earl."

After hearing that bad news, the picket line job was even sweeter. I still earned my union wages, they filled my car with gas every day, and my only responsibility was to take a dozen picket signs to four locations in the morning and pick them up in the evening.

As the picket captain, I was only paid for four hours a day, so I worked all I could as an oiler on smaller projects. We didn't get as much overtime on those jobs, but along with being the picket captain, and having worked on the dam for about a month, I had earned enough money for nearly two years of school. That put me well on my way to paying nearly every dollar for my own college education, which has been a life long source of satisfaction.

The road from Eugene to Cougar Dam ran through Nimrod, Finn Rock, and for the family of the kid who was killed, the town of Misery. Uncle Carl did his part; he kicked the operator out of the union. But talk about luck—I may have avoided serious injury because of the guy who put a piece of metal on the end of a grease gun that could stop a rock-crushing Leviathan.

Luck occurs when you can't connect the dots to certain events that add up to extreme good fortune. But more often, it occurs when preparation collides with opportunity.

CHAPTER 5

College years

The die was cast. If I didn't make the team or flunked out, I had only one plan: join the Navy like Larry, Moe, and Scott. I would never return to Eugene as a failure.

The '59 Ford station wagon looked pretty good as it pulled up behind Hewitt Hall on a hot August day in 1961. It's harder for mothers to let go of their children, and Mom cried a little bit, but Dad added some comic relief. When we shook hands, he said, "It's not that I don't hate to see you go, but I just cut my grocery bill in half." That pretty much sums up the emotional side of our family. We loved each other deeply, but we weren't warm, group-hug kind of people.

The second floor of Hewitt was deserted. I was the only football player on the floor. I carried the small family suitcase in one hand, my tanker jacket in the other, and my football shoes were tied by the laces and were slung over my shoulder. It took three minutes to unpack:

2 pairs of Levis
2 Pendelton shirts
2 plaid summer shirts
1 high school football jersey

5 pairs of skivvy briefs
5 J.C. Penny white T-shirts
1 gray workout T-shirt
1 shaving brush in a mug with shaving soap
1 Gillette double edged razor with 1 pack of extra blades
1 conical-shaped bottle of Old Spice aftershave lotion

I surveyed the closet. Three-fourths of the small space was left for whomever my roommate would be. As I walked out of the dorm to head over to the stadium to check out my football gear I met up with a player who would become known as "Sweet Sammy."

After the usual introductions Jim Cannal asked, "Howsh your grades?" he lisped through a freshly missing bottom tooth.

"Not my strong point. And you?"

"I'm gonna schtudy like crazy because I'm going to be a PE teacher and coach."

Cannal seemed to know a lot about Linfield and was convinced by coach Spiegelberg that even though he rarely played on the Medford team, he would eventually be a starter at a small school. Academically he was at my level, but he was convinced he could get good grades. I thought, *If this guy, who talks like a country bumpkin, thinks he can make it, I'll make it easy.* But he did say he'd have to "Schtudy like crazy," and "scho" would I.

Bob Kane, one of my coaches at South, had said "Players in good shape get noticed." So, for the last two weeks of summer I had trained hard every day after work. I wanted to be in shape for the first requirement of practice: the mile run under five minutes and thirty seconds.

Practices were divided into several stations, with each teaching a football fundamental through lots of agility and conditioning. Every practice ended in wind sprints. "We might get beat by a better team, but we will not be beaten by a better conditioned team," coach Durham often said. We all bought into that and barfed in silence. I ran hard, like coach Kane said, and it did get me noticed. I moved up the depth chart.

On the fourth day we suited up in pads. My first contact drill was called the "Meat Grinder." The defensive player stood between two big dummy bags. From five yards away, the offensive player would run at him and try to block him out from between the bags. The offensive players came in rapid-fire succession until he was knocked out from the bags. The first defender between the bags was Hugh Yoshida, a defensive half-back all-American. As quick as a gnat he slipped side to side making the first few blockers look silly. Only the shear numbers of five or six guys nearly at the same time could knock him off balance. (Yoshida went on to become the athletic director at the University of Hawaii. The Yoshida stadium is named in his honor.)

Tom Younker, an all-American defensive end, was less subtle. He ripped the first couple of guys with a forearm to the face mask then clubbed a few more on the back of the helmet until he was overwhelmed by so many bodies he had no chance. It was our favorite drill.

My guy was a smallish half-back that I could easily block out from between the bags. *I'll give him a cross-body block and knock him out right away. After all, I'm from South Eugene,* I thought as I eyed Jack Deines. Apparently, Jack hadn't read my press clippings and didn't know how good I was. As I laid out for a cross-body block, he wound up his forearm. He didn't move. He whacked me right behind the helmet where the ear meets the neck.

"Son, are you alright? Son, are you going to be okay?" Coach Roy Helser was looking down at me through his Ben Franklin spectacles wanting to know how many fingers I saw, where I was, and the other usual stuff one asks a person who's just been cold-cocked.

Like a boxer rising on rubbery legs from an eight count, I staggered to my feet and woozily went to the end of the defensive line for my turn between the bags. I had just learned how effective the forearm shiver could be. *What's good for the goose is good for the gander,* I hazily reasoned.

I had watched Barry Fulman play in the Shriner's All-State game. He was a big tackle from South Salem. He started his charge at me, but before he could get fully extended, I did to him what Deines did to me. I took a step in front of the bags and rocked Barry with a forearm. Blood gushed like a geyser from deep cuts that opened up his left eye socket. He looked like he had been sliced with a razor. My forearm had wedged between his facemask and helmet. I apologized to him as I watched the blood pour out of his helmet onto his jersey. He was a bloody mess, and I was relieved when he said he could see out of the eye.

Coach Helser gave me an "I see you learned something today" kind of look. He knew I felt terrible, and after attending to Barry, he said, "Look, son you can't feel sorry for the guy across from you. That's football."

The all-state player, who was used to pushing other guys around, never played again. His eye injuries healed up in a few weeks, but he had lost his stomach for the game.

After two weeks of daily doubles, I was on the varsity depth chart. I was second as a defensive halfback and fullback, first on the punt team as the lifeguard, the lone guy who stands just in front of the punter and I was on the first kick-off team. Nothing dramatic, but I was on the team.

On Friday afternoon, the last day of daily doubles, a freak

play took place. I got awkwardly tangled up in a block and again dislocated my left shoulder. At the hospital, Dr. Van Zyle announced that I was out for the season. The shoulder would have to be surgically repaired over the Christmas break, but "That's football."

I got out of the hospital on Monday, the day the rest of the freshman arrived. With my arm in a sling I met guys like Ken Lummus, a Bay Area kid with slicked-back hair; Fred Loffer, the son of a barber from the other bay area, Coos Bay; Phil Judson, a preacher's kid; and my roommate, Wayne Carlson from Greeley, Colorado. We were all instant friends and did everything as a fair-sized group. Right away, we claimed ourselves to be the best dorm floor on campus. Our motto became "The boys in Hewitt do it, faster and more efficiently." We made the goofy slogan stick by winning the intramural flag-football championship and a few guys getting 4.0 GPAs.

My freshman year had such an impact on my life that when it came time for our own kids to go to college, the rule was; they could go to any college they selected, but they had to live in the dorm their freshman year.

Freshmen registration meant two days of standing in long lines. We took entrance tests for English and math. I couldn't believe I passed them both with high enough scores to stay out of the preparatory, or "bonehead," courses. Those classes didn't count for college credit, but you had to pay for them just like the other classes.

Fifteen credits was a full load, but you could take sixteen without an extra charge. It seemed like a bargain, so I always took the maximum. Like most freshmen, I started with the required classes: English, Western Civilization, Psychology, Life of Jesus (which I expected to be advanced Sunday school.) I rounded out my schedule with what I thought would be softies like, Speech Fundamentals and Physical Education. In college, there are no

Mickey Mouse classes. All of the courses required a term paper, and in speech, each talk involved almost as much research as a term paper. Every class required reading a ton of books and you were not spoon-fed religion. I got all Cs except in PE and Speech, and eked out a 2.37 GPA. I was ecstatic. I knew I could pass the courses and stay eligible for football.

The football team went on to play in the Camelia Bowl for the national championship in Sacramento. A few of us from the dorm made the trip. It was the farthest I had ever been from Eugene. I loved it. We barely lost the game, but the trip was great.

In the spring, several of us piled into what Lummus called his "chicken-fat yellow" '57 Chevy and went to Tijuana, Mexico. We epitomized the ugly American, or at least college kids gone wild. We have laughed about those stories for years and will continue to do so until we're all gone. A golden oldie song tickles your ear; a favorite old story delights your heart.

On warm spring weekends, trips to the coast became a regular occurrence. I had joined the Theta Chi fraternity, which added to the mix of fun. You can probably guess what happened to my barely-getting-by grades of the first semester. Yup, they dropped to a 2.03 GPA. I was still eligible, but I wasn't proud of the grades.

Mom and Dad didn't say anything about my grades. I was paying the college tab by myself. It was on my shoulders: grades, finances, football, the entire works—I relished it.

The high-paying summer job I was counting on evaporated during the school year. The union did away with their summer student program, so now I was like every college kid out there, scrambling for a job.

One day, while Dad was on a telephone job, he stopped at a

construction sight and asked the foreman if he needed an extra hand. "He said he can always use a hard worker, so you get out there tomorrow and apply," Dad told me.

The foreman was a young, tough man who was trying to get the most from a small job to get promoted to larger projects. It was not a union shop, and I received laborer's pay, which was half of what I had made the summer before. There was no overtime pay, but we worked long hours, so I still made a lot of money.

My main job was being the flagman. This is the worst job I have ever had. Time passed agonizingly slow as I controlled traffic with the stop and slow sign. The sun beat down and my feet got hot while standing on the pavement of the McKenzie River Highway that runs between Eugene and Springfield. That was nothing compared to the boredom that numbed my mind.

During the three weeks I worked on this job, thousands of drivers gave up control of their cars to my sign. They couldn't get by me until I flashed them the "SLOW" sign. The few times the boss gave me other jobs, like jumping into a water-filled ditch and shoveling a blockage away, I couldn't wait to leap into the quagmire. It made me as happy as a pig in mud.

I had no idea how visible being a flagman was until after the job ended. In college, I hitchhiked a lot, and nearly every year, a few people would pick me up and ask, "Weren't you the kid that used to be the flagman up on the McKenzie highway?" That unforeseen fringe benefit of the job got me quite a few rides because people already knew who I was.

The pipeline job ended when the natural gas line was connected to a sawmill that would use the gas for its drying kilns. That's the life of a construction worker: you work yourself right out of a job. Most of the laborers had other jobs lined up, but I needed a job quick.

The next day, I applied at a plywood mill where Mom and Dad said I might have a shot at vacation relief. A friend from their square dance group worked at the company and knew the foreman. This was a sure thing, because "it's not what you know, but who you know."

"I was sent by Duane Williams. My name is Bob Ferguson, and I'm here to apply for your vacation relief job."

The foreman's shirtsleeves were rolled up. He was slightly balding and good looking. He was tanned from working in the yard, filled with energy, and exuded a persona that screamed "I worked my way up, and you can too." He cut a large swath in the mill yard.

"Who told you we had an opening?" he asked.

I must not have said his name distinctly enough. I sharpened my diction because dropping the name of somebody influential was all important. I said, "Duane Williams."

"Who's he?" the foreman asked.

"I, er, uh, er, well, I think he works in the office or something."

"I don't know anybody that works over there. We don't mix much. I get most of my vacation help from the guys who work here inside the mill, but I'm missing a guy who's out sick and I need another man. Can you go to work right now?"

My dictum of "It's not what you know, but who you know" came crashing down. But I became a big believer in being in the right place at the right time. That is something you can personally control. The more you spread yourself around, the more opportunities you will find. I adopted a new motto, "The harder I work, the luckier I get."

"Yes sir, I came ready to work. I've got my hard hat and gloves in the car."

"You don't need the hard hat. Go fill out the application in the office and I'll show you how to feed the dryer. You married?"

"No, I'm going to college and need to pay my own way."

"We've got a couple other college kids here. I get a little

pressure from the owner. He's a big Oregon Duck football fan. You play football?"

"Not at Oregon. I go to Linfield College, but I do play football."

"What school is that?"

"Linfield. It's just a small school."

I don't know why, I was proud of my school and our football team, but I half apologized for not playing in a big-time program.

"The kid you're filling in for today goes to Oregon. He's already got a full ride from the school and doesn't really need this job, but we need to get the work done here in the plant. I'm feeding the dryer myself; I'm filling in for him. So you got a full ride?"

"No, our school can't give athletic scholarships. They gave me a pair of shoes and some jobs during the year, but I need to make as much money as I can during the summer."

"Can you work a double shift today?"

"I'll work any shift you want, and I'll be here every day. I need the cash."

"We're not union, and you won't get paid any time-and-a-half. Still interested?"

"You bet," I said.

"Good, because if you do what you say, you'll make enough money for school, but if you put me back to feedin' the dryer by callin' in sick or something, you'll be out of here like this Oregon kid who's going to be gone as soon as I can get to a phone. I don't care how good a ball player anyone is. I've got a mill to run."

The goal of paying for college myself was still within reach; all I had to do was work hard. Come to think of it, that's how any of us reach our goals.

The blue-collar mill workers were a hard-working and hard-playing bunch. They could have cared less if you were a football player. They wanted the work done on their shift because their jobs were tied directly to the profitability of the mill. My hard-working, laborer attitude fit in well, but they liked to call me "college boy." It was part sarcasm, but I think it was part envy.

They ran crap games, played poker, and held cockfights, but arm wrestling was one of their more bizarre betting sports.

"Hey, college boy, get in here on the arm wrestling match." I did all I could to avoid the situation. This was a no-win situation for me. If I won, I would hurt the image of the mill champ. If I didn't join in, I would be seen as a college kid who thinks he's too good for the mill games.

Some bets reached twenty dollars. This was big money. These guys would have to work a full day to cover their bet. If I won or lost, people were still going to lose hard earned cash. I was trapped. Looking at the size of the biceps on my opponent, I didn't see how anybody could bet against him. He was as shocked as I was when his arm hit the table. He demanded a rematch. The odds shifted in my favor. Two matches were for money, the third for fun. He lost all three. The mood was more somber than a funeral parlor as they slumped back to work. The champ had been beaten by a snot-nosed college kid.

The work was boring and the summer long, but my last day of working at the mill finally arrived. I pulled into the parking lot for the day shift. As we stood in line to get our pay cards punched at the time clock, there was a buzz. Winks and nods were exchanged. I had no idea what it was all about. At noon, I was ambushed. A final arm wrestling contest was a must. This time, all the odds and bets were in my favor. Another no-win situation, but I was going to be gone after the shift was over so I didn't care. *Slap* went the back of my hand as it hit the table.

"I've been practicing twice a day, every day, against a post, so I knew I could beat you," the champ said. "Wanna go again?"

"Nope. You're the champ and you beat me too easily. I guess I should have practiced."

Those that lost money on the first match got their revenge, the champ had earned his status back, and for a day I could withstand the taunts of, "How you gonna play football with those wimpy arms, college boy?" They would be laughing about my defeat for days, maybe months, but I would be back on campus and they would still be at the mill, with no other job in sight.

My daughter Rachel had a full-ride scholarship for basketball and one day she whined, "Why do I have to work during the summer when my school is paid for?"

"Because you'll need extra money," I lied.

After looking hard for a job, she ended up doing the dirty work of restoring burned out properties. She realized that this was the best-paying job a young person with no education could get. She returned to school with a new appreciation for the value of a college degree. She learned for herself what I preached: "The summer job is part of a college education; you learn what you might be doing the rest of your life if you don't graduate."

I learned that self-realization is a better educator than a thousand sermons.

After sitting out the previous season I would have to compete for a position on the '62 football team like any other freshman. After a decent showing in daily doubles I played on special teams, but wasn't able to beat out anyone for a starting position, but when guys got hurt, I filled in. The first four games, the coach started me at four different positions. I started at defensive halfback, then a game or two at fullback, one game at defensive end, and one at linebacker. It helped to be versatile. I started every game, but never did win a permanent slot.

We were conference champions, but there was no playoff system to go to a bowl. A team had to be undefeated and untied to get invited to the NAIA championship round. We had one of each to larger NCAA schools, but they still counted against our record. Only four teams out of nearly 300 schools would get invited to the playoffs. I had a solid season, but nothing stellar.

After a great freshman year in Hewitt Hall, Fred Loffer, Jim Hogue, and I had decided to room together in a tiny room at the Theta Chi Fraternity house. Hogue was a clothes horse, and he took up seven-eighths of the closet. Fred and I shared the six hangers that were left, but we needed only four for our few threads.

The bunks were old military spring-style stacked three high. Being a light sleeper, I wondered if I would get any sleep. After practice, I was bushed, and trying to study without falling asleep was tough. I studied more during the hours between classes, and as my study habits improved, so did my grades. I began to enjoy the academic side of college. Learning became fun.

The house was noisy, and it was impossible for me to sleep at night. I needed to figure out how to get back to the dorm. I had been trying to get Babe Edman to come to Linfield for some time. His parents wanted him to go to college, but he knew he could work in the family furniture store and do very well without a degree. His motivation for college was zero.

Babe could have been an outstanding athlete. He could hit a Whiffle ball better than any of us and he had a soft shooting touch with a basketball, but he excelled when it came to field goals with a football. During high school, we made a goal post about half the size of a real one by putting up a stick on each end of his sister's swing set. He could consistently split those narrow uprights at thirty yards, which was outstanding for a high school kicker, but he never turned out because he didn't want to do "all of the running and other football stuff."

Babe's parents cajoled him into applying to Linfield, and he was accepted. I told him if he got in, I would room with him. It was an easy way for me to get some sleep by moving out of the frat house. After the Christmas break, I was back on second floor Hewitt rooming with Babe, but nobody from my freshman year was still there—life had moved on, as it always does.

After only two weeks on campus, Babe skipped Friday's classes and went home to bowl in a tournament. Bowling had taken over his life. In high school, he had won a local TV tournament that lasted several weeks and he was dubbed a "teenage bowling sensation." He was hooked on bowling. When he realized that in college just a few missed classes and assignments means failing grades, he gave up on school and spent all of his time at the lanes. He left school before the semester ended and flunked out with a zero GPA.

To raise money for his bowling habit, Babe had sold his golf clubs to other students in the dorm. When his dad, Lloyd Senior, came to pick up all his gear, he asked me to "round up everybody that's got the clubs and I'll pay them off." Babe has the lovable personality of a panda bear, and nobody has ever been able to stay angry with him past a nanosecond. So it was no surprise when Mr. Edman said, "You know Bob, this is the third time I've bought this set of clubs."

All the clubs were retrieved except for the woods. Walt Edmonds wouldn't sell them back.

"Mr. Edman, I sold the woods to my set and can't get them back. A deal is a deal and Babe needs to learn some consequences."

Walt graduated in three years and is an appellate judge in Oregon. He had the makings of a judge way back then—hard, but fair. Babe had the makings of a good business person even without a degree. He has taken the family store to new heights and new locations and, no surprise here, he is nearly a scratch golfer.

Bob Ferguson, see Coach Durham read the note posted on the outside of the coach's office. It was an effective method of communicating with his players. Word would get around, and a player never failed to get the message. We checked the board every day.

"McMinnville needs a director for their park program this summer. Are you interested? It probably won't pay too much, but it would look good on your resume," coach Durham said.

I had taken his "Recreation Management" class that semester. The class was basically read a book about recreation management, discuss it, and then write a short paper. Dennis Vitale, aka, The Blob, our halfback from Seaside, was taking it because he needed an easy grade to stay eligible for football. I was taking it to learn all I could about recreation programs in general because I wanted to be a camp director. The book had only a few ideas for summer camps, but was chocked full of ideas about park programs. My term paper project was designing a daily park program, so I had part of the job already done.

The mill foreman had already told me he would hire me again, but "vacation dryer feeder" would do nothing to jazz up a resume. The title of Park Director would make it sing. My life after college had direction and purpose; now I could add some experience. I mulled it over for an entire fraction of a millisecond before I said, "How do I apply for the job?"

"You're a little young at twenty years old, but Paul Durham thinks you can do the job," said Joe Dancer, the city manager.

"I've had lots of experience as a camp counselor. I took coach Durham's 'Recreation Management' class, where I designed an entire park program. I would love to have the job, but how much does it pay?"

"Two hundred and fifty dollars."

"Per month?"

"No, for the summer." His answer flattened my swelling exuberance.

"Boy, I'd love to take the job, but school costs so much. I don't think I can take it. What does the job entail?"

"There're several parts to the job. The main job is running the park program from noon to five every weekday."

"Well, maybe I can get a job in the morning and after the park closes."

"Another element of the job is running the men's softball program on Tuesday and Thursday nights. That also includes lining the field and umpiring the games."

"Wow, that's a lot of work for only two hundred and fifty dollars for the whole summer." I thought, *He's trying to take advantage of a twenty-year-old who desperately wants the job. I'll send up a trial balloon.* I responded, "I'm sorry, but I've got to figure out how to pay for school, so I don't think I'll be able to take it unless you can pay more money."

"I'm sorry too, but that's all we've got in the budget." My trial balloon had fallen faster than the Hindenburg. But he went on: "There's another $250 dollars, but we will pay that to your assistant. She also has to run the tennis lessons twice a week in the evening while you run the softball program."

I'd have an assistant? That's another resume point, I thought.

"I've already hired her. Do you want the job or not?"

Negotiations were over—I lost.

I did some quick math. It was easy; the numbers were small. After I paid for room and board during the summer, there wouldn't be a plug nickel left for school. I still had some money left over from my well paying jobs of previous summers. I would have to cobble together some other jobs and see if I had enough cash to cover the money pit called tuition, books, and fees. Those costs were fixed, but room and board I could do something about.

"Yes, I'll take it," I said, trying not to sound too eager.

This opportunity was too good to pass up. It meant less money now, but this resume title plus supervising an employee would mean more money later.

"Fill out this application and bring it back," he said.

"Can I fill it out while I'm here? It's a long walk to the dorm I live in."

"I thought all college kids have cars these days. You can borrow the city pickup to get the equipment to the park and the lock-box at the ball field, but you'll need to get there on your own after that. Come and see me the day before the park opens and I'll arrange it."

How was I going to find a place to stay and eat for nothing? I convinced a couple of my fraternity brothers that I should be able to stay in the frat house over the summer in exchange for replanting the humongous, weed infested lawn. They agreed to bring it up at the next meeting.

With the housing problem almost out of the way, I had to get my meals free. I stuck my head inside coach's office door that was almost always open, "Coach, can I see you for a few minutes?"

"Fergy, I'll take your case right now," coach Durham said

"Coach, I got the park job, but it pays so little I'll be struggling to pay tuition next fall. If I had a job where I could work for my meals this summer, I can make it with some extra work after the football season."

"Go see Milt Robbins at the hospital. He might be able to help you out." He cordially waved me out of his office as he picked up the phone and began dialing.

Milt was a Linfield alum and the administrator for the two

hospitals in McMinnville. He had been quite an athlete in his day and was always getting jobs for athletes. He set me up. For three meals a day, I would mop three floors of the hospital four days a week, and one day a week I would mow and edge the lawn. The breakfast was good and the cook would even fry me up four or five eggs any way I liked them. I stoked up on breakfast because lunch and dinner were the epitome of institutional food, but I had the basics covered and I got all the milk I wanted.

Getting to live at the frat house for nothing became tricky. I found out how bloodthirsty some of the so-called "brothers" could be at the meeting discussing my proposition. Especially if they had money, they thought I should pay the usual thirty-five dollar monthly rent. Some thought I should put in the lawn and still pay some money. I was going to be the only person staying at the house, and I should have suggested I would housesit for the safety of the frat. One of the brothers even said I was taking advantage of the fraternity.

"Okay, forget it," I said at the meeting trying to avoid any-more hard feelings. "I'll make the same offer to one of the other houses. I need a place to live, and being brothers and all ..."

"I can't believe I'm hearing all this," Fred, my old roommate, said. "A brother needs a place to live, he's willing to do what none of us are willing to do, and we're giving him a hard time." Fred was a natural leader, and he showed off his powers of persuasion. "This lawn will need to be tilled up, raked, tilled again, leveled with a roller, planted, watered, and tended to all summer. As the house manager, I checked into what it would cost to replace the lawn, and we don't have enough money. Fergy only wants a place to sleep, which costs us nothing."

He carried the day. The vote was unanimous. But I should have listened to Fred tell what it would take to put in that gigantic lawn. It was harder work than I ever imagined it could be.

The food at the hospital was marginal, and I skipped lots

of meals. In the end, I would have been better off getting one good, part-time job and pay for room and board elsewhere. The work would have been easier and the food better, but we have to accept the decisions we make and work through them. It was temporary. Milt and the coach had gone to bat for me. I had to follow through.

A pearl of wisdom I heard somewhere says, "If it doesn't kill you, it will make you stronger," but who in the heck wants to keep testing that theory? It's like "Hitting yourself in the head with a hammer—it feels so good when you stop."

My schedule for the summer of 1963 would be:

AM

06:30 — Go six blocks from the Theta Chi house to the hospital for breakfast, then hustle a quarter mile over to campus

07:30 – 9:00 — Geology class, then grab a donut and coffee at Riley student center

10:00 –11:45 — Trek over to the hospital to mop floors and eat lunch, then dash the quarter mile to the McMinnville City Park

PM

12:00 – 5:00 — Run the park program and hustle back to the hospital for dinner

5:30 – 11:30 — Get to the softball field a mile or two north of town on Tuesdays and Thursdays, chalk the field and umpire three games a night. On my off nights, I would study for geology and work on projects for an arts and crafts class I was also taking.

The logistics were daunting; a car was out of the question, but a solution presented itself. Steve Richardson was a wealthy Seattle kid. He had just graduated and was leaving for Naval Officer's Training School. He owned the classiest bike I had ever seen, a ten-speed Schwinn Continental. We had been good friends, so he sold it to me for a pittance of what it cost. That bike propelled me all over town with twin benefits: I got everywhere quickly and my calves and thighs became the strongest they had ever been, which would be great for football.

A lot of people thought Steve was a snob because he was outspoken about athletes who had the "jock" mentality of thinking that crudeness should pass for humor. He reminded me of Cary Grant and was the first true gentleman I had ever met.

Later that summer, a group of us went up to his wedding at a big Seattle church and a reception at a golf course. It was by far the most splendiferous occasion any of us had ever attended. True to our frat-boy form, we swilled expensive champagne like it was beer, ate our first caviar, and wolfed down little sandwiches like it was our last meal. The sit-down dinner, orchestra, and toasts were superb, and Steve looked like an English nobleman.

Steve breezed through Naval Officers Training and became a jet pilot. It was about a year after attending that spectacular wedding that we got bad news at the frat house. The cable slinging his F-8E "Crusader" off the deck of an aircraft carrier snapped and his plane slid off the end. The massive ship could not stop, causing his death. His body was not recoverable. I can only imagine the heartbreak the loss of such a stellar young man must have brought to the doorstep of his parents and young wife. The Vietnam War had now hit home with full force.

The bike that Steve sold to me at way below its value made it possible for me to get a great job and have a fantastic summer. He is still remembered by me and all who knew him.

"Are you rich?" the park kids asked. They had never seen a bicycle like mine.

"No, but I've always been lucky. That's how I got this job at the park."

"What will we be doing?" tiny Suzy Lyons asked.

"Well, I see you have a dog, so on Friday, why don't we have a pet day? Everybody can bring their pets, and we'll decorate them for a parade, and we'll have prizes."

This idea was lifted directly from the textbook for the recreation class. It was the first direct link between the real world and my education. The parade boasted several dogs of various sizes, a kitten in a wagon, a turtle, two mice and crepe papered bikes.

My assistant, Sharon Price, was a PE teacher who had just graduated from Oregon State and knew nothing about recreation, but it wasn't "rocket science." The program was ours to design from the ground up, with neither guidance nor interference from the city fathers. Kids poured their energy into baseball, checkers, chess, songs, nature hikes, darts, box hockey and plain old play. It was the perfect first job for a resume, but there was a continuous nagging thought: *How am I going to get enough money to pay for school?*

Mr. Dancer hadn't told me that running the softball program also included recruiting the sponsors for the teams. That was another huge slice of time for such a miniscule salary. But with my stumblebum luck, it turned out to be a great plus. I met a lot of business owners in town, and for the rest my college years, occasionally one of them would call me for a well-paying odd job. They knew they would get their money's worth.

Umpiring the games was a nightmare. I wasn't very good at it, and after a few weeks, riots were nearly breaking out. I learned a few new cuss words, and a lot of adjectives were uttered to describe my eyesight. Enough! I came up with a solution: each team would take turns umpiring games. If they didn't, their team would forfeit. That rule immediately smoothed things out. As a twenty-year-old college kid, I had learned one rule about solving problems: put the complainers in charge of the things they complain about.

A college friend, Dick Withnell (now the "Car King" of Oregon,) was working as an intern at the newspaper. He took a lot of pictures at the softball games and featured our park event days along with a small article in the *News Register*. The stories had mothers from all over town bringing their kids to our program. The park bustled with activity every day.

I was a part of the community. People would wave as they saw me riding my bike from one job to another. I invited several boys from the park to stay at the Theta house. They brought sleeping bags and pillows, and I brought candy from the park. They seemed to have a lot of fun.

In mid-summer, I had a short fling with Vicki Bergren. She worked in the deli department of the supermarket her dad owned. I was totally infatuated—with her deli skills. She was a nice girl, but extraordinary at making sandwiches with meat, cheeses, and breads I had never heard of. To me, cheese was Velveeta, something my brother and I occasionally used for fish bait. She romanced me with such gastronomical delights as pumpernickel bread slathered in mayo, piled high with pastrami, and topped with exotic cheeses from the Netherlands. We enjoyed each other's company, but were only mildly romantically involved. I never had to pay for the delectable lunches she put together. She believed in the old adage, "The way to a man's heart is through his stomach." I did all I could to support her belief. Her creations were a welcome break from the drab hospital food.

Nearing summer's end, after geology class, Ken Lummus and I walked into the small student union one day to find several people staring at me, winking and whispering, to each other. One was a married graduate student in my arts and crafts class. We hadn't said too much to each other during the class, so I wondered what was going on. Sitting in a short-backed wooden booth next to them was a well-dressed, pretty girl reading the *Linfield Review*. She didn't even look up. Ever since we had been freshman together in Hewitt Hall, Ken and I never missed an opportunity to make a pass at a lone girl. We moved our donuts to her table.

She was the sister of Judy Harrison, the married student in my arts and crafts class, and she would be coming to Linfield in the fall. By the end of the conversation, I had made a date to see her that night after the softball games. Her nickname was Arty, which we thought was a strange name for a girl.

I turned off the field lights, hopped on my bike, and rode several miles to a trailer court out on Three Mile Lane where Arty was staying a few days with her sister.

"Is Arty home?" I had trouble saying her boyish sounding name, but she was no boy.

"Ardis has already gone to bed, and you can't come in this late," Judy said.

"I've ridden a long way, and she knew I would be late because I run the softball program."

"It's too late for me, and I would have to chaperone you, so that's that."

You bet your sweet bippy that's that! She's off my list for good. What kind of name is Ardis anyway? I thought.

She drove her sister's big, black Buick Wildcat convertible and wore her hair piled high in a stylish beehive look. Her white pearlized sunglasses contrasted with her tanned skin. When she stepped out of the car wearing a white blouse over a flowered turquoise bikini, she had everybody's attention, including mine, and she knew it. I let her back onto my list. Ardis now seemed like a wonderful name for a pretty girl.

The McMinnville City Park was shady, but she found a spot where the rays of the sun beamed down on her tan body like a Greek sun goddess directing the rays to her luscious form. I ogled her from afar. The kids wanted to know if she was my girlfriend. "Not yet," I told them. She strolled over to the snack shack to buy a candy bar. All eyes were on her—and me, as I gave her some change for a Coke.

"I'm sorry about last night. My sister thinks she still has to baby-sit me," Ardi said.

"That's okay. I like real long bike rides late at night." She had me mesmerized.

It was Friday night, and there were no softball games, so Ardi picked me up at the frat house in her sister's fancy car. Vicki had stashed a delectable corned beef sandwich in the fridge for me, so I brought it along. We drove out Baker Creek Road and found a sparking spot. We shared that delicious morsel using the hood of the car as a table. Ardi broke an awkward silence, she fluttered her eyelashes and said, "You make a great sandwich."

Now was no time to lie, so I said "Thank you." It was a warm summer night, and the radio was on a top-tunes station. As we kissed, The Platters sang their classic, "One starry night we fell in love ..."

During the first week of the park program, Sharon and I could see that we could make a little extra money by selling candy and pop. I stopped in at Mr. Dancer's office and asked if the city would loan us forty dollars to get it started. We could split the profits. He sternly lectured me about city funds and the total impropriety of such an arrangement.

Sharon and I put up our own money to buy the first forty-dollar load of pop for the Coke machine. We already had a burgeoning business selling the candy I bought at wholesale from Vicki's dad. The machine added a lot more business. The small equipment shed had a plywood window that could be raised up to create a candy store. We gave the kids a candy bar and a pop to run the "snack shack." The kids signed up days in advance to run the snack shack; for a few of them, it was a special treat to get a few sweets. We gave away a candy bar to the finder of the softball in the tall weeds or the chess piece that went missing in a pile of games. We never lost a single piece of equipment. We thought the small enterprise was a great addition to the park program—until the day we went to turn in the park gear.

"I understand you made quite a bit of money from the candy and pop machine," said a grim-looking city administrator whom I had never met and who failed to introduce himself.

"We did make some money, and we are splitting it," I said.

"And you made this money on city property on city time?" he asked.

"We never looked at it like that I guess, but that would be true."

"Then you'll have to give that money to the city, where it rightfully belongs."

Sharon and I stared in shock at each other. We had made well over $600, and I was counting on my three hundred for school. It was obvious we were being legally mugged by someone who was sitting in Mr. Dancer's office chair.

"Have we broken some sort of law?" I thought it was odd the bullying stranger didn't tell us his name.

"Well no, but it's the principle of the thing. That money was made by city employees on city property," he said.

"There is another principle here as well."

I remembered Walt Edmond's words when he kept Babe's golf clubs: "a deal is a deal."

"I asked Mr. Dancer at the start of the summer if the city would loan us the money to get it started and split the profits. He said that wouldn't be appropriate, so we put up our own forty dollars and got the machine installed. We took all the risk because we only made money if all of the bottles got returned." I felt the back of my neck getting hot. "Now you want all of the money without putting up a nickel?"

"Legally, it belongs to the city," he said.

"We also gave away a lot of pop and candy to the kids working the snack shack, or for finding lost softballs and other equipment. We didn't even lose a piece to a jigsaw puzzle."

I paused and took a deep breath. I didn't feel we should give an inch. He didn't respond after my pause, so I continued. "We made most of this money in the evenings and on weekends when people would come down to the park to picnic. We gave the kids treats to clean up the mess left by all of those people." He was unmoved by our generosity to the kids. I gathered steam. "We were only paid $250 each, and you knew you underpaid us. I'm sure you read about some of our successful events in the newspaper." I rehearsed in my own mind what I would say next. "I can't speak for Sharon, but unless you can show us that we have broken the law, then I'm keeping my part of the money because I need it for tuition."

"I'm with Bob!" Sharon said.

Mr. Dancer walked into his office and the stranger arose from Mr. Dancer's chair.

"They don't want to give the money back," the tough guy said.

"Theoretically, it should be city money, but we don't have any way to force them to give it up," Mr. Dancer said.

We had them. "We really enjoyed the park program, and I'm

sorry this has become an issue. I'll have the pop man take the machine out right away."

"No, no, I heard what you said about the machine being used on weekends. If the citizens enjoy it, there's no need to take it out." He turned and spoke to the grump. "I think they showed us how to make a little extra cash, and this is the first time we didn't lose a bunch of equipment. As far as I know, the kids were the only ones keeping the park clean. Those newspaper articles created a lot of good will in the community. I think it's okay for them to keep the money."

I grew braver. "Well, we still own the forty dollars worth of pop in the machine, so we'll need to be reimbursed for that. I'll have the Coke man stop by for you to sign on for the machine."

Mr. Dancer took out a cash box and handed each of us a twenty dollar bill. That small victory taught me a lesson: when you are right, stick to your guns, even against city hall.

Over the decades, Ardi and I have visited that little park where our romance blossomed. We drink a Coke from a machine that dispenses cans and still makes the city money. We listen to our Platters tape playing "One starry night we fell in love ..." and I remember in detail the two-piece swimsuit. On one such visit, she asked me that universal question that all wives eventually ask their husbands at three thirty in the morning. (I can assure all of you women out there that you will get a better response from any question while your hubby is enjoying a plate of bacon and eggs cooked to his liking rather than in the middle of the night.)

"Dear," she says. "If I die ..." Wives always pause at this point because it is such a sensitive subject. "Will you make those corned beef sandwiches for our friends who come to my service?"

Football is a friendly engagement in a war that delivers an

exhilarating high. The feeling of contact that comes from hitting someone head-on heightens the survival instincts. It is probably close to the tribal urge to enforce your will upon another tribe, with each person doing his specific job in unison with the others. Tribal instinct or not, I couldn't get enough of it. There were no scholarships, fame, or professional football prospects. Nobody ever said it, but it was understood, "love the game or go home."

I am hardly unique when I say that I would trade a lot of tomorrows for another game day. The wife of a football coach once asked her husband, "Do you love me more than you love football?" That question is right up there with, "Does this dress make me look fat?" He knew he was on thin ice when he answered, "No—but I love you more than I love basketball."

Every year the sweet smell of new-mown grass rattles my old bones with the desire to start daily doubles. I relive the hope for a national title like I had back in '63. We thought we could run the table and make it to the playoffs. Being the second-leading scorer in '62 and scoring the only touchdown in a six-to-zero game, I was the heir apparent to the starting fullback position. I had worked on evading tacklers and dreamed about continuing my record of never getting thrown for a loss. It was my time to shine at fullback. I couldn't wait for practice to start.

Bill Smith, an all-American junior college transfer, won the mile run going away. When we started running offensive plays without pads, I was stunned and incredibly hurt. Smith started on the first team without so much as having run a contact drill. He had been handed my position without beating me out. I was devastated and humiliated in front of my peers. Strangely, even though I would be relegated to the second team for at least two years, the thought of quitting never entered my mind. But I wanted to bawl like a baby, loud and hard.

In the long run, he did me a favor. I hurt my knee and lost a lot of lateral movement. Like the year before, coach Durham tried me at a lot of positions—linebacker, defensive end, defensive halfback, and safety—but there was always someone who was better. Mid-season, against Lewis and Clark, coach Durham started me at the middle-guard position. The light turned on. I learned to read the offenses and could react faster than any opponent could move. My stumblebum luck had not deserted me.

We didn't make it to the national playoffs like we thought we would. We played one game literally during a hurricane; we tied, six to six. Then we were beaten by a much larger NCAA Division II team, which knocked us out of post-season play. I was as disappointed about not getting to play a few more games as I was about losing our national ranking.

On campus, Ardi and I were an item. She loved to watch the football games. She never saw me play fullback, so I never mentioned my huge disappointment. Besides, I garnered lineman of the week for twenty-one tackles against Willamette University. After playing only half the season at middle guard, I still led the team in tackles. Life was superb.

The spring semester of '64, I joined another team—the speech team. The speech club traveled more often and in better style than any sports team. I had taken all of the speech classes I could, so Professor Craig Singletary said I could join the debate team the second half of the year.

I focused on Lincoln-Douglas debate and impromptu speeches. Roy Gronquist was my debate partner. While I played football, he attended all of the debate meetings to put together the pro and con sides to the debate topic, which that year was capital punishment. It took a lot of research to develop a good argument. Every two-person debate team had a debate box jammed with three by five index cards that had quotes from books, magazines, and news papers. We dove into the box of massive information carried by a team of two girls who went on to beat Harvard to win first place in the Women's National Debate Tournament.

Building the debate argument was a cooperative effort of the entire team, so borrowing their information was not plagiarism. We had their same material, but our skills didn't get us close to winning a tournament. We were amateurs against experts. By the time we started debating, all of the other college teams had been at it for an entire semester. One of my regrets is that I debated for only two years. It was easily one of the most useful activities in which I ever participated.

On road trips we had grand pinochle games, and Professor Singletary didn't mind that Gronquist and I piggybacked on the work that others had done. Doctor Singletary was inducted into the Linfield Hall of Fame for his service of forty-five years as the PA announcer for football games. I was one of the five speakers at Coach Durham's funeral service. Afterwards Craig came up to me and said, "That's one of your better ones. I'm giving you an A plus."

"The park program was so successful last summer that Mr. Curt Ramsey, a professional in the field of recreation, has been hired as the new director. His salary will be $3,000 dollars for the summer, which begins the Monday after the last day of school."

The *News Register* article was a slap in the face to Sharon and me. But we had the satisfaction of knowing that no matter how much he got paid, he would have a tough act to follow. To this day, I run into kids from that program who remember the little ribbon they got from a Friday special event. At a Linfield football game a few years ago, a middle-aged man said to me, "You may not remember me, but you made me and a lot of other kids love Linfield." As a matter of fact, I didn't remember him, until he said his name. "I'm Mark McCaully. You let a bunch of us kids stay at the Theta Chi house one weekend."

"It was fun having you kids over. What are they all doing these days?"

"The Lyons boys went on to play college baseball, and Gary even played on a national championship softball team a few years ago. They own the Lyons vending company in Tualatin." I knew of the multi-million dollar company, but didn't know it was run by the Lyons kids from the park.

"I've just come back from Colorado," Mark went on, "and I'm going to be their office manager. They have taken care of their parents and the other eight children." Then he said something that pleasantly surprised me. "All of us kids at the house that night have kept in touch. When we get together, we talk about how fun that summer was and how boring the park program was the summer after you left. Not even a pet parade."

That puffed me up for a week. I had always wondered how the "professional in recreation" had fared. Now I knew. The amateurs had done pretty well—for amateurs.

With the park job unavailable, I began applying for summer jobs that would pay a decent wage, look good on the resume, and afford a cheap to no-cost living situation. I landed a job at Luther Burbank School for Boys. The school was on Mercer Island, just east of Seattle, right on the edge of Lake Washington. The job title was impressive, Group Life Supervisor. This meant I would be in charge of juvenile delinquents who lived in a "cottage," a euphemism for a dilapidated Tudor mansion with a dormitory-type sleeping porch.

I sold my bike to one of the frat brothers who thought I should have paid to stay at the house. Since he thought everybody had plenty of money, I jacked the price up way above what I had paid for it. I bought a cheap DKW motorcycle that had over 100,000 miles on it. It had a small sturdy engine, looked like a BMW bike, and got sixty miles to the gallon. It would do, but now I had to figure out where to stay.

Ardi and I were pretty serious and wanted to see each other over the summer. She would be living at the Erikson's beach house on Samish Island, an hour and a half north of Seattle and working in a cannery. Her dad would be working the night shift on the Seattle Monorail and tending to his candy vending route during the day so their Seattle house would be empty most of the time. I would use the spare bedroom in the basement. It was agreed that I would paint the house and mow the lawn for rent, but I would have to figure out my own meals. It was perfect because I would get at least one meal a day at the school, and usually two.

I felt like one of the Hell's Angels Motorcycle Club riding that bike on the freeway up to Seattle. My hair blew in the wind; I looked cool, but I was scared to death. How can you tell if a motorcyclist is happy? By the bugs in his teeth. That was me, but it wasn't the bugs that got to me, it was the constant, pelting rain. It rained twenty-nine straight days in June, and it seemed like that much in July.

The do-gooder stuff I had learned in college sociology classes didn't seem to change the behavior of delinquent kids. Firm discipline, to the point of rudeness, seemed to be most effective. It wasn't lost on me that many on the staff were ex-military sergeants with command voices. Some of the kids were eighteen while I was only twenty–one, so I had to act a lot older. Unlike at camp or the park, I had to be a disciplinarian. There were a few scuffles, but nothing serious.

My main job was to make sure they got up in the morning, were tucked in bed at night, and ate three square meals in between. With my park and camp experience, I was the supervisor selected to take the kids to recreation venues around Seattle. That was fun. We went to Sea Fair, movies, Golden Gate Park, Barnum and Bailey Circus, and every other activity that came to town.

We created a few activities of our own, like a camping trip. It would be just me taking eight kids camping for four days. Two of them were older kids and one was in for killing his parents. I wasn't sure I wanted to do this, but I was the logical choice, and I would get four paid days off in return, something they called "compensatory" time off.

"Okay, Manuel, here's the deal. You're the oldest and the biggest, and you're the one that wants to go camping more than anyone else." I was using a piece of advice I had learned from one of the other counselors: use the cottage bully to your advantage. "It's going to be your job to keep everyone else in line, or we turn around immediately and come back to the cottage. Are you okay with that?" I said.

"Yes, as long as I don't get blamed for everything."

"You won't, but this can be a lot of fun if we keep everybody out of trouble."

That bit of strategy paid off. We had three days of hiking, roasting marshmallows, and telling stories around the fire like any other youth group. We had two large tents. No way was I going to sleep in a tent with these kids. That temptation might prove too much for them to handle. They crowded into one while I put obstacles in front of my door to discourage a sound beating if they should get an odd notion. I smelled cigarette smoke the first night and yelled at them to put the smokes out or we'd be going back to the cottage in the middle of the night. I didn't smell it again—Manuel knew I meant it. He took charge of the cigs.

After three days of fun, I felt very smug about my ability to cajole eight delinquents into getting along together without any bullying. I woke up the fourth day, ready to break camp. I stepped out of the tent and was jolted wide awake. The van and the kids were gone! The headlines raced across my mind: "Irresponsible Supervisor Lets Kids Escape." But was I irresponsible? The keys were in my pocket. The little buggers had picked the lock, hot-wired it, rolled it down the hill so I wouldn't hear it start, and left—without me!

I flagged down a man in a passing car and explained my rather awkward situation. He agreed to drop me off at the nearest phone. A few miles down the road, I spotted the van at a swimming hole the kids had wanted to stop at on the first day. It was a beautiful spot, with a deep pool and smooth rocks about ten feet high, which made a natural jump-off point. With the usual concerns about liability, I couldn't let them, but they would not to be denied. They showed great ingenuity in taking the van, but their plan didn't go beyond the swimming hole.

The van was parked in plain sight, and they had taken off all of their clothes right there where they parked. They were skinny dipping with obvious delight. I was envious. What kid doesn't want the once-in-a-lifetime freedom they were enjoying? "I can handle it from here," I told my ride. I put their clothes in the van and let them swim another half-hour, and then I honked the horn. They went into variations of the fig-leaf pose, hands folded across the crotch.

"We need to be back for supper, so get your bare fannies up here and get dressed. If you don't, I'm leaving with your clothes." They hopped to it.

"You're not going to tell on us, are you Mr. Ferguson?" Manuel said.

"Let's see how breaking camp goes. If you guys give me all of the cigarettes you've been stealing around the campground, I'll think about it."

The kids broke camp like Boy Scouts. They were courteous, kind, helpful—and I threw a sizable pile of cigarettes into our last fire. It was not in my own best interests to relay the events to the cottage supervisor. He already thought I was too young and not severe enough with the kids. The delinquents knew I was a softy and had taken full advantage of me for three months. By the end of the summer, I had to leave my personality at home and assume the behavior of a drill sergeant—like the other staff. This was not a career choice for a fun-loving extrovert.

It seemed to always rain that summer, and it got a little risky riding the motorcycle. I had a good scare when I was traveling through Seattle's Harlem. At a stop light, a great big, drunk, black guy jumped on the back of my bike. After a short ride, he wanted me to take him back to show off for his friends. I told him if he didn't get off at the next light, he would be riding with me to Mercer Island. He hopped off and flashed me half of the peace sign.

One night shortly after the unwanted rider, I was coming home from work when a car on my right didn't see me and ran a stop sign. I was able to jerk my leg out from between the car and the bike before I slammed sideways into the driver's door. It was a small miracle that I had no injuries, but the bike was a contorted mass of metal.

The insurance company settled up the next day and paid me twice what I paid for the bike. I used half of it to buy a 1952 four-door Chevy sedan. Let it rain, I didn't care.

The rain did stop, but even that brought a new challenge. Ardi's dad, John, left me a note to get the house painted during the dry spell. The house was mostly brick, so I hastily did my first house painting job. I believe the emphasis should be on the word "hastily." John, being a perfectionist, repainted it within a few days, but said nothing to his daughter's boy friend.

I filled in as many shifts as I could so I saw Ardi only once during the entire summer. Again, I made enough money to pay for another school year without asking the folks for help.

I was glad to leave that job, and I wasn't sure I had scraped any scales off the rhino hides of the kids—except one. As I walked out to my car on the last day, Elijah Ford, a twelve-year-old black boy who had been a ward of the state since he was eight, ran out to the parking lot. He put his arms around my waist and with big tears in his eyes he said, "Mr. Ferguson, I sure do hate seeing you go." That made everything worth it, even the near heart-attack shock of waking up and finding the van and the kids gone.

The thermometer rested at twelve-degrees and thirty mile per hour winds created an icy chill cold enough to freeze the beak off a penguin. It went right through our lightweight, team blazers. On December 6, 1964, in Fargo, North Dakota, we stepped off the plane into weather that physically and psychologically intimidated us. We had made it into a playoff game against Concordia College of Minnesota, which we would dub the "Ice Bowl." We were taken straight to the field for an afternoon practice to get us "used to the cold." This was a Thursday, and we would be playing on Saturday. It was impossible to get acclimated to weather fit only for a polar bear in such a short time.

After we checked into the hotel, we began scrambling for sweatshirts, gloves, extra socks, and long underwear for the game. We practiced on Friday. No amount of clothing could keep us warm, but we bought more.

On the day of the game, it was five degrees outside with a mild wind. If wind-chill factors had been reported we would have seen that it was fifteen below zero and the field was frozen hard. We had so many clothes on, we could hardly move. When we came out of the locker room, we looked like a team from the

University of Pillsbury—a bunch of fat little Dough Boys. The coach had rounded up some big butane heaters and put them behind the benches. That was a mistake—some guys wanted to warm their buns by the heaters instead of playing.

For extra protection from the cold, the Concordia Cobbers had the ear holes on their helmets taped over. That was it. They ignored the cold and wore tennis shoes for the icy field conditions. They looked tough. They were tough. They kicked our thermal-covered hind-ends.

On their first play of the game, they ran their big fullback, Nick Heidi, right up the middle. He was as ugly as a mud fence. His round, Coke-bottle glasses sat on a slightly bleeding nose and a black mouth guard, made him look as fierce as he was. *Smack!* I forced my face mask into his right knee. *Thwack!* I thought I must surely have damaged his other knee with my chin. He carried the ball twice for eight yards, right over me. It would be a long day. They were a better team than us. No matter what the weather, there was no way we were prepared for the battering ram they used against us all day.

At the awards banquet that night, the emcee summed up the entire game: "The winner of the MVP award is Nick Heidi. He gained 153 yards on twenty carries—for a lot of people that's a pretty good season."

The spring semester of '65, I got a job at Maclaren School for Boys in Woodburn, an hour's drive from McMinnville. I rode with another man from Mac, Fred Glanville. He had a brand-new Volkswagen Beetle, so I paid him for gas. It worked out well for us both. On the days he wasn't working, I would drive my '52, two-tone green Chevy, which everyone took to calling "The Pickle." I didn't like to drive while I was taking sixteen units and working full time on the night shift at the boy's school. Two of the nights were over the weekend, so my job didn't interfere with my classes. As sort of a night watchman I could study on the job and by exchanging shifts with other staff I was able to make all of the debate tournaments.

Eventually, Fred got transferred to the day shift, so I had to drive all of the time. I got into the habit of falling asleep at the wheel. One night while driving to work, I fell asleep and ran a stop sign at a T in the road. The car jumped a small storm ditch, and I found myself between two rows of walnut trees. I turned the Pickle around and jumped the ditch again and went on to work. I was cutting it way too close. I told my boss at the school that day that they would need to find someone else.

I picked up a weekend job at the plywood mill on the edge of town. I was back to feeding the dryers. I wouldn't have as much money, but I would be alive to spend it.

A dream was coming true during the summer of 1965, and I could hardly wait. The executive director of the Easter Seal Society, Jim Torson, hired me as the assistant camp director to Gary Benson. Gary would be going into insurance at the end of summer camp, and I was slated to become the camp director after my graduation in December. Like a sponge, I absorbed everything I could about the camp to prepare for my new job. Gary saw the camp as a vacation before entering the insurance game. He was a nice guy, but had no passion for the job. That was great for me. I supplied what he lacked.

I made it a point to never read the newspaper, but Hank, the caretaker, pointed to an article that said Johnson would increase the draft numbers to support the war in Vietnam. In jest, I began singing that World War II tune, "Over There." I was sure that working for a non-profit was the same as being a teacher and would make me exempt from the draft. My unfailing, Ferguson stumblebum luck would again see me through.

"Ferguson, get 'em in a huddle and call a play," coach Durham said.

Another dream, to call the defensive signals, was now a reality, but I was caught off-guard. Weakly, I said, "Huddle up, guys. Okay, let's try a slant left. Readyyy, break!"

"That's not how you call defensive signals. Now huddle up and do it again!" coach said.

Wow! He must not have liked slant left, I thought.

"Okay, fellas, how about if we try a slant right," I said.

"Ferguson you sound like you're askin' 'em to vote. Just give them the command, slant right!"

Eureka! I got it. I knew what he wanted, and I was ready to take charge of the huddle.

"Get in there, Schweitzer, and call the signals!" coach said.

"Slant right," Schweitzer commanded.

I never called another play. My three year dream of being a defensive captain was shattered in more pieces than a crystal vase dropped from the Space Needle.

That was not the only bad start to my last year of football. Out of the corner of my eye, I could see them zeroing in on me for a crunching double-team. Fred Von Appen had never forgiven me for not becoming a shaved-head football fanatic like himself. One time, he tried to give me a cheap shot, but I knocked him bottom side up. Now, we were playing against each other in the alumni game at the start of the season of my senior year. Fred and the other guard, Jerry Grossen, played for the alums. They teamed up to lay the wood to me.

They didn't find me so easy to knock down, but in the process I hurt my ankle and knee. I was unceremoniously hauled off to the hospital during the game in Ol' Joe Groves's '54 Ford station wagon with him at the wheel puffing on a Camel cigarette.

I would miss four weeks. That put a lot of plans on hold. My picture was on the front of the press book, and football schedules touting me as an all-American candidate. Now I would be lucky to repeat as all-conference. It wasn't so much the injury that bothered me, but this would be my last season to ever play football, I wanted to play every single down. My passion for the game would never be satisfied, and to miss nearly half the season was gut-wrenching.

Wags, a.k.a. Wally Greene, told a story at a reunion in 2006 that summed up the passion that Linfield players bring to the game: "I was in seeing Doc Van Zyle. I'd just broken my arm for the second time, and I asked him to put on the type of cast that would let me play in Saturday's game. He erupted." Wally was more animated than a Disney movie as he captured the obsession of those days. "He threw his pen across the room and yelled, 'What in the Sam Hill is the matter with you people? Ferguson was just in here on a knee he shouldn't even be walking on, and he wants a brace and a clearance to play. Now you've broken the same arm I just fixed a few months ago. Don't you know there's more to life than football?'"

There really wasn't, but the doctor couldn't understand that. Luckily I missed only three games because we had a bye week. We had one tie, but were still invited to the national playoffs. In the first game against Sul Ross State, I blocked two extra points and we came from behind in the fourth quarter to tie the game at 21-21. I had never blocked any before, so it was the right time. We won it on a field goal with time running out!

That put us in the Champion Bowl in Augusta, Georgia, where we got spanked by St. Johns, from Collegeville, Minnesota. They scored on their first possession, but I blocked their first extra point to keep the score six to zero. I thought we could stay with them—I hadn't realized they were just warming up.

It was the same emcee for that night's banquet as the previous year, and before he handed my runner-up plaque to me, he said, "This next guy must have set some kind of record. He blocked three extra points in two consecutive games. The first two helped get his team here tonight." That sounded strange. I didn't know anyone had really noticed, especially a league VIP.

For the second year in a row, I led the team in tackles, played well in the championship series, and was selected to the AP Little All-American team and their All-Coast team, which included larger schools. My most coveted award was being voted the best defensive player by my peers. That more than made up for my debacle at calling the defensive signals.

My football days ended way too soon. I hadn't played enough to get it out of my system, but I've got a plan. When I die, I'm going to be buried completely suited up with helmet, cleats, and pads ready for a football game. After *The Head Coach* lets me through the Pearly Gates, I'm going straight to the field and get in the game. I know we'll get to play every Saturday for all eternity, but I don't want to waste a single minute of forever by having to take the time to suit up.

"Greetings, You are hereby ordered to report for a pre-induction physical …" The letter went on to tell me I would be receiving my draft notice in January. It was already mid-December. Being a camp director was not like being a teacher. I had to face the music, which was off-key.

The Vietnam War was heating up, and every male graduating from college was diving for cover—including me. I spent the remaining two weeks of school appealing to my draft board, trying to extend my student deferment so I could take some education classes and get a teaching degree. They denied my request. I checked into reserve units in Eugene, but they were full. Spots had been taken by students from the University of Oregon, many were football players recruited from California. I could not wriggle out of the military, but I did not want to be drafted. Getting drafted would be a slap in the face to my dad and brother who had enlisted during their time to serve.

Being an officer appealed to me, so I signed up to take the Naval Officer Training Test. It was given in downtown Portland at the old U.S. Post Office building. It took place the day after one of my last college finals, which had been followed by imbibing copious amounts of adult beverages. I was so sick, I wasn't sure I could pass the test. It was worse than the SATs.

"Sir, can you tell me how long it will be before you know if I've passed the test and been accepted into your Officers Training School?" I asked after handing it in.

"That takes about six months. They have to correct it and all," said the officer.

"I'm going to be drafted in about five weeks; I need to know before that. Can they give this a priority?"

"No, it just takes time, but you can sign up as an enlisted man and then, when the test results come back, you'll be flagged for OTS."

"What happens if I don't pass?"

"Then you'll serve four years as an enlisted man."

This wasn't an option. I didn't want to wait to be drafted. A few of my friends had taken that route; it seemed like a waste of four years of college not to use your education to get the best job available. Under the circumstances, being a military officer— was the best job.

"I Want You," read the door-length poster featuring the classic pose of Uncle Sam with his finger pointing at me. Yes, he wanted me, and I had to make a decision. The people inside the small room had closely cropped hair, blue trousers with a red stripe down the sides, and perfectly pressed khaki shirts filled with ribbons on the left chest. They were spit-and-polish Marines. I liked the way they all jumped up when I walked into the office.

"Do the Marines have an officer's school?" I asked the lean Marine with three chevrons over the top of two rockers. Even the most unknowledgeable civilian would know he was a sergeant.

"Yes suh, we sure do." His Southern accent was as thick as country gravy.

"How long will it take you to find out if I passed your test?"

"About five minutes."

"How long does the test take?"

"It's a timed test. You get half an hour, but most finish it in about twenty minutes. If you have a college education, the Marine Corps doesn't waste time giving you that test like the Navy does. They'll find out if you're officer material at OCS."

"When can I take the test?"

"Suh, you can take it right now if you want. We don't set up special days to take it; it doesn't take that long." I liked the way he called me suh.

The test was easy. The sergeant put a page dotted with small holes over the top of my answer sheet that had twenty-five little circles filled in with my number-two pencil. He checked a few wrong, but in less than half an hour, I knew I was eligible for OCS. I liked the way the Marines did business. I liked their military bearing. They were professional soldiers.

My investigation into the military branches had been marginal, but after I took the test it seemed that everywhere I looked there was a story about Marines. Mostly they were about Marines getting killed, and I began to have second thoughts about doing the last thing that would make me a Marine—being sworn in. College was ending and life was getting serious. Like the Navy hymn says, "Say farewell to college joys, we sail at break of day."

Ardi had an opportunity to become a stewardess, something she had always wanted to do. She applied, was accepted by United Airlines, and would begin training at about the same time I would enter OCS. We both felt that with the uncertainties clouding our lives, this would be a good plan. If we really loved each other, it would last.

I didn't know anyone in Vietnam, or even know anyone who knew someone who was there. It had never been a serious thought, but the war began to plague my thinking.

I stalled the swearing-in as long as I could. The sergeant wanted me to come to downtown Portland and get sworn in. I was afraid of the future. Bragging too much about joining the Marine Corps left me no choice. The sergeant knew I had been stalling him with second thoughts, so he came to McMinnville. He swore me in, and I signed the papers. There was no turning back. It was time to embrace the decision, move forward, and do my best.

"How ya runnin' son!" coach Durham said to one of his players who responded, "Ninety percent, working on a hundred coach." People enjoyed him because he was truly interested in their well being, then he turned his attention to me

"Fergy, I heard you joined the Marines," he said as he walked through the small student union.

"I was going to be drafted, so I outsmarted 'em and joined up with the best," I said.

"Egad, are you sure you outsmarted them by joining the Marines?"

"The Navy wasn't going to know if I was in their officer's program for months. I didn't want to get drafted to do something I feel is a responsibility."

"I understand that part, but good Lord, the Marines? You'll probably go to Vietnam; they seem to be doing most of the fighting."

"There are lots of different jobs in the Marines," I lied. "I expect my Ferguson luck to land me a soft job, maybe even here in the U. S." I knew that was a monster fib.

"I wish you well. There are not enough trees over there for even the generals to hide behind, from what I've been watching on TV, so be careful."

Daily the media reported casualties from the frontlines. The images were graphic. The bodies were somebody's kids, and they were dead. But I thought it was only hype.

I went home for Christmas and enjoyed it as much as possible. The two Johns, Babe, and I got together one last time. We all went to Christmas Eve midnight service at Grace Lutheran. It wasn't at all like vacations past. John Dirlam was in grad school at UCLA, Babe was running the family furniture store, and John Blair's parents had fallen on some hard times and moved to Astoria. J. B. had the responsibility of paying the mortgage on their house, so he dropped out of Oregon and took a job with Lane County. In a few days, I would be headed to OCS.

Our youth had vanished like a pleasant dream you awaken from only to remember you have an ugly day staring you smack-dab in the face.

CHAPTER 6

Marine Corps

It was a date filled with dread, but there was no way to avoid the colossal change in my life that January 10, 1966, would bring. I shivered as much from fear as the early morning cold as I sat in the small, prop-driven airplane on the tarmac at the Eugene Airport. It would be a quick trip to Portland to catch a cross-country flight to Washington, D.C.

I hugged a large yellow envelope containing my original set of orders with eighteen copies ordering me to report by midnight to Marine Corps Base, Quantico, Virginia for Officers Candidate School. The horror stories I had heard about boot camp drill instructors had me wondering why I ever joined up. My dad and brother both told me to hang onto my packet for dear life. If I lost it "Call the Red Cross at once," they said. I had the number in my wallet.

The door to the small plane opened again and let in a fresh blast of freezing air, along with a young man who was also holding onto the same kind of yellow packet I was squeezing. He glanced at me, then my packet, waved his envelope, and said, "Quantico, by any chance?"

"Yup," I said as we began laughing about the amazing coincidence. Mike Riley was a basketball player at Linfield, but neither of us had any idea that the other had joined the Marine Corps. He was originally from Bend, but his parents had moved to Eugene, so we had the same draft board. He had also discovered that the reserve units had been "Californiated," so he joined the Marines under the same circumstances as me. We both breathed a sigh of relief at having a traveling companion, somebody to share whatever lay ahead.

It took over ten hours to get to Washington, D.C. and we grabbed a shuttle bus to the train station. It took some time to sort through the massive schedule that lit up a gigantic board behind the ticket counter. We figured if we took the ten o'clock train to Quantico, we would arrive half an hour before our required midnight check-in time. We bought tickets and adjourned to the bar. It was crowded, but off in a corner was a big round table with five guys sitting around it with large yellow packets on the table.

We held up our envelopes and joined the happy party. "No sense getting there early," a voice with an East Coast accent said.

We were feeling pretty good by the time we boarded the train. We spent the hour-and-a-half trip finding out where everyone was from and guessing what might be ahead for all of us. We were certain of only one thing: it would be the toughest ten weeks imaginable.

The train tracks went right by the guard shack of the Quantico Marine Corps Base. It was below freezing as we piled out of the train. The guard stamped our orders, took one of the copies, and handed the rest back to us. A voice bellowed, "Over here, youse maggots. You're mine now, and Mommy's not here to wipe your noses. Youse miserable human beings fall in on me."

We looked at each other not quite knowing what to do.

Having been a Cub Scout, I at least knew to stand at attention in front of the short little sergeant. The others followed suit.

"Stand at attention when you fall in," the sergeant yelled. The inebriated snickers stopped when he said, "Drop and give me twenty-five pushups, laughing boys."

We had been ordered to climb aboard the Marine Corp's most popular mode of transportation, a canvas-covered truck with benches called a "six-by-six." Once aboard, we whispered our comments about the sergeant—after making sure he was well out of earshot. We watched him pace near the guard shack. A few minutes before midnight, a taxi pulled up, and out stumbled a drunk person. He was trying to make it to the shack before the strike of twelve, when he would be considered AWOL. The cab driver had not received his full fare, so he hopped out and angrily approached the inebriated passenger, who was holding a yellow packet.

We didn't need to hear the conversation. The cabbie held out his hand which held only a few dollars, and the snockered candidate-to-be showed the driver an empty wallet and turned his pockets inside out.

"Candidate Drunk is broke. The guards won't let him in the gate until he pays the driver." The sergeant's breath steamed out of his mouth as he spoke. "He's going to be AWOL in exactly five minutes, at which time it will be my personal pleasure to escort him to the brig and make sure this scum-bag never becomes an officer in my Marine Corps—so what are all of youses going to do about it?" We had no idea what to do. "Candidate Drunk needs another thirty dollars for the cab fare. He will need a little help getting on the truck and you now have about three minutes left before he's AWOL and all of youses start doing a hundred push-ups for not coming to the aid of one of your own men."

Wallets opened up, cash was gathered, and a couple of guys on the end of the truck ran to the gate to pay the money. They heaved Candidate Drunk onto the floor of the truck. He promptly hung his head out the back of the rig and left a trail of barf as the big diesel rumbled toward the barracks. That was our first lesson at OCS: never leave anybody behind—ever—no matter what your personal risk or cost might be. That code of conduct would be drilled into us over and over again during the next ten weeks. Years down the road, I would learn its importance.

There were already people in bed when we arrived. The platoons were selected by the arrival times of the candidates. The first forty-eight men formed the first platoon, the next forty-eight made up the second, and so on. Everyone in our platoon had had the same idea: arrive as late as possible. This filled our platoon with characters like Candidate Drunk, who was from a wealthy family in Kentucky that raised race horses. Along with four other platoons, we comprised the first OCS class that would be conducted during the cold Virginia winter.

"You slime balls find a bunk, strip to your skivvies. Put those civilian rags back in your suitcases, then stand at attention in front of your bunk. You wretched excuses for men have two minutes. Do you hear me!?"

"Yes sir," uttered a variety of meek voices.

"I said, do you hear me, you slug-eating imbeciles? And youses better answer as one!"

"Yes-yes-sir, yes sergeant," came more mixed replies.

"Which one of youse mental midgets called me sir?" The sergeant stormed over in front of the candidate that raised his hand and got nose to nose with him. "I am a sergeant in the United States Marine Corps. You will not call me sir. You will say 'yes, sergeant' or 'no, sergeant.' Is that perfectly clear, Mary?"

"Yes, sir—I mean, sergeant."

The sergeant went ballistic with a string of swear words that would make a truck driver blush. "You look like a girl, that's why I called you Mary. I'm going to ride your fanny and make sure a Mary doesn't become an officer in my Marine Corps." He turned his wrath on us. "You have three minutes to use the head and climb into your bunks for some shut eye. If every one of you isn't in bed, we'll do some more pushups. Is that clear?"

The little sergeant had a big voice.

"Yes, sergeant," we said nearly as one.

"Fall out, youse college creeps."

Everything moved in a blur. It's amazing what you can accomplish when pushed. I had no idea where Riley was bunking, and I didn't see him again for a week.

At 0500, we were awakened by a riding crop rattling around inside the squad bay garbage can wielded by our sergeant. "Doesn't he sleep?" Whispered someone.

"Youse maggots have five minutes to fall in outside for physical training."

The squad bay flew into a flurry of action. I threw on a pair of pants, a pair of tennies, and my full-length rain coat was small protection against the cold. I was amazed at how little time it took for all forty eight of us to do exactly as he said. The barracks were arranged in a U, and we were in a side barracks. We were the only platoon out for early PT. We realized then that our sergeant was more sadistic than the others.

The sergeant arranged us in three rows according to height, with the tallest people at the front and the shortest in the back. He ran us through the "daily nine exercises," which included jumping jacks, pushups, sit-ups, and ended with grueling squat thrusts. After a few instructions about marching, we were dismissed and ordered to take showers and shave.

"Listen up," yelled candidate Davidson. "If you have to use the head, do it now, you won't have time for the next three days."

He wanted to be a mustang, a Marine officer promoted from the enlisted ranks. He had earned his college degree through a program the Corps had for up-coming enlisted men. He was squared away and he was right about the three days.

We formed up again in the middle of the quad. My place in line was easy to find: a kid from California who was slightly taller than me stood to my left. The long, blond surfer-hair on candidate Sunderman was easy to spot in the line.

It was still winter dark when a cacophony of rhythmic, guttural music started as the five sergeants began marching their troops to morning chow. Each gave the same command, but each was unique. "Ateeeeeeeeeeeeeeeenhut," said one in a tenor voice. Another across the quad bellowed in a rumbling bass, "Teeennnnhut." A baritone emphasized another vowel: "Aaaaaaaaaatennnhut."

The cold air crackled with five different versions of "Your left, your left, your left right left," but none of them clearly pro-nounced the words. The cadenced, sing-song voices of five ser-geants calling out their marching orders was strangely beautiful, fun to march to, and left an indelible impression. I knew I was in the Marine Corps with professional soldiers. They took pride in the inimitable voice commands that kept their platoons in step. The military had no desire to homogenize this part of military drill. The more exceptional a sergeant's voice, the easier for his troops to hear his commands in the mass of five platoons. We waited in the chow line for half an hour in freezing temperatures. "Hurry up and wait," someone groused.

It was getting light as we marched from the mess hall to the uniform shop. The fatigue uniforms only needed to be an approximate fit because every one would lose twenty pounds, but they took a lot of time getting the right fit for our boots. A Marine moves on his feet, but despite great care in sizing, everyone developed ugly blisters.

The haircut took only seconds, but when I ran out of the barber shop, I had no idea where to line up. The blond surfer-hair was gone. The sergeant noticed my confusion. "Do you need an invitation, candidate?"

"No sergeant, but I don't see the candidate I was next to."

"Didn't you look at his face, candidate?"

"Yes, I did sergeant, but …"

"But, what, candidate? You think I was going to let a Goldilocks in my Marine Corps? Everybody drop and give me twenty-five because I have to nursemaid this candidate back into formation."

That night, we wore official olive-drab boxers and T-shirts as we stood at attention in front of our bunks. The sarge yelled, "Inna rack!" Bodies jumped into their bunks—except me. I had no idea what "Inna rack" meant, so I stayed at attention. "Outta da rack," commanded the sergeant. Feet hit the floor, and everyone had to do another twenty five, which were now getting harder, because I flubbed up. "Inna rack," came the order. I was the first on my bunk lying on my stomach and watching the sergeant play his game with us.

"When I say inna rack, I mean, inna rack and at attention." I put my hands down to my sides and stiffened. I had no idea how to be at attention on a bunk. I was enjoying the game until he came over to my bunk. "Are you laughing at me, candidate?"

"No sir, I mean no sergeant. I'm just smiling."

"Oh, that's good, candidate. Do you think this sergeant likes to be eyeballed and smiled at? And why aren't you at attention?"

"I am, sergeant."

"You are a numbskull, candidate. When you are at attention in your rack, you are on your back, candidate Numb. Outta da rack," he said to the room, "and you can all thank candidate Numb here for another twenty five—now!"

The sarge's game was no longer fun. When he said, "Inna rack," I was the first on the bunk, on my back, and at attention.

He turned off the lights and walked out without saying a word. I was too scared to move. I slept at attention.

The next day was more of the same. The sergeant would harass us about trivial matters, make every candidate look stupid, and then make us do push ups. During one formation he got serious.

"Candidates, the little piece of paper you've just been given is your Marine Corps life. Those six little numbers on that piece of paper next to your name is your serial number and *you will* never forget it. You have exactly sixty seconds to memorize it at the end of which you will eat that little scrap of paper and God help you if you haven't got it memorized."

It was inevitable that a few people would forget their number. It was re-written on typing paper. After they memorized it again, of course, they had to eat it in one minute. It could not be done. In the spirit of leaving no one behind we were all obliged to eat a piece to help out our fellow Marine.

While having lunch with some college cronies a while back, I said, "093911. Anyone know what that is?" "606315" said another and the service numbers of several present were easily repeated. We have all forgotten a lot about our service days, but I have seldom found a military person who doesn't remember his service number.

My college mate, Mike Riley and I did not see each other until Sunday, when we were given a half-day of liberty. After doing our laundry, a group of us went to Diamond Lou's, a small tavern filled mostly with Marines.

"Were you candidate Numb that first night?" asked Riley. "I was too scared to look down that way or he might get on me."

"Yeah. How was I supposed to know that you have to be on your back to be at attention in the rack? At least he doesn't call me Candidate Mary like he does that other candidate."

We laughed about the harassment, like his giving us ten minutes for all forty-eight of us to shower in three stalls. "I think the sarge must have gone into his office and cracked up after he told all of us to do ten pushups in that tiny shower room," someone said. "I'll tell ya, when he told us a second time, I grabbed a little slice of floor and didn't look up," said another class member. The beer and the freedom of a few hours from incessant badgering was delightful.

"I don't know how he expects us not to laugh when he's yellin, 'Candidate Mary, you're shaking like a small dog trying to pass a peach seed.' Now that was funny," said Riley.

The time passed too quickly. We headed back to the barracks, wondering what the hike scheduled for the next day would bring. We had watched an army training film about a forced march. It looked like a bunch of guys out for a stroll wearing their combat gear. It would be a piece of cake. We awoke to a foot of snow. We were certain the hike would be cancelled.

"All right, youse maggots. Today we get to enjoy this beautiful weather. Make sure you have an extra pair of socks in your packs. You'll need them."

Jerry Bennett and I drew stretcher bearer duty for that first march. Our job was to stay ten yards behind the last platoon. One of us carried the stretcher, and the other carried both rifles.

The march was nothing like the training movie. The platoons were to keep twenty yards between each other at all times. The first platoon dictated the pace of the following four. On the first hill, we walked, just like the movie. On the downhill side, the first platoon switched into the OCS shuffle, an in-step jog. It started a ripple effect. The second platoon had not yet crested the hill, so to keep the twenty yard space intact, they ran up the last part of the hill. The third platoon was just at the beginning of the hill, so they had to run up the entire hill. By the time the ripple effect reached the stretcher bearers, we ran, slipping and sliding, the entire three miles.

Jerry and I hit it off by helping each other on that first punishing run, and by the end of the day I'd given him the nickname Ben and he called me RE. We had other nicknames, but we liked those and nobody else ever used them.

For every tiny infraction—calling the sergeant sir, or not getting down in pushup position fast enough—the sergeant would give you a chit that had checkboxes: Good, Average, and Unsatisfactory. "That is Unsat, candidate. Here's your chit." I was the first in the platoon to get one as candidate Numb. I was sure I was going to wash out.

The thought of failing to become an officer worried me. It would be difficult to face my family and friends. Eventually, everybody began to get enough chits to wallpaper the squad-bay, but the threat of getting booted out of OCS was very real. One candidate relieved himself during the long wait in the chow line. The yellow snow gave him away, and by the time we finished chow and got back to the barracks, he was gone. "Officers do not make spectacles of themselves," the sergeant said.

Riley, Ben, and I, on one of our few liberties, went to Washington, D.C., to see the usual sights, like the Lincoln Memorial, the White House and the Capitol building. We topped it off by going to some sort of a nightclub in a large hall. Most of the party bunch were students from Georgetown University and surrounding schools. The music was loud and the girls too young—or was it that we were too old? It didn't matter; we had to stay focused on getting through OCS.

A lot of the physical training was fun. The obstacle course consisted of climbing over walls, jumping over a series of waist-high logs, and other barriers. The confidence course, though, did have a small element of danger. It involved diving out to grab a rope and swinging to the other side of a pond and running down steeply slanted logs. A misstep could mean a serious injury. It was the same fun stuff I had liked to do as a kid, but got spanked for.

It didn't matter what athletic shape you might be in, because the physical training broke every one down to an even playing field. It made football daily doubles look easy. Some candidates were gung-ho Marines; I wasn't one of them, but I gave it my best effort in these drills.

Everyone in our platoon was a college graduate, two had been practicing attorneys, Candidate Mary was a psychologist, and many others had left good jobs. With everyone being successful in the real world, the worst thing we had to do was rank each other as leaders. We were given a whiteboard with lines on it and a grease pencil. We wrote the name of each candidate in descending order for their leadership ability. Bunkmate rated bunkmate. Then we put our names at the top and placed the boards next to our racks. We looked at everyone's board. It was difficult to rate one of your friends, but it had to be done. The top ten and bottom five were easy to pick. Riley, Ben, and I usually rated in the top ten.

Al Johnson bunked next to me and was rated by nearly everyone in the last five slots. He was married and held an education degree, but he hadn't yet found a teaching job, so he was eligible for the draft. He joined the Marines because he wanted to be in with the best. He was a nice guy, but he had a less commanding presence than I did in my first defensive huddle. For a teacher, this was an admirable trait, but the Marine Corps could ill afford to have an officer who might waffle. Football is a game, killing is not. Not every person can be an artist, a poet—or warrior. We all liked Al—but as a civilian.

Right after the rating exercise, we were hustled outside for marching practice while the bottom five were called into the sergeant's office. When we came back, they were gone without a trace. The peer evaluation was repeated three times. Each time, men were dropped from the program. The sight of empty bunks made us work harder.

After one forced marched, a candidate who had tested well in every assignment went into the sergeant's office and told him he was going to kill himself if he didn't get out of the Marine Corps. The sergeant marched him out the door without having him return to get his gear.

Back in the barracks, the sergeant said, "If anybody else wants to kill himself, for the record, I don't care. But you're not going to give my Marine Corps a bad name by doing it on my time. You'll get your chance to die soon enough."

The squad bay was silent. The candidate had been a hippie, but he was well educated, physically one of the best, and he was in the top ten in peer rankings. The best any of us could figure out was that he wasn't getting his regular drug supply, so he took a desperate measure to get out.

During one of our endless "hurry up and wait" sessions, Riley asked, "Sergeant, why did you let Endicott get off so easy?"

Sarge gave an answer that gave me chills. "In the entire history of the Marine Corps, nobody has ever been drafted. We expect the men who join us to add to our legacy of integrity, courage, and sacrifice." He looked at each of us squarely in the eyes as if to say, *And you guys better not louse things up.* He held the attention of everyone within earshot. "We knew Endicott was faking it, but he didn't have the character to uphold that tradition, so he was given a less than honorable discharge. The MPs escorted him right out the front gate within the hour. We want only the best in the Marine Corps."

We were standing in a chilly, late-February mixture of rain and snow waiting for noon chow. The usual banter had ceased as we soaked in the sergeant's words. In the cold drizzle, we experienced a warmth in our souls that comes from the pride of membership in a special group.

Near graduation, we went out on an overnight bivouac. It was the OCS's version of cowboys and Native Americans (I don't think that offends anyone). We had blanks in our M14 rifles, and I drew the night watch on the perimeter. The temperature had dipped below freezing, so I climbed into my sleeping bag up to my waist and sat with my rifle pointed toward the field of fire where the attack would probably come from.

A shadow moved, and I flattened my silhouette in my foxhole. *Pow ... pow ... pow.* "Hey candidate, you're dead," I yelled at the running Marine. "Hey, you! You're supposed to fall!"

"Stuff it, candidate! You missed me," he yelled as he kept advancing.

Our sergeant expected us to hold the line, or we would do millions of pushups. The enemy's sergeant expected him to overrun and conquer. They must have been threatened with more pushups than us, because they didn't play by the rules. None of them stopped.

After they passed my position, I fell asleep. I didn't wake up until just before dawn when the truck horn honked signaling an end to the exercise. I reached for a drink from my canteen, but the water was frozen solid. *At least Vietnam won't be freezing,* I thought. I was sick of the snow and cold.

A few days after the bivouac, we flew in a C-130 to Cherry Point, South Carolina, to attend an air show. I had never thought about being a pilot, but the air crews talked about a climate-controlled environment. The memory of that frozen canteen was still fresh in my mind. At the end of the show, we were given a chance to sign up for the air wing. Planes that could be heated sounded cool. I signed my payroll signature, Robert E. Ferguson, with lightning speed before they could change their minds.

A few days later, we took the physical exam for the air wing.

It was far more rigorous than the military induction exam. Some guys found out they were colorblind or had a hearing loss. I found out I had literally no depth perception. One of the tests for this was looking into an instrument similar to something you would see in an optometrist's office, with three vertical bars on a white background. The task was to determine which bars were closest or were evenly lined up, and so on.

"Dr. Heath, will you please step in here and take a look at this? I don't know how, but this candidate is cheating."

"Respectfully, sir, I'm not cheating. I can't help it if I got them all right."

Both doctors gave me a puzzled look. "I haven't seen a score like this in twenty years. What I can't figure out is, why are you trying to fail this test?" Now I had the puzzled look. "You missed every single question," Dr. Heath said.

They tested me again and decided I was an anomaly of nature. It washed me out as a pilot, but not as a navigator. Depth perception was not needed to see a radar screen.

A few days later, six of us found out we would be going directly to Pensacola, Florida, for flight training: three pilots and three navigators. Jerry Bennett and I were on the navigator list. We would not be required to attend the six months of Officers Basic School in Quantico, where Marine officers learned to wage a ground war, fire sophisticated weaponry, jump from helicopters during vertical assaults, and learn about massive air power. I was ecstatic about going directly to Pensacola. While learning to jump from helicopters and blowing stuff up sounded fun, it couldn't compete with going to someplace warm.

Spending Sunday at Diamond Lou's had become a ritual. Our last visit after the ninth week was the most hilarious. We recounted the many screw-ups we all made, but got an especially good belly laugh out of Candidate Westering's colossal blunder on the parade ground.

As we marched, the sergeant would give commands to adjust our rifles so they were all lined up perfectly at the exact same angle. The commands he used were meant to pull the butt of your rifle inboard, outboard, down, or up. As he marched the demonstration column by the rest of us, Sarge would shout, "Inboard on your butt, Woosley," and Woosley would move the butt of his rifle to the left. It was easy to see how the sergeant got all of the weapons tilted at the same angle.

Being the shortest man in the platoon, Westering was at the end of the column. He held the butt of his rifle so far out from his body it pointed back toward the sergeant's head, who was giving his commands from the rear of the column.

The sergeant yelled, "Westering, down on your butt." No adjustment was made. "Westering, I said down on your butt!" Still no adjustment. The sergeant ran up next to him and said, "Westering, down on your butt, and I mean now you imbecile!" Candidate Westering lowered his butt—by bending his knees and marching like a waddling duck. We laughed hysterically and the sarge didn't give us push ups—he was laughing too hard.

Westering had been an attorney before joining up, and we wondered how he could be so inept at following orders. He washed out during the peer evaluation. The last time we saw him, he was peeling spuds at the OCS mess hall, but I'm pretty sure he got assigned to a legal job.

At our first inspection, we used the Marine Corps Field Book to arrange our bunks in exactly the same manner as a picture in the book. Each article of clothing had to be folded to precise specifications. The boxers and T-shirts had to look on one bunk exactly the same as they did on another. We used a ruler to get them to comply with the strict dimensions. Some of the guys who could afford it used a laundry service each week. Candidate Boyer was one of them. When the sergeant came to his bunk, he became incensed.

"Boyer, these skivvies aren't even close to being correct. Didn't you read your field book?"

"Yes, I did read it, sergeant."

"Then why would you fold your skivvies like this?"

"I didn't fold them, sergeant."

"Then who did, you maggot!?"

"The laundry folded them, sergeant."

We received twenty-five pushups for unrestrained laughter.

The much-anticipated graduation date of March 18, 1966, came to pass. "Thank you, gentleman," I said as I returned the salute of our two platoon sergeants. It was a tradition that a new lieutenant would pay a dollar to the first enlisted man that salutes him. They stood together at the end of the platform saluting each new lieutenant together. It was an odd moment. They had been our mentors and tormentors, but now they were fellow Marines who called me sir. That was the first time I had seen them with their ribbons on their chests. They both had several rows, and I recognized Purple Hearts and Bronze Stars. We had been trained by the best of the best. They were crackerjack Marines. But it was not a sad departure.

OCS tested your mettle up to a point, but we shot blanks and were never in any real danger. I don't know what happened to most of the men who went on to become platoon leaders, but I do know about a few of them. Candidate Fitchner was gung-ho during OCS. He wanted to be a big bad Marine and wouldn't even consider "being in the wimpy air wing." He growled and snarled like a bear during PT drills, while climbing over walls on the obstacle course, or any other time we did anything arduous. He was fearless in everything—as a candidate.

When Fitchner's platoon first encountered enemy action in Vietnam, he fell down on the ground in a fetal position and started crying. He was frozen and unable to give any commands to his men. Nearly his entire platoon was lost. He was court-martialed for cowardice in the face of the enemy.

I don't know what his punishment was, but personally, I don't think he should have been punished at all. First, it is impossible to tell how anybody will react until you are placed in a combat situation. Next, there is the matter of the thousands of cowardly draft-dodgers who fled to Canada and were eventually given amnesty. Finally, Fitchner is not a criminal, and he will punish himself for the rest of his life. Enough is enough.

Phil Anweiler was at the other extreme. He was a small, quiet kid from the South who spoke with a soft drawl. He became a Radar Operator and was comfortably in a fighter squadron when he volunteered for a front-line position as a Forward Air Con-troller. He distinguished himself in combat by calling in air strikes so close to his own position the shrapnel fell on top of him. As he came out of the field from his FAC tour, I asked him, "Why in the world did you volunteer for such a dangerous job?"

"I wanted to be a real Marine and be able to say I had scratched with the chickens."

Those Southern boys always had a down-home flavor to their talk, and such a strong sense of duty that I have wondered out loud, "how in the world did the Confederates lose the Civil War?"

Jerry Bennett and I had a three-fold mission: erase the memories of harassment at the hands of drill sergeants, forget the frozen ten weeks of OCS, and put the recent officer status that the United

States Congress had conferred upon us to good use. This meant regaling the ladies.

The Officer's Club at the Pensacola Naval Air Station reminded me of a plush country club. It had a large pool, two tennis courts, and was adjacent to a golf course. A lot of military personnel retired in Pensacola because of the base accoutrements.

The ammunition Ben and I used to complete our assignment was a recipe called a Salty Dawg. It was a concoction of grapefruit juice, vodka, and crushed ice served in a beer glass with a salted rim like a margarita. The Dawg had become our favorite drink after seeing two Blue Angel pilots order it the previous night in the O Club. It was cheap and tasted like trouble when taken in large doses.

The mid-March sun warmed our winter-pale, twenty-two-year-old, rock-hard bodies while our brains pleasantly fogged over from our newly discovered libation. It looked like a breakfast drink, which made it the obvious choice for a late-morning cocktail as we lounged by the Olympic-size pool.

The club's hi-fi speakers played Big Band sounds along with favorites by Elvis and Waylon Jennings. Country-Western music was a military favorite and easily won out over the music of the Beatles. The warm air and a creeping numbness put us in a near catatonic state. The deep immersion into such pleasure made OCS seem like it had happened in a previous life, not within the last three days.

OCS had galvanized our friendship from that first forced march as stretcher bearers. We were now prepared to sacrifice, life, limb, and hangovers for one another. We were making the most out of our last day before starting the required pre-flight class that preceded the pressure-packed, sixteen-week Radar Officer's program.

Two girls flitted in like butterflies and alit close by. "Would you ladies like a drink?" Ben asked the prettier of the two in his baritone voice that was Southern Comfort smooth.

"We'd be deeelighted," answered another drawling voice from a Southern belle. We moved our lounges next to theirs.

There's always one pretty and one ugly, I thought.

"My father's an admiral. Are you going to make the military a career?" the homely one asked me in a tone that was icier than the water that had been frozen in my canteen.

Homely and a snob to boot, I thought as I took a swig of the liquid remedy for ugly. "Well, I think I want to see if I can make it through the RO program first," I responded.

"Of course, you know it's very hard and many flunk out," she said.

"So I've heard, but OCS was hard, too. Out of forty-eight guys that started in our platoon, only thirty-three graduated," I said in an aloof voice to let her know I felt up to the challenge.

Her tone made me shiver in the warm sun, but Ben and the Southern belle were warming up. It didn't hurt that he was one-fourth Commanche Indian with high cheekbones, a dark complexion, a six-foot frame, and killer good looks. His Oklahoman "aw shucks" personality made him a hit with the ladies.

Ben was moving in to get the lady's phone number while I was saddled with a girl resembling a bug-eyed snapper with the personality of a prickly blowfish. Just when it looked like I would be stuck with an obnoxious companion for the day, the situation changed.

A young Naval cadet in his dress white uniform approached Ben's girl and said, "Hi Mary Beth. We still on for tonight?" He ignored us like we were some of the pool furniture.

"Well, of course we are. Gloria and I just wanted to get a little sun today. These gentlemen were kind enough to buy us a drink," she said in a syrupy Southern accent. "Is your friend coming, too?"

"He'll be here. He's the best diver on our swim team," the white uniform replied.

Ben was turning red, but said nothing.

The cadet walked out onto the end of the diving board and began to jump like an Olympic diver testing the three-meter board. He looked silly in his dress whites on a diving board, but it was obvious he was an expert diver. He was cocky, but he backed it up. He was more comfortable on the end of a diving board than most of us are sitting in a rocking chair.

"What's your friend's name again?" the Snapper asked the cadet in a pleasant voice that had eluded her all day.

"Cadet Danielson. His father's an admiral, too. He probably knows your father," the cadet replied while still springing on the end of the board.

I now understood the point about her dad being an admiral. She only dated cadets or academy graduates. She was the military's version of a gold-digging social climber.

The cadet was smooth and charming. He looked superb in his dress whites, while Ben and I were dressed in plaid Bermuda shorts that would have been thrown out by any respectable thrift shop. Even in his uniform, you could tell the cadet was an athlete who could bend his body into a pretzel and hit the water in a ten-point dive.

Ben looked like a bull ready to charge a matador. He was filled with the planet's entire supply of testosterone. I had once seen him in that state in Diamond Lou's when some townies began bad-mouthing Marines. Riley and I had to get him out of there for the safety of the two hecklers. You never dance on the pride of a Southerner.

"Don't do it Ben," I said. "I've seen that look before. These cadets are guests of the air base and it would be ..."

"Darlin', would you hold my Dawg? This Marine has a mission to accomplish," Ben said, interrupting me.

The belle stammered, "Well, we weren't really sure if things were still planned for the night with the two cadets and ..."

"Shucks, don't pay it no never mind. We understand," he said in his good ol' boy voice as he handed her his drink.

"Pay it no never mind my derriere," I mumbled. I knew better. Ben was a man of action, and there would be no stopping him. His honor was at stake. They had played us for suckers, and that was a big blow to the egos of two Marine lieutenants.

"Admiral's daughter, you better hold mine too," I said handing her my glass while grabbing our OCS duffle bags with our extras in them.

The cadet bounced high in a graceful diving form impressing the girls. While he was midair, Ben pulled the old neighborhood pool trick: he jumped on the back half of the diving board, giving it an extra large gyrating bounce. We were dashing through the pool gate when we heard the splash. Mission accomplished.

Despite the justice of it all, Ben might have bought some trouble. The cadets were the crème de la crème of the Naval Academy and were attending a luncheon in their honor at the O Club. They were pampered the entire week in hopes they would become Navy pilots. Ben might have to face some serious music.

Ben's escapade had proven at least one thing. In only ten weeks, not even the U. S. Congress could make a gentleman out of a dirt farmer's son from a family of twelve children. He was rough around the edges, but that's what made him Ben.

We reported at 0700 the following morning for required tests to get into the pre-flight school that preceded the RO program. The senior man of the class was Walt Samura, a Marine first lieutenant. He was the senior officer in charge of taking roll and marching the group to classes. After roll call, he asked with an extra bit of authority in his voice, "Anyone know anything about Navel Cadet Hockinson, who was pushed into the pool at the O Club?"

"He wasn't pushed, sir," Ben said reverting to his loud OCS voice.

"You know something about this, Lieutenant Bennett?"

"Yes sir, I was in the vicinity, but he wasn't pushed." Ben carefully selected his words. In the Marine Corps your honor is everything. Even the smallest lie could end your career. We liked that concept—it kept out the phonies.

"Lieutenant Bennett, your integrity is at stake here. It's hard for me to believe nobody pushed this cocky son-of-a-sea-biscuit into that pool. Had he been drinking?"

Samura had given Ben a slight opening for redemption, and Ben knew it. "Yes sir, a little, but you know the Navy. Even a little is too much." There were a few chortles, as the class was half Navy and half Marines. Good-natured ribbing was a given.

"Then I'll report to the CO that he had been drinking and no one pushed him in. In case you were wondering Ben, the admiral wanted to know, in his own words, 'what did this prima dona think he was doing in his dress whites on the end of a diving board when he had a date with my daughter after the luncheon?' "

Samura's impersonation of the admiral was perfect. The formation cackled without fear of pushups. We were now officers. We formed up and marched off to another obstacle to becoming a Radar Officer—math tests for pre-flight.

The testing began with three different types of math exams. I panicked. I felt Mrs. Applegar perched on my shoulder, with her horns and forked tail, whispering into my ear, "How dumb are you anyway?" The first test was entirely on the use of a slide rule. I had no idea how to use a slide rule, but I took it out of the case and tried to make some sense of it. I marked every answer C. The worst I could get on an ABCD response sheet was twenty-five percent. I was so flustered from that part of the test I choked on the other two, which were basic algebra and geometry. I was the only person in our class of fifty-five who flunked.

I thought I had flunked out before I even got started, but I would be allowed one retake. I went back to the Bachelor's Officer's Quarters with a series of Self-Instructional Manuals. I poured over them night and day for a week, and then retook the test. The ghost of Applegar was there, but smaller this time. I flunked. I washed out, so I had to go see the base commander and explain why I again flunked the test. I figured he'd say, "How dumb are you, anyway?"

"Before I sign your orders sending you back to Quantico, I want to hear what you have to say for yourself, lieutenant."

"Sir, my answers on the first test were all guesses, even the ones I got right. On the second test, even though I didn't pass, I knew all of the answers that I got right. It seems like the Marine Corps has already invested a lot of time and money in me, sir. I'll make that investment pay off if I can have one more chance."

"Lieutenant, I've never given anyone a third chance, but I like your answer. This is your last chance, but if you don't get eighty percent, your orders will be waiting for you at the guard shack. Do you understand? "

"Yes, sir. I won't let you down."

I was given another set of Self-Instructional Manuals. I left my room in the BOQ only for meals. I put Mrs. Applegar in the closet.

Each exam was a little bit harder, but as I looked at the questions on the third test, they were not a collection of mysteries like they had been on the first two. They made sense, and I thought I had a good chance of getting a maximum score. I knew I had passed before it was even corrected. The ghost of Mrs. Applegar went *poof,* into thin air—forever.

Ben, Roger Meadors, who we had met during the pre-flight week, and I moved out of the BOQ into a three-bedroom house we dubbed the Snake Ranch. Roger had a car, and we began to run around together. The house had the things we were looking for, a barbecue and privacy, and something we weren't looking for: a gazillion cockroaches. We tried everything to get rid of them. Bug poison was like a fertility drug to them and they multiplied faster. We put crumbs on the kitchen counter and, in the dead of night, flicked on the light and clobbered them with rolled up newspapers. They scoffed at our commando raids. We were no match for these tiny beasts that had survived droughts, famines, and whatever killed off the dinosaurs and turned rain forests into underground pools of oil. They would survive us. We gave up and learned to live with the little prehistoric buggers.

The Radar Officer's School was rigorous. There were 116 tests in sixteen weeks, and you had to pass each one. If you flunked, you were given one retake. Flunk that and you were out, or flunk any two tests and you also got bounced. I seemed to pass each test with the bare minimum score at the very bottom of the class, but I never flunked.

While I was struggling with the RO program, on the other side of the continent Ardi had completed stewardess training, was flying all over the country, and had the world by the tail. About midsummer, United Airline employees went on strike, so she and her roommate, Carol Wright, traveled by bus from their waterfront apartment in Seattle to Pensacola.

Ben and I picked them up at the bus station in his new Aztec red Chevy Super Sport. It cost him a payment of $150 per month, which happened to be the exact amount of his newfound wealth—flight pay. The predatory dealers just outside the base gate sold any car you wanted, including Corvettes, for that exact amount—as long as they were the beneficiary of your $10,000 GI life insurance policy.

The trip had taken them three days, and they apologized for the usual girl stuff, like not wearing makeup, but to us, they were eye-candy. Ben and Carol were mutually smitten. Love at first sight. Why not? She was pretty, and he was a man's man. Together they would make beautiful babies, and the country needed parents like them.

Ben showed a tender side with Carol I hadn't seen before. His mamma had taught him how to treat a woman with admiration and respect. He was the gentleman Congress had made him. Ben's bedroom had two beds, so we put the girls in his room, he took the couch, and we chaperoned ourselves—for the most part.

With the female distractions at the Ranch, Ben and I stayed after classes to get our studies done. The pressure of RO school was intense, and we had put too much effort into the program to wash out because of hormones.

Cars were never a big deal to me and I wanted to begin saving, so I bought a 1957 four-door, black Pontiac, for which I paid $400 in cash. I was keeping my flight pay. It was a huge car that we dubbed the "Batmobile." My car was always good for a laugh, but it was to be our carriage to the Change of Command Ball. Ben and I hadn't planned to go, but I told Ardi about it. She and Carol thought it would be fun, so they brought their formal gowns cross-country for the event. The Batmobile was the only logical vehicle.

The ball was a spectacular formal affair. Ben and Carol's eyes were fixed only on each other. They looked like Prince Charming and Snow White dancing at the castle. Ardi and I were past the wooing stage, but our commitment to each other was renewed by getting engaged.

The United strike got settled, so they had to fly back the next morning. The ball was a magnificent finale to their visit.

Together, the four of us stayed up all night at the Ranch, but separate in our coupled thoughts. The girls would be heading back to terrific jobs, and we had to get on with the two toughest classes yet to come: electronics and navigation. These were the classes that flunked out the most people, and we had already lost over a dozen students.

Shortly after the girls left, a once-in-a-lifetime opportunity came along. Ben, Roger, and I were selected as escorts for the Miss Universe Pageant. This was an extraordinary opportunity, but the timing was off. It required that those selected have in their possession a full complement of dress uniforms—the whites, blues, khakis, and greens—and a ceremonial sword. We only had the whites we bought for the ball and the dress greens from OCS. Another fly in the ointment was that one could not be married or engaged. I had just given Ardi an engagement ring and Ben's new romance with Carol made him not want to go. We were in trouble.

By flipping coins, I was selected to approach the CO to get us out of this gig. We hadn't been officers long enough to earn enough money to buy all of the uniforms. I had forgotten all about the forms we had signed when I first checked into the base. I embellished the truth just a little bit. I put down that I could speak Spanish and German *fluently.*

"Don't I know you, lieutenant?"

"Yes, sir. You let me take a third math test for the pre-flight school."

"So how are you doing?"

"I'm doing fine sir," which was preferable to, "I'm last in the class."

"I'm glad I made the right decision. So why are you here today?"

"It's this form, sir, I'm engaged," I blurted out.

"You didn't put on your form that you were engaged," he said.

"Yes, sir—I mean, no, sir. I mean, I wasn't engaged at the time I filled it out, sir, and that part about the uniforms, sir, I ..."

"You signed this document, which states that you have a complete set of uniforms. Why are you talking to me about uniforms?"

"Well sir, that is, I mean, yes sir, I signed it, and it is my intent to buy them as soon as I have enough money, but I came here right from OCS and ..."

"I know they taught you about Marine Corps integrity at OCS, lieutenant, so I'm sure everything you said in this document will be true by Friday."

"No sir—I mean yes sir, my uniforms will look good by Friday." I was just glad he hadn't asked me about the part on the form where I answered that I spoke fluent Spanish and German.

Ben and I got loans from the bank, while Roger called home for the needed dollars. Then the three of us scrambled to get the uniforms fitted and bought our swords. As the events unfolded, it was worth every penny.

We were flown in a military transport to Miami. We stayed at the world-famous Fontainebleau hotel for free. They treated us like royalty. There were two parts to the pageant: the coronation of the queen and then the Queens' Ball, where we would serve as escorts. There weren't enough seats in the Jackie Gleason Theater for all of us to go to the coronation, so I stayed at the hotel bar for a barbecue.

We each knew the country of the girl we would be escorting; I had drawn Miss Sweden. I thought it was nice when she made the top five. In usual dramatic pageant style, they strung out the suspense. When they announced her as Miss Universe, I almost gagged on a chicken leg.

It was my turn for fifteen minutes of fame as the escort of Miss Universe at the Queens' Ball. Bulbs flashed, TV cameras rolled, and I had a bad case of stage fright. As she took my arm to walk down the stage to the dance floor, I leaned over and said to the most beautiful woman in the world, "We need to smile for the cameras."

Through ventriloquist lips that didn't change her plastic smile, she said, "Don't you think I know that?"

Those were the last words she said to me all evening. We started the dance, but after about five steps, Bob Crosby, Bing's son and chairman of the pageant, cut in. It went like that the entire evening.

We sat at the head table, and I tried to make some small talk. The duke and duchess, along with an ambassador or two from Sweden, were at our table. They bought expensive magnums of champagne and toasted the most beautiful woman in the world. Each man at the table spent a bundle on champagne. They all looked at me when it was my turn. I couldn't begin to afford the hundred bucks they were shelling out, and I certainly wasn't going to spend it on Miss Plastic Smile of the Universe. I excused myself from the table and asked Miss Sweden's chaperone to dance.

The Associated Press took a picture of me and the newly crowned Miss Universe that was shot around the world. Not all of the newspapers picked it up, but my hometown did, as well as the *Seattle Times*. Myrtle, my future mother-in-law, saw it and wanted to know why I was escorting Miss Universe while engaged to her daughter. She didn't understand about the Marine Corps and the pickle I would have been in if I hadn't followed through.

Emmett Carson, a frequent visitor at the Snake Ranch, had been in our platoon in OCS and was in the aviation program for pilots. Just after the pageant, Roger, Ben, and I along with a few other Marines had driven to Farmerville, Louisiana, to participate in his military wedding. The crossed-sword arch was impressive to the small town and made the front page of the local scandal sheet. On the way back from his wedding we stopped for a night of jazz in New Orleans at Pete's Place, Pete Fountain's jazz joint.

Emmett had a degree in electrical engineering and we had him come out to the Ranch, for an all-night cram session with several of us before the electronics exam.

The test was as hard as we had expected. There was a crowd looking at the scores posted next to the classroom door. I heard my name mentioned. Being dead-last in the class, I approached with trepidation. The group made a path for me. I looked at the bottom of the list—I wasn't there. Had I already washed out? My eyes kept moving up. There I was, at the very top, with nearly a perfect paper! I had stunned everyone, but Ben had flunked. He had to retake the exam the next day. Emmett had flight school pressures, so I did the best I could to help Ben. He couldn't get a handle on reading a schematic diagram. Somehow, I understood that subject, but it was a disaster for Ben—he failed again.

"My whole family's been so proud of me. I don't know how I'll face 'em," Ben said, as he fought back tears while turning in all his school books.

"Ben, they're still proud of you. You're the first family member to graduate from college. I'll always be proud of you." The words came hard to me. "You've come a long way from that small farm house packed with twelve kids back in Frederick, Oklahoma. When we get through with this war, I'm coming out to meet all of them." We shook hands. I ached to hug him, but there's no hugging in the Marine Corps.

Ben thought he would be sent back to Quantico for six months of basic school. But by the end of the day, he had orders to a two-week artillery school, and then was to immediately report as a Forward Observer for an artillery base somewhere in Vietnam. A very dangerous job, but Ben would face it head on. I was positive of that.

The day of our graduation was bittersweet. We had taken our last class that morning, a two-hour navigation problem that could not be solved without getting lost. You had to find your position again and continue on. It required every chart, slide rule, and formula we had learned, and it was impossible to complete. Nobody reached the final destination. It was specifically designed to make you perform under stress. The top man in our class flunked it.

We chose to delay the O Club graduation ceremony for three hours to wait for the smartest guy in the class. His flunking had to be a fluke. We received the unthinkable news: our number-one man had not even come close to passing the retake. Under pressure, his smarts went south, but that was the purpose of the exam; can you perform under pressure? He was in the Navy, so he would now have to learn about boats and probably never see the war up close.

Ben had written to me twice from Vietnam. His last letter read, "We are taking casualties every day, so I hope I get a letter from my ol' swimming pool buddy in case one of those rounds has my name on it. That would use up one of my nine lives, leaving me only eight more for Carol when I get back to the world."

It wasn't like Ben to write such a letter. It held a sense of desperation. I quickly wrote him a letter, trying to keep things on the light side, about how the nightlife at the Snake Ranch wasn't the same without him—and it wasn't.

Ardi called me in tears. Carol had called her from Hawaii where she was waiting for Ben to arrive for his seven days of R and R. Carol had gone to Hawaii a week before Ben was to arrive and made plans for their wedding that would take place as soon as he got there. It was there she received the life-wrenching news from his family—Ben had been killed in action. She was terribly in love with him and didn't marry until her mid-forties.

Ben's death hit me hard. I hated the Marine Corps for sending him to Vietnam without first going to Basic School. It seemed like they punished him for not passing the electronics class. He was the first casualty from the Ranch.

I hoped my letter had reached him before he got hit. It was returned sixteen days later, unopened. Stamped in big, red letters on the back was the word "DECEASED." I had to sit down. It cut deeply to know one of my best friends had not received my letter telling him how much his friendship meant to me. I opened it and read my last line, "Ben, when we get through this war, I'm expecting you to be in my wedding, so make sure you keep your sword sharp and your powder dry."

In September of 1967, Jerry Bennett was being ripped apart by an enemy rocket on Hill 66 in the Republic of South Vietnam. He was as physically tough a Marine as I ever knew, but steel beats flesh every time.

Once in a while, I order up a Salty Ol' Dawg, and let my thoughts drift back to that sunny day at the pool. I laugh about our fun times, I use his one-liners like they are my own, and my second son is named Ryan Bennett Ferguson. Friends like Ben rub off on you so hard, their memory warms you for a life time.

When Ben shipped out, Paul Gee, another RO, took his place at the Ranch. With his flight pay, Paul bought a VW station wagon. He and I ended up in the same squadron in Vietnam.

He was smart as a whip and liked all of the technical aspects of being a navigator.

Paul Gee was killed about two years later while on final approach to the Da Nang air base after flying a mission to electronically jam surface-to-air missiles for a Navy flight. He was in an EF-10 B aircraft; its escape hatch is a chute in its belly that you slide out to exit in an emergency. Below two hundred feet, there is no escape because the personal parachute will not open in time. He and his pilot were on final approach at Da Nang when they simply went down. They had no chance of survival.

Rusty Ray was another member of the Ranch for a short time. He moved in while he finished up his helicopter training. Flying was his passion, and he brought a couple of radio-controlled airplanes to the Ranch. They were too big to keep in the BOQ, but our garage was just right. In Vietnam, his chopper was shot out of the air during a routine medevac mission, which underscores the point that; nothing in a war zone is ever routine.

Jess Haggerman was the sixth Marine to move to the Ranch. I had met Jess several times when I went to visit John Dirlam at Pacific Lutheran University. I didn't know he had joined the Marines until we ran into each other at the Pensacola BOQ. He was already in chopper school, and he loved to fly the whirligigs. He was good at it. In Vietnam, he became a pilot's, pilot, logging more than a thousand combat hours. After he mustered out of the Corps, he flew six months for the CIA. He loved the precise flying required on dangerous missions.

After returning to the U.S., Jess joined the Army Reserve to fly choppers on the weekends, even though his day job was flying helicopters for Weyerhaeuser. When Mount St. Helens blew its top, Jess is the person who rescued the three loggers the next day. Out of all the news media clamoring to get aboard his chopper, he grabbed one person out of the crowd. That person happened to have been from *National Geographic* magazine. In their spread on the eruption, there is a picture of a man walking up the decimated hill leaving deep footprints in the ash like it was snow. That picture is of Jess.

Jess still gets interviewed when the anniversaries of the eruption take place. To my surprise, one day he was in the video I showed to a class where I was substitute-teaching.

Six Marines lived at the Ranch at various times; three were killed, and I was wounded. Despite flying some hairy missions, only Roger and Jess escaped Vietnam unscathed. As a group, the cockroaches fared much better than we did.

After we completed RO School, Roger left for radar intercept training. I was still harboring a passion for football and tried out for the base team and got myself attached to the Special Services unit. That was a great time. My sole duty for three months was to play football! We had no championship to win, we only practiced a few hours a day, the weather was always good, and we had a party after every game. At halftime, the locker-room air was thick with cigarette smoke.

Nobody was committed like they were to their college team and we won only two games. We beat the University of Mexico City twice; once in Pensacola and once in Mexico City. UMC had the best concept for sports I've ever seen. They had two teams, one that traveled each week and one that played at home every week. Their heaviest players only weighed 150 pounds, so they were both easy wins.

It was fun to play again. There were no training rules, no wind sprints and you haven't lived until you've seen a football player coming out of a locker room with a cigarette jutting through his face mask.

On paper, we had some good players who had started for West Point, the Naval Academy, and other big name schools. The amazing thing was, most of them would have struggled to earn a starting spot at Linfield.

I played tackle and weighed in at 200 pounds, the maximum weight limit to be in the air wing. It was the best I ever played. I was the fastest I had been in years and I knew more about football than the other players because I had played for a great coach.

The next training put us in an airplane in Glencoe, Georgia. The object was to use all of our math and navigation skills to run intercept missions and shoot down other planes in mock dog fights. The training would be shorter but more intense. It consisted of twenty-six flights, with each Radar Officer running five intercepts on each flight. If you flunk two intercepts on a flight, you were given a "down" for that flight. Get two downs out of the twenty-six, and you're gone. The academics were easier, but the flights were pressure-packed.

I quickly learned that there are different kinds of intelligences that exist within our brains. An entirely different set of skills was required for this training. Act and react was the name of the game. The RO had to picture the enemy bogie in the sky like he was looking at an airplane through a window and then use all of the academics to shoot him down or be shot down. I excelled in the dogfights. It seemed easy for me. My star was rising, and I was helping the others.

The dynamics of the training group changed. Several of the RO professor types who were excellent at the pencil and paper tests didn't make it past the first three hops. Those of us who were left seemed to be generalists with fast reflexes and quick thinking patterns. There was a high correlation between athletic backgrounds and intercept success.

The climax of my training came on my twenty-fourth hop. The bogies we had been chasing flew straight and level. This time, they would try to shoot us down. The stakes were high.

The flight consisted of shooting our opponent down with a rocket called a Sparrow. It rode a radar beam to the front quarter of the enemy aircraft. My job was to tell the pilot the direction and the number of compass degrees for every turn. For the purpose of making the exercise harder, it was assumed we missed with the Sparrow and had to out-maneuver the other plane, get behind them, and shoot them down with a Sidewinder, a heat-seeking missile that would fly up their tailpipe. It was a game of wits, one on one.

During my first run on my twenty-fourth flight, our electronic compass went offline. It was one of the most important pieces of information for calculating headings to tell the pilot to fly. I now had to rely on the magnetic compass, which was more of an approximation. I could read the altitude and range of the bogie from my radar screen, but from there on out it was seat-of-the-pants navigating.

We twisted and turned as they tried to shoot us down, but in the end I won all of my battles that day. The RO who ran his intercepts after me couldn't get the hang of it and was dropped from the program. It wasn't that tragic. He became an air traffic controller and got a cushy job after the war, In retrospect, he made out quite well.

The shadow of Vietnam loomed larger, and Ardi and I decided not to be engaged. As Marines, there was no question where we would be going. On the one hand, I didn't want to leave a young widow behind. On the other hand, I didn't want to die without knowing life's greatest pleasure of being together as man and wife.

With war reports becoming more gruesome on a daily basis, Ardi and I decided to put our personal lives on standby.

We were not the type to live together before marriage, even though we were beginning to see it everywhere. Pride in ourselves and upbringing would not allow it, no matter what the future held. This war didn't affect everybody in society, only a few of us. The vast majority of our friends were still in school, or had teaching jobs providing them with exemptions from the draft. A few of the men were able to join the reserves, and a few got drafted. Almost for certain the reservists wouldn't go to Vietnam, but they rolled the dice and took their chances. They had their lives to live, and I had mine. I came to embrace the idea that not everybody should go to war. Teachers were making major contributions on the home front.

Because of the need for ROs in Vietnam, the training was to continue over the Christmas holidays. But due to a scheduling SNAFU, on December 23, 1966, I found myself flying military standby to Eugene to spend Christmas with the folks. There were no direct flights from Georgia, so I caught a military flight to Denver. From there, I would have to fly standby through Seattle. Ardi was living in a lakefront apartment, having the fun of a lifetime as an unengaged stewardess.

"Hi Ardi, this is Bob. I got bumped off of standby, and I'm in Seattle—I, uh, er, so I thought I'd give you a call and see how you're doing."

She let me stammer—a lot. The conversation was painfully awkward. I wanted to see her, but I didn't want to impose on her new life. Her "Hello" had icicles hanging from it.

"I hadn't planned to come home, but things didn't work out at the training command, so I'm flying home, but I'm stuck in Seattle until morning." There was a Pause. A long embarrassing pause.

"Isn't that too bad?" Her breath froze my earpiece.

"I flew in a military plane to Denver and on United to here, and you know airplane food, so maybe you'd like to get some dinner with me. This won't surprise you, I'm still broke, but maybe we could get a burger."

"What for?" An arctic blast hit my ear drum.

"You know we're probably not the only people ever caught in these circumstances, and it's a little hard to really get things right all the time, but I've seen the inside of every bar in Glencoe, Georgia at least twice, and I didn't know what I had until you sent the ring back." The ball was in her court. I decided to wait and see if there was any melting going on.

"I'll fix you something here," she said tepidly.

"Taxi! Oh, taxi!" I yelled from the curbside phone.

When I reached her place, she was wearing a robe that she had made. It was a full-length Chinese dress made of a soft, red felt material with a Mandarin collar. A gold strip of embroidery ran from the top of the collar just under her chin to the bottom of the floor-length gown. She looked spectacular, but romance did not ensue. We were married six days later.

After a three-day honeymoon in Fort Lauderdale, we moved into a furnished apartment in nearby Brunswick. The remaining few weeks in Georgia were fun. Ron Robson and I were ahead of the other ROs in the training, so we had a little slack in our schedules. He came over every night on the excuse of watching the TV he had loaned us. It was a six-inch TV and you had to sit directly in front of it to see anything. It was like Ron said, "It's so small, we'll have to take turns watching it."

Ardi and I babysat a few times for the new baby girl of Doug Avery and his wife Cindy. They lived in our apartment complex. Their child didn't look anything like Doug, which was good; in OCS, the sergeants called him "Candidate Ugly."

His ancestors had been officers in the Revolutionary War. His mother's name was "Lou Doug," and Doug himself was as

Southern fried as chicken. Like all of those good ol' boys, duty to country is not an obligation, but a birthright. In May 1968, Doug's A6-A aircraft was lost just north of the DMZ. His family did not get a final report until 2002, when they read about the discovery of his remains in a local newspaper. (This would be a good place for the reader to dog-ear this page and go to http://refugeministries.us/avery/ and learn more about a great American—and bring a hanky.)

Ardi pinned the RO wings on Ron and me after the graduation ceremony which completed our flight training. It wasn't as fun as the OCS or Pensacola graduations. People were already dead or currently in harm's way in Vietnam. The war was real—and we were headed into the teeth of it.

After posting stellar scores in running air to air intercepts, I hoped to get into a fighter command. The luck of the draw sent me to a photo-reconnaissance and electronic countermeasures squadron. Ron was sent to a fighter squadron at Cherry Point, North Carolina.

Recon missions tended to be long, with a lot of technical preparation. But the location of the squadron, sunny El Toro, California, made up for any complaints I had about the assignment.

Ardi and I sold the Batmobile and flew to Seattle. We upgraded to a 1960 Chevrolet Impala hard top—a blue and white beauty. Spending money on a new car seemed ridiculous to us; after all, it hadn't been that long since I was riding a motorcycle in the rain. We now had all of our bills paid off and were starting to move ahead a little bit in the savings department.

Part of the fun of military life was that there were no secrets. Everyone knew exactly how much everyone else got paid. If a lieutenant and his wife were driving the big car, living in a fancy apartment, and wearing big wedding rings, they were either in debt or had rich parents. Nobody cared. Your worth would be based solely upon your contribution to the squadron.

Most of the officers lived in apartments with a pool, but Ardi and I chose a tiny duplex tucked into a small corner of Tustin, California. The only amenity was a shared laundry room with quarter-gobbling machines. We filled it with furniture bought in a retirement complex in Laguna Hills. Ardi's great aunt and uncle, Anna and Hubert Morel, lived there. They had told us about all of the seniors who were selling high quality furniture at low prices as they downsized from large homes to condos. One weekend, we picked up a local *Penny Saver* circular and scoured their neighborhood for bargains. We bought a coffee table, dining room set, and lamps. We used all of it for decades before passing everything on to family or friends.

My day job at the squadron consisted of flying photo-recon training missions. My collateral duty was supervising the parachute loft: all of the chutes in Martin Baker ejection seats had to be regularly checked and hung in a tall loft to keep their suppleness. It was easy duty. The enlisted men running it were young and eager to do a good job. They were apprehensive when they heard a young officer would be in charge, since a few of the young officers had let their new supervising authority go to their heads.

The para-loft kids were a good crew. I didn't want to spoil it, so I did something quite unlike an officer; instead of the usual terse commands, I took a page out of a book which I had been reading, Dale Carnegie's *How to Win Friends and Influence People*. Carnegie makes the point that you get more productivity from people when you let them be in charge of their own work. I began my first day as their new boss by saying, "Okay, gentlemen, I'm here to work for you." That simple statement got around to the other enlisted men and put me in good stead with all of the troops in the squadron. Carnegie was right and I made that book required reading for my kids at early ages.

The squadron training was rigorous, but the emphasis was on helping us be better navigators. The tests didn't flunk you, but were designed to find your weak points. On a mission, only a perfect score would do. We flew night hops to targets a few hundred miles away and snapped pictures of giant bull's-eyes on the ground. The idea was to get the target in the center of a photo frame.

To build our navigation skills, we took cross-country flights all over the country. On one occasion, I flew with the CO, Colonel Percival, up to McCord Air Force Base near Seattle to have dinner with his parents and my in-laws. After our dinner, the RF-4B put on a spectacular nighttime display as we hit the afterburners on takeoff as we headed back to El Toro. The flames shot out the back about a hundred feet with a deafening roar. I think that was the first time John and Myrtle considered me something more than a Cro-Magnon football player. And maybe even a suitable husband for their daughter. (At our fortieth wedding anniversary, Myrtle did whisper to Ardi, "I think Bob might work out.")

The CO knew the para-loft ran itself, so he also put me in charge of Special Services. My job was to put together the squadron athletic teams and get the enlisted men military rates for Disneyland, Knott's Berry Farm, and Sea World. It was like running the park program in McMinnville, except the kids were older.

I started a little coffee and donut stand we called the gidunk ("gi" rhymes with knee and "dunk" as in donut.) It resembled the park snack shack, but for adults. It became a big hit and started making money. We used the profits to buy things for the athletic teams, but we began to make too much money. The CO asked me to keep two sets of books: one for the general inspector that would show sales under the allowable amount that a squadron could keep and another set for how much it really made. Money issues were one of those petty, small ways in which you could get into big trouble in the military.

The day I left the squadron to ship out to Vietnam, Colonel Percival called me into his office and told me to bring both sets of books. When I handed him the one set I kept for the inspectors, he swore more than the DI at OCS . He lit a big cigar, blew some smoke rings, and stared at me from under thick, bushy eyebrows. I knew something was about to hit the fan.

"I'm going to talk to you like a Dutch uncle. You let me down by not keeping two sets of books," he said.

"I made sure the one set would meet the inspection requirements. Honestly sir, I bought a couple of kegs of beer for the enlisted men's picnic, and I loaned some of the money to enlisted guys who were a little short, but we always got paid back. I thought that kind of stuff in any set of books would get me in hot water."

"Fergy, I gave you a near-perfect fitness report. The only person with a higher report in the squadron was my second in command, and you were just a shade below him. You can have a great career in the Marine Corps, and I hope you stay in, but you should have told me what you were doing."

"Thank you for that report sir, but may I speak freely?"

"Of course. That's why you're here."

"Sir, I'm a little shocked that my fitness report would be so high, since you're always chewing me out for something. I never see you chewing on the other lieutenants."

More smoke rings, more thinking; I assumed another load was about to hit the same fan.

"You know—you're right, but it's because they don't have your potential. They wouldn't begin to see what Special Services can do for the morale of the men. As officers, we work hard and we need to play hard, but so do the troops. You're the only lieutenant in any squadron I've ever been in who's done something to keep up their morale." He held the cigar between his index and middle finger, which were pointing at me for emphasis. "Do you know we've had our highest rates of reenlistment ever? Not only that, but that sergeant Fish you recommended for OCS is now a lieutenant at Pensacola earning his wings. That's why you got a high fitness report. Now, I want you to carry your good work to Vietnam and think about staying in the Corps. I hope to be seeing you over there before you rotate back, but I'll be keeping an eye on your career." (Sergeant Fish had a great career. After his tour in Vietnam, he went on to become the personal helicopter pilot for Vice President Spiro T. Agnew.)

I left Colonel Percival's office feeling great. He was one of the brightest people I had ever met, and he had finally said I had done a good job. Maybe he should have read the part in Carnegie's book that says, "Be generous with your praise and lavish with your approbations."

A few weeks before my conversation with the CO, Mike Riley stayed overnight with Ardi and I in our Tustin apartment. He had just returned from his thirteen-month tour in Vietnam, where he served as a platoon commander. He was filled with stories about the country, his men, the people, and his part in the war.

"We had missions we went on every day that ranged several miles from our base, but we really didn't get into too much fighting," he said. I wondered if he was giving me the real deal. "We only lost one guy, and he was only wounded. He tripped a booby trap wire hooked to a 500-pound bomb, but the VC had buried it so deep the blast went straight up. He was stunned from the concussion, but all he got out of it was a broken ear drum." It seemed funny that such a big bomb didn't kill him. "We had all hit the deck, but he just stood next to the giant hole and said, 'What happened?'"

It's an odd thing to laugh about a near death experience, but Riley, his troops, and the kid with a new hearing problem did just that.

"Did you ever get ambushed?" I asked, expecting to hear horror stories.

"Nope, the closest we ever came to it was one day; we were on a recon mission. We're just walking along and all of a sudden, we see six dinks just 'diddy-boppin' along with their rifles slung over their shoulders. They were talking like they were taking a walk in the park, and we were kinda doin' the same thing." His body was animated as he showed how they carried their weapons. "By the time they saw us, we had wasted three of them and the other three threw up their hands to surrender. It was all over in a few seconds. It was just dumb luck they didn't hear us." I was pretty sure he was being his usual, modest self.

"I brought an AK-47 home as a souvenir, and my kids gave me something." Riley reverently took a plaque out of his duffle bag that his platoon had given him before he left. The inscription read: "To 2nd Lt. Riley for his extraordinary Leadership in the Republic of South Vietnam. To all who see this, know ye that he shall forever be the Skipper of Riley's Raiders." The plaque was handmade on the fire-base from scraps on hand, but he cradled it caringly as he looked at the platoon picture in the middle of it.

"I hope all of those guys make it out. The three VC we captured told us they were a few days ahead of a North Vietnamese Army battalion. The NVA are every bit as good as soldiers as anyone we can put in the field. I'm afraid our casualties will jump when we start fighting them."

The sun found us still talking about leadership styles, Fitchner's reaction under fire, losing Ben, and how much more serious life had become in the two years since we'd left Linfield. Riley was carrying a large yellow packet like the one we carried on the day we reported to OCS. He was on his way to San Diego for a one-year assignment training platoons headed for Vietnam, after which he would muster back into civilian life.

Mike Riley distinguished himself with his country and his men. He could prove it with the most impressive plaque I have ever seen.

CHAPTER 7

Vietnam–Squadron VMCJ-1

It was the era of civil rights, and the women's movement was just emerging. The U.S. Supreme Court had ruled that United Airlines could not require stewardesses to quit because they got married. UAL snubbed that decision, and Ardi was forced out of her job when we tied the knot back in December. It would have been a great job for her while I was in Vietnam, and we could have used the extra cash. On the other hand, it was an opportunity for her to go back to Linfield so she could finish her education degree in the thirteen months that I would be across the pond.

I took two weeks leave to get Ardi situated before I left for Nam. We rented a small apartment in McMinnville. It was a nice, safe place for her to be. Carl and Kathy Heisler could be counted on for moral support, and Jim Wickerd, who was working at a local gas station, promised to keep the Chevy running. Our life was so well-planned, nothing could go wrong.

It snowed the night before I was to leave. I got up early and put the chains on the car. I couldn't be late. We made it to the Portland International Airport with some time to spare. We held each other tight until it was time to part for what seemed would be a lifetime.

My plane flew a Great Circle route over the North Pole that included a stop at Elmendorf Air Force Base in Anchorage, Alaska. I dashed into the terminal just so I could say I had been in Alaska. It took seventeen hours to reach Okinawa, where we were scheduled for a one-night layover and then fly straight into Da Nang Air Base, Republic of South Vietnam.

The Tet Offensive had just started, and the Viet Cong were shelling the Da Nang runway. Our flight was delayed for three days. An Air Force lieutenant and I rented a guide, who drove us all around the island of Okinawa. On the fourth day, we planned to see a bullfight. The Asian contest is different than a Spanish bull fight; for instance, there is no matador. The bulls fight each other until one is knocked silly, but there is no killing. Much more sensible, I thought. I was eager to see it and avoid another day in Vietnam, because my thirteen-month tour of duty started the day I left Portland. I now had only 392 days left.

A knock on my BOQ door at 0400 brought me back to reality. The Da Nang runway was repaired, and I would be leaving at 0630 for the war effort. My gut started to knot up. I slid a note of goodbye under the door to the lieutenant I had planned to go with to the bullfights. He had orders for thirteen months of duty on Okinawa. His biggest worry was if his car would arrive safely. I've always thought ninety percent of the guys make out well during a war. Only ten percent do the actual fighting. He was the ninety, and I would be the ten—but I would be the lucky one in that ten percent.

Their glazed-over eyes were engulfed by dark circles. The gaunt figures were incapable of neither sorrow nor joy. They were old. Their youth had been a casualty of war.

They waited on the Da Nang tarmac to travel to the world I had left behind. Some had come straight from a night ambush; their faces still had the remnants of camouflage grease. Their tattered utilities were sweat stained; a few had wet boots from crossing a creek to make it to the landing strip. They unloaded their weapons and put them into large metal bins. I couldn't tell nor did it matter which branch of the service they came from. They had fought until the very last day of their rotation date—and survived. They would get on our airplane one way or another. To stay a single day longer could be fatal. They wished us good luck as we exited and they readied to board. They made me thankful I was going to the air wing and not the bush. No glazed-over look for me.

All of Da Nang looked to be in chaos. The air reeked of dirt, diesel, sweat, and unfamiliar spices. There was a line of trucks loaded with soldiers in combat gear and Vietnamese civilians with all their worldly possessions wrapped in blankets and woven baskets. Getting to squadron VMCJ-1 might take me a while. I asked a sergeant who looked like he was in some sort of authority how to get to the Marine side of the air base.

"Lieutenant, the best thing to do is just ask one of these truck drivers where they're headed. Sooner or later, you'll find one going your way."

It was a war zone, and we were all in it together. Every driver I asked was eager to help if he could. Finally I found one going my way, but I have no idea where the Vietnamese family with a small pig in a basket was headed or why they were aboard a military truck.

After hitching a few more rides, I arrived at the VMCJ-1 living area. It consisted of two rows of hootches facing each other, with a walkway of wooden ammo crates down the middle to keep your feet out of the mud during the monsoons. *This is going to be a long year,* I thought as I looked at the humble accommodations, *but thank God it's not the bush.*

I had missed the real heavy monsoon rains, so I was arriving at a good time. The flight crews lived five men to a hootch. They were oblong huts with a four-foot-high plywood half-wall and tent canvas and netting extending up to a pitched roof covered with corrugated metal. Everything about the hootch accommodated the utilitarian four-by-eight sheet of plywood, a building material that created the hootch dimensions of roughly, sixteen by thirty-two feet. The bunks were the standard spring cots with a thin mattress, covered with mosquito netting that hung from the ceiling.

In mid January, Vietnam is humid and warm but not hot. Everything felt damp and smelled like mildew. Sleeping space was at a premium. I ended up bunking in the rack of an RO who had recently been killed. His RF 4-B over-rotated on takeoff, and the plane fell tail-first back onto the tarmac. He and the pilot safely ejected, but the jet had been loaded with extra fuel. The draft from a giant fireball pulled the RO back into the inferno.

Many in the squadron witnessed the gruesome sight of Tom Grudd dangling, twisting, desperately trying to steer his parachute away from the flaming rubble. He descended slowly into a horrific, fiery death. The pilot survived and watched the scene as he drifted safely to the ground. I can only guess at what his thoughts must have been—the crash was caused by pilot error.

Despite Grudd's death, life went on. This was the liveliest of the officer's hootches in the squadron. The front of the hootch had been configured to house a full-size fridge for keeping ample amounts of cold beer and wine. A game table and stools made from the all-purpose ammo crates made it a natural gathering place for a lot of the officers. The hootch commander was Wil Foster a tall, small town kid from Merlin, Oregon and the only pilot in the hootch. Dan Richards a short, wiry blond from Florida, contrasted with the seriousness of Ron Rusthoven. Todd Vangermeersch, a skinny hockey player from Rhode Island rounded out the mix of gregarious personalities that attracted flight crews from the other hootches.

Like the mosquito netting that hung from the ceiling, the ghost of Tom Grudd shrouded my rack. Vangermeersch and Grudd had been good friends. He resented my taking Tom's place, and he made no bones about it. It created a strain between the two of us as taut as a stretched rubber band. It didn't take long for anxieties to snap. I was unaware that I had been using a pillow that Grudd's wife had sent him. I was lying on my rack using it as a headrest while reading the *Stars and Stripes* newspaper. Smeersch, as we called him, walked over and yanked it from under my head and I cracked my noggin on the rail of the bunk.

"That's Tom Grudd's. I should have sent it home to his wife," he said.

"Hey, Vangermeersch, all you have to do is ask! You want me outta here, you go find me another bunk and I'll move. But you understand one thing—I wasn't here when Grudd died, and I'm not taking any more guff off of you, so stow your sarcastic remarks or be ready to defend your skinny self. That's all I'm going to say."

"Smeersch," Wil Foster said, "as the hootch commander, you've been out of line. Fergy didn't even know Tom. This is going to cost you that bottle of Mateuse wine you've been hoarding in the fridge. Fergy and I are going to drink it. You can join us if you're up to apologizing."

Smeersch moped and paced, as we drank his expensive wine.

"Well, I may as well have a little of my own wine," Smeersch said.

By the time we'd killed half a bottle, Smeersch and I were good friends. I had lost Ben, but he just left and then died.

Smeersch had helplessly watched as Grudd was slowly pulled back into the firestorm. War exposes raw nerves, but you cover them up, move on, and save your fight for the enemy.

The mission of VMCJ-1 was two-fold: photo reconnaissance, and electronic countermeasures. I was involved only in photo-recon. The countermeasure guys electronically jammed enemy radars, including surface-to-air missile sites.

The squadron letters and number appeared on the side of our plane, and we were proud of them. The V meant it was a fixed-wing aircraft, the MC stood for Marine Corps, the J was for reconnaissance (I never understood why it wasn't an R), and the 1 meant we were squadron one of three Marine reconnaissance squadrons.

We flew 24/7 using cameras that could spot a nickel on the ground from 5,000 feet. We used infrared film for night missions in the RF-4B. This aircraft identification made sense. The R stood for the reconnaissance version of the F-4 fighter, and it was model version B. It had a needle nose unlike other F-4s, which had a bulbous front end. No guns, no escorts, just the world's fastest flying jet and our wits for protection. "Kill 'em with fillem" was our motto.

Our lives consisted of: sleep, fly, eat chow, have a few beers, and repeat, every day. Someone in the hootch was always flying, the morale was great, and probably like all wars, the humor was exceptional. The tedium was broken up by sports, cards, and endless games of Acey-Deucey, with lots of evening camaraderie at our refrigerator. The laughter was tempered by knowing that daylight would bring another round of danger.

My first in-country hop was a familiarization flight. The purpose of this assignment was to get to know the major landmarks and quirks of the air base and ended with a short, safe mission. But every hop in a war zone is a combat mission. I would be flying with Major Fallon, and we were given an easy target to photograph. I planned and re-planned the navigation of that first flight. It was impossible to sleep. I was scared. I hoped I wouldn't wet my flight suit strapping into the plane.

We had completed the familiarization portion of the flight, and, from my back seat, I was in charge of the rest of the mission. I had selected a small inlet on the coastline as the initial point of entry for the target.

"Major, come to a heading of 240 degrees over the mouth of that inlet."

"Roger," said Major Fallon.

"Maintain 500 feet altitude and 300 knots." The speed and altitude was just right for the camera we were using, which would make the enemy stand out as big as centerfold models.

"Roger." He maneuvered the aircraft to the precise speed, heading, and altitude.

A piece of cake, I thought as we rolled in on the inlet. It was an easy first mission. I pushed all of the buttons to start the cameras rolling for a perfect run.

Wham! My head hit the right side of the canopy; the G-forces scattered my pencils and maps. *Whap!* I hit the left side of the canopy, followed quickly by another smash from the right. I checked the gauges—no alarms. I couldn't eject; we were going above the 200-knot limit. To eject at 300 knots would be fatal. The wind shear would shatter your face mask like a hundred-pound sledge hammer swung with full force.

"Fergy, did you see that?"

"See what?"

"Those tracers about the size of golf balls coming up at us."

"No, I was looking at my camera gear. Are you sure?"

Smack! I hit the ceiling.

"Don't tell me you didn't see that one. It went right by your canopy."

"I was trying to get my maps and didn't see anything."

"Ya know, I need a witness to substantiate that we are being shot at."

"Major, you've got your witness. I know you're not bending this aircraft around for the fun of it. I've never pulled Gs like that."

We lined up for the run again and completed the mission. Back in the big, steel, U-shaped revetments that housed the planes, Major Fallon did his post-flight inspection. He was staring at the small dial in the wheel well. "Look at that G meter. It's pegged at ten Gs—the wings are supposed to fall off at nine." He patted the plane's wing like it was his pet dog. "I'm glad this baby can't read."

We earned an air medal that day for completing the mission under enemy fire, which I never did see. If that was an example of what flying in Vietnam would be like, I knew some of us wouldn't survive. Tom Grudd was the only crew member lost so far, but as this small war heated up, we all knew in the back of our minds it was only a matter of time.

Day-to-day flying was fairly safe. We went out on a mission, took pictures, came back, and had the film developed. If we spotted enemy troops, bombing raids were immediately launched. The B-52s based in Thailand would be rolling within the hour, and they would carpet bomb the area. These Air Force missions were called "arclites," and they were devastating. Sometimes they used anti-personnel bombs that exploded three feet off of the ground and sent out shrapnel in all directions. In the drop zone, small trees looked like they had been cut off with a giant chainsaw at about a yard high. It was disgusting to think of what they did to flesh. Within a few days, we would recon the area again and there would often be another road snaking around bomb craters. The enemy was ingenious, persistent, and had an unending supply of men.

We were a high-tech squadron, using side-looking radar and infra-red cameras for night missions. After the ground had cooled, we would fly over suspected enemy positions where we could spot the heat from the engines of enemy trucks and small cooking fires. When our film was developed, it looked like small clear dots on a piece of film negative. That was the bad guys. Past intelligence told us that a half a dozen soldiers would be gathered around each cooking fire that dotted the film. By counting the number of fires, it could be estimated rather accurately the number of enemy in that vicinity. A few phone calls and the massive air attacks from Thailand would be rolling.

For the air crews, it was a sanitary war. We never saw the blood and guts from those bombs. We had decent meals, hot showers, cold beer, and a little Vietnamese "house mouse" to do our laundry every day. I knew I had made the right decision to stay out of the grunt war. I wasn't cut out for it like Riley was, but I envied him for being a "real" Marine.

One day it was my turn "in the barrel." Our mission was to drop into the thick clouds and heavy rains pounding the A Shau Valley and photograph the winding road that ran the thirty-mile length of the valley basin. It was a major supply route for the Viet Cong. On my five-by-six-inch radar screen, it was a dark void shaped like a meat platter ringed by bright green feedback from the surrounding 3,000-foot mountains. We were an all-weather squadron and would be the only birds flying that day. The trick was to get into the valley as close as possible to the southern mountains, descend to 250 feet, and follow the twisting road at a blazing 500 knots. At that speed and altitude, we would be a screaming surprise to anyone on the ground. We could get in and out of the valley before they could get a bead on us with small arms. It was safe from that standpoint, but my navigation had to be perfect. If I was a few miles short, we would "buy the farm" on the side of a Vietnamese mountain.

We punched through the cloud cover close to the sloping hills at the south end of the valley. The pilot hit the throttles, pushing our speed to 500 knots. The speed was exhilarating; not being able to eject doubled the "pucker factor." I switched on the forward-looking camera mounted just under the nose cone of the aircraft. All I had to do now was hold on and tell the pilot when to pull up so we didn't hit the northern mountains while he fixated on the winding road.

The valley floor was littered with burned-out vehicles, theirs and ours. The hulk of an A-1 prop-driven plane sat next to a crater-filled airstrip. A few years earlier, an Air Force pilot was shot down, but his wing mate, Bernard Fisher, landed on the airstrip next to him as the VC closed in. The downed airman scrambled into the second seat of Fisher's plane while taking heavy fire from small arms as they lifted off the pock-marked airstrip. Fisher's well-chronicled rescue exceeds any fiction you can read. Just seeing the downed A-1 was an inspiration. Fisher, a mild-mannered Mormon, received the Medal of Honor. The success of our mission stood on their shoulders—the location of that plane was a checkpoint on my low-level navigation map.

These were our most dangerous hops, but they were the favorite of all the crews. There was a satisfaction in completing a mission we had trained for. It was like getting into the big game after you practiced long and hard for it. A lot of our missions were flown at 2,000 feet, took over three hours to complete, and consisted of flying a grid of flight lines to map a specific area. One of these milk-run missions was to fly along the Demilitarized Zone and photograph surface-to-air missile sites. The SAMs were portable, which meant we had DMZ missions every day. Occasionally, a crew would have to take evasive action from a fired missile by diving straight toward it to get inside its turn radius. Those who had seen them said they looked like a big telephone pole coming up at you.

Since we flew the recon missions alone, there were never any witnesses to the loss of our air planes. They simply didn't come back. We didn't know if they were lost from ground fire, a SAM, pilot error, or a mechanical malfunction. We had sixty flight crew members; we lost six but recovered four more that were shot down from ground fire.

Shortly after we moved into the new, air-conditioned Quonset huts, my roommate, First Lieutenant Ariel Cross, went missing. I held out hope beyond all reasonableness that he might have survived as a prisoner of war. Years later, a visit to a traveling Vietnam War Memorial told me otherwise. The Corps kept Lt. Cross and his navigator as MIA. He is listed as a major on the Vietnam Veterans' Memorial Wall.

My ninety to ten percent ratio was almost perfect. I was lucky to be on the ninety percent side of that equation, and after all, ten percent is miniscule—unless it's your friends.

"If you're a gung-ho Marine, get on a table and tap dance," barked Colonel Parker. There were grins on all of the faces inside the busy Marine Corps Officer's Club at Da Nang Air Base. They looked around for the CO, not knowing what to do about the bizarre command. We were all gung-ho Marines, but tap dance on the tables?

The CO repeated himself. "I said, anybody that's a gung-ho Marine, get on a table and tap dance! That's an order!"

A riot erupted. The seventy-plus aviators in the club scrambled to the top of the thirty plywood tables and did their version of a tap dance. Beer spilled, wrestling matches ensued, a few tables were broken, and there were some skinned knees and elbows.

I came out from behind the bamboo bar with the microphone and said in the CO's voice, "As you were, gentlemen." Laughter exploded, drinks were gulped, and backs were slapped as they caught onto the prank. The joke lasted for days. "Are you gung-ho?" someone would say, and anybody nearby would tap dance.

My O Club shenanigans earned me some points with my fellow officers, but it also caught the eye of Major Tanner. He was short in height, shallow in humor, and devoid of personality. He had forged a mediocre career by kissing up to his superiors and kicking the seat cushion of the guys below him. Military types like him could advance—but only so far. The respect of your men was necessary to get beyond a lieutenant colonel. "Colonel Parker, I'm sure you heard about the ruckus Lieutenant Ferguson caused at the O Club, and some government property was destroyed," Major Tanner said. "In my opinion a brawl at the club is conduct unbecoming of an officer."

"Thank you major, but we've just completed a pretty hairy operation," Colonel Parker said. "When we work hard, we play hard. The other squadron commanders tell me their boys all thought it was a hoot, and nobody got hurt." He paused to let the tattle-tale quality of the major's complaint sink in. "If you're referring to the broken tables as government property, I saw Fergy and another lieutenant fixing them. But your point is well made. I'll talk to Lieutenant Ferguson." He chewed on the ever-present cigar stuck in the corner of his mouth. There must have been an unwritten regulation somewhere requiring Marine COs to smoke cigars then chew them right down to a stub.

As he posted the following day's orders in the hootches, Corporal Magnus relayed this conversation to me. He told it with more relish than a neighborhood gossip.

"I'm surprised Major Tanner would criticize a fellow officer in your presence, but thanks for the scuttlebutt, Corporal Magnus." I handed him a six pack of beer. "Keep your ear to the ground, and I'll keep you in beer. Major Tanner isn't my immediate supervisor, so there's nothing he can personally do, but I don't need him volunteering me for the CO's naughty-boy list."

"You're in good shape for now, lieutenant, but you'll need to be squared-away around Major Tanner," Magnus said as he popped the top and chugged a beer in our hootch.

Corporal Magnus was a young black kid from Georgia, and he was probably surprised that a white officer would socialize with him. He was a product of the racial bias I had seen when I took my intercept training in Glencoe only a year earlier. Blacks still drank out of separate water fountains, had segregated seating in theaters, and rode in the back of the bus. Discrimination was no longer legal, but a sign in a Glencoe Laundromat read, "Any nigger coins used here will be donated to the Ku Klux Klan." In the squadron, we only saw his skin as Marine Corps green.

Colonel Parker had read my El Toro fitness report, and once again, I was the Special Services Officer. In a war zone, the morale of the men is a priority. I organized a lot of sports activities and a few keg parties for our enlisted troops. Since we worked around the clock, we had some midnight volleyball games under a bright moon. It was a fun diversion.

Major Tanner hated fun. He was all work, no play, and never joined in the festivities. He seemed convinced that fun times did not promote proper military bearing. He was incensed that

I provided kegs of beer for the enlisted men, many of whom were not of legal drinking age. I couldn't have cared less what he thought. These troops could not be compared to the kids back home living life under the roofs of their parents. Besides, he was not my boss; I answered only to the CO, and that rubbed more salt into his self-righteous wounds.

Sheer joy overtook me when Major Tanner was transferred out of the squadron and up to the Air Wing. The wing command was the administrative arm for several squadrons. He was put in charge of transferring personnel to different jobs within Vietnam. He wouldn't even be living in our squadron area anymore. I was ecstatic.

It was about that time I had moved into one of the air-conditioned Quonset huts with Ariel Cross. The huts had been walled off down the middle, with two men living on each side. It was more comfortable for sleeping, but the configuration broke up the camaraderie and festivities of our old hootch.

After returning from a night hop, I was looking forward to some rack time in the air-cooled space. Cross had left for an afternoon hop, and I had slipped into a dream about being back in the world with Ardi. The loud knock on the door interrupted the best part of my dream. I opened the military-green door of the hut and said, "What's going on, Corporal Magnus?"

"Lieutenant, I just came to tell you that you need to report to Major Tanner at wing headquarters ASAP."

"What's the gouge, corporal?" I asked.

"Don't know, sir. Even the CO didn't know what it was about, but he did say he hated to see you go up to the wing to some office job."

"You know, corporal, I've been here seven months and flown seventy-five combat missions. After that flight two nights ago with major Goller, I'm ready to fly a desk for a while." It was standard procedure to fly for half of your tour and then move to a ground job. "He's going to get somebody killed trying to get a Distinguished Flying Cross."

"You guys didn't complete that mission, did you sir?" Magnus asked.

"Nope. I chickened out at the last second," I said.

It was similar to the screaming day missions in the A Shau valley where I used the downed plane for a check-point, but this had been a night mission using flares that popped like giant flash bulbs. There was a high overcast so there was absolutely no light. It was like flying inside a giant basketball; conditions were perfect for vertigo. You could be flying upside down and not know it except for your instruments.

"The guys that had us on radar said we were clear to descend into the valley, but my gear said we hadn't crossed the southern mountains. My radar got fuzzy at the bottom of the scope." I was trying to give a plausible explanation rather than confess to the panic that had gripped me, causing me to delay our descent. "We didn't drop into the valley for another fifteen seconds, and I knew with the first flash that I had missed the southern part of the road. I'd like to do it again," I lied. "But this time, I'd listen to those Navy boys who had us on radar. Their gear was a lot better for that mission. But that was the first time I'd ever worked with them."

"Major Goller and Captain Daniels completed that mission last night. They're going to get the DFC for it," Magnus said.

"I know. I gave Daniels my maps. He's an old salt, and he's worked with the Navy quite a bit. It would have been a piece of cake if I had just let them guide us, but I wasn't sure how good they were."

I'll never know how that mission might have affected anyone on the ground. I chickened out, and I hope to God it didn't cost anyone his life. I've kept that repugnant truth buried. Confessing it now does not give me closure; there is no such thing. This admission does not give me a cathartic relief. I suppose such a haunting is a byproduct of war, but I have learned to live with it.

To change the painful topic I said to Magnus, "When does the major want to see me?"

"Right away, sir."

"That's a shame. I'd have a beer with you, but if he smelled it on me, he'd probably have me court-martialed rather than giving me another job."

Looking squared-away for the major was my best chance at a good job within the wing. I changed into clean, olive drab, many-pocketed utility shirt and pants. I gave a quick shine to my jungle boots and hopped a ride up to wing headquarters.

Major Tanner was smiling like a Cheshire cat.

"Lieutenant Ferguson, you will have completed your thirteen- month tour of duty here in Vietnam in almost exactly six months."

"Yes sir, but I'm a long way from getting short."

"Your rotation date back to the world is the same as two other officers, but they are pilots."

There were some pilots who tended to treat ROs as second class citizens, and Tanner was one of them. I knew I would not be getting any kind of a plum job, but I wasn't prepared for what he said next in a tone of gleefulness.

"I'm transferring you out to the field to be a Forward Air Controller," he said slightly chorteling.

His words stunned me. The rule of thumb in Vietnam was that when you get to wing, you give the best jobs to the guys in your squadron, not the worst. It was very bad form to do otherwise.

It wasn't a death sentence, but FACs had a very high casualty rate. The FAC went out on operations with the grunts and worked with the kids who got the glazed-over looks. When they came under fire, the FAC assessed the situation from the forward point of attack and called in artillery or air strikes to get them all out of a sticky wicket. It was a dangerous job meant for gung-ho Marines, not someone like me who had been trying their best to avoid going into the bush.

"But major, there's only a handful of ROs qualified for photo-recon, and it's a critical billet. Is another RO on the way to replace me?" I could have guessed his reply.

"I don't know, and I don't care. In two days, you're going to FAC School in Okinawa, and then reporting to the Fifth Marine Division for assignment." An evil smirk crept over his face like a sadist enjoying someone else's pain.

"But major, I've been here over six months. I'm scheduled to meet my wife in Hawaii on R and R in three weeks, and I never did go to basic school."

I pulled out all the whining stops. Sweat stung my eyes, but it wasn't from the hundred-degree heat. It was from my humiliation at groveling on my knees to a spiteful human being.

"War is hell, lieutenant. Be sure to take all of your gear with you. You'll be reporting directly to the field after you get back from the school." His eyes sparkled with glee as he smugly watched me fill with the terror of going out with the grunts.

I did have the satisfaction of knowing he would never become a good CO—he was too self-righteous to ever smoke cigars.

Any place in a war zone is dangerous, but the FAC billet had a casualty rate even higher than platoon leaders, a billet I had avoided like the plague. It now looked like I had jumped from the frying pan into the fire, but I fully expected my Ferguson bumbling luck to hold true.

The five-day FAC School on Okinawa was a blur. Tactics and weapons during the day, write a letter home to the wife after dinner, then go to the O Club to listen to Asians impersonate

Elvis and Hank Williams. They couldn't speak a word of English, but they sounded just like the stars.

The first day, we were each given a FAC kit. It contained what looked like two plastic playing cards that had the essentials for running air strikes and calling in artillery. Another item was a twelve-inch square of fluorescent pink nylon fabric. The idea was to put the ultra-bright square on top of your helmet and stand in an open area so the planes could identify your position. I could handle this, so I stayed at the club too long every night, wrote letters to Ardi, and dozed during the classes. I reasoned, *What could they do, send me to Vietnam and make me a FAC?*

I was given orders after completing the school and learned that I had been assigned to the company commanded by none other than Captain Charles Spittal Robb, President Johnson's son-in-law.

"A piece of cake! He has to be the best-protected Marine in all of Vietnam," I yelled jubilantly into the muggy Okinawa air.

I immediately wrote a "don't worry" letter home.

> *Dear Ardi,*
>
> *I know I've told you that being a FAC is a dangerous job, but as usual, I lucked out. I'm attached to the company commanded by President Johnson's son-in-law, Charles Robb. You know they won't let anything happen to him. Of all the places I could have been sent, this is one of the safest.*
>
> *The FAC tour is now only for three months, then I will get my R and R in Hawaii in September. For seven days we can get reacquainted.*
>
> *As always, loving and thinking of you,*
>
> *Bob*
>
> *P.S. Bring the bikini you wore to the park, hubba, hubba!*

My first chore was to check into battalion headquarters on a big hill somewhere not too far from Da Nang. By the time I arrived, they had already served dinner in the mess hall. Out here in the bush, I would have to suffer until breakfast. In Da Nang I could have grabbed a snack out of our fridge. In the colonel's office, I met three other lieutenants checking in to become platoon commanders. They had just finished basic school at Quantico, and they looked young and green in their new jungle utilities.

The colonel's top sergeant filled us in on where each of us would be going, along with a little scuttlebutt about each location. One of the lieutenants had the unfortunate name of Charles Robb. He would be going as far away as possible from the other Robb to avoid any confusion. Lieutenant Jim Kelley would be joining his platoon in the field, where they were already out on an extended mission. I learned that I was going to Hill 37 to replace a FAC who had been killed by a sniper. Lieutenant Sharpe was going to the same hill to become a platoon commander.

The news got worse. "I don't know why they keep Captain Robb in the field," said the sergeant. "We've captured some North Vietnamese regulars on a suicide mission with orders to assassinate him."

The sergeant minced no words about Robb's presence getting Marines killed, and I was now scared spit-less. I hoped the other three lieutenants didn't notice my fear, but they may well have been thinking the same thing. We had good reason to be scared.

The colonel finally showed up at 0100 hour and gave us a briefing until 0300 hours, then met us for breakfast at 0530. He rode the chopper that dropped off each of us at our new duty locations. "When did the man sleep?" we wondered. His sergeant said this was a typical day for the colonel; he loved being in the field with his men. He looked like he had been born with a cigar in the crook of his mouth as he deftly rolled it from side to side as he talked.

Second Lieutenant Robb was dropped off on Hill 59. Second Lieutenant Kelley jumped out of the chopper and ran into the edge of the jungle to find his men. Second Lieutenant Sharpe and I were dropped off on Hill 37, fifteen miles southeast of Da Nang. I was the old-timer of the three. I had been in two years and was a first lieutenant at age twenty-four.

Captain Robb was a very abrupt person and rarely smiled; there was no idle chit-chat to break the ice, and he talked only military business during lunch. We ate B-rations, a military version of what you might take on a mountain climb and about as good as most school lunches. The canned, sliced ham, reconstituted potatoes, canned veggies, and fresh bread made for a decent lunch. The food reflected the captain's terse military demeanor: "adequate, but without flavor," I mumbled.

Captain Robb clearly saw the Vietnam War as a means to advancing his military career or as a launching pad into politics. He could have played it safe and stayed in a supply company on the docks of Saigon, but he wanted a line company. We all respected him for that. Despite the fact that his presence was getting Marines killed, there was no animosity towards him. He was out here with the rest of us, "scratchin' with the chickens."

My FAC team consisted of three corporals and a sergeant. My plan was to have two men go into the field with me every day while two stayed on the hill to handle radio communications. The headquarters was an underground bunker covered with corrugated steel and sand bags. A tall drink of water standing nearby introduced himself as Corporal Carson, part of the FAC team.

He was a happy-go-lucky kid who had just turned nineteen. At six feet, four inches tall and a strapping 220 pounds, he was an eating machine.

"I love the Marine Corps, sir. Going out on our two and three day operations is just like a camping trip back home, but I get more to eat here."

I wondered what his "back home" was like if Vietnam seemed better. He liked being in the field humping the forty pound radio and any extra chow he could scrounge. I always gave him my C-ration cans of lima beans and ham. C-rats were packed with nutrition, but they were definitely survival food. He mixed them with a little Tabasco sauce and acted like he was on a Sunday school picnic. He seemed oblivious to the extra danger that surrounded radio operators—they were a first priority target for snipers.

He was a contrast to Sergeant Dixon, a small, wiry kid who was a few weeks away from rotating back to the world after he voluntarily extended his tour an extra six months. No Marine extends unless they are gung-ho, so I was surprised at our first meeting.

"I'm not going out in the bush anymore, lieutenant." I didn't respond to his affront. "It's gotten too hairy out there with all of the attacks in our sector." Dixon made this declaration as though he was in charge. "My first year was nothing like this. If I'd known the Tet Offensive was going to kill this many of us, I never would have shipped over. I've done my part." I thought he had just been testing my authority, but he felt entitled to tell me how things were going to be. "Captain Bischoff was okay with it before he bought the farm, so I don't see why his replacement shouldn't be."

I never liked to order people to do anything. I preferred to get them to do it on their own, but I didn't have time to argue, and he needed to know that I was the CO of the FAC team.

"Well, I guess you have done your share, but I need you. There're only four of you instead of the usual five. You will be rotating every other mission in the field."

He knew that when an officer said "You will be," it was an order.

"With all due respect, sir, I suppose you're going to stay on the hill, sir, while we go out every day. Is that right, sir?"

I let his sarcasm slide by. "No, Sergeant Dixon. As long as there are only four of you, I'll be going out every day as long as my body can take it. I've got to learn about being in the bush. I know you're a short timer, but I don't want to get myself or anybody else killed because my second in command wants to play it safe on the hill."

I paused. I wished I had been puffing on a big cigar. I would have blown a few smoke rings and flicked a few ashes on the ground. I had just discovered why COs smoke cigars: it gives them time to think. This was awkward; we just stared at each other. A few thick smoke rings would have cleared the air for him and let him know something else was going to be hitting the fan.

"I need you to get me oriented on how things really work out there," I finally said. "You and Corporal Carson will be going with me on tomorrow's mission. Draw your rations and ammo and be ready to launch at 0530."

"Aye, aye, sir!"

His mocking tone sent the message that he didn't like taking orders from a green lieutenant, but I didn't give a hang what he liked. I was his immediate CO. That was my first real order that I had ever needed to give.

At 0500, I was nudged awake by the corporal of the guard. Trying to get some sleep on the late Captain Bischoff's cot was like trying to catch a nap while waiting for the guillotine to drop. I was more scared than before my first combat flight. I thought about Fitchner falling apart when the action started and getting his men wasted. I was as afraid of being a coward as I was of taking a bullet.

It was billed as a simple re-supply mission of a Special Forces compound that protected a little village named Thuong Duc, located about eight miles northwest of Hill 37. We would be attached to Captain Robb's company of about three hundred men. In addition to lots of troops, we traveled with two tanks and eight armored personnel carriers called amtracs, short for amphibious tractor. They looked like a giant steel shoebox with tank treads and a .30-caliber machine gun mounted on the front deck. We were a well-armed force protecting four or five trucks filled with supplies ranging from bullets to beans.

Our convoy stretched out over half a mile. Our biggest worries came from ambushes and land mines. We swept the road with metal detectors as we advanced and left men every so often to guard the road so the VC couldn't slip back in behind us and mine the road for our trip back. Those soldiers had a tough job, sitting in the heat all day just waiting and watching, watching and waiting, for nearly ten hours in dehydrating heat.

Plink went the round as it hit the side of the tank. It's true; you never hear the one that gets you. Bullets travel faster than sound, and a bit of time passed before we heard the unmistakable *craack* of an AK-47 Russian-made rifle. Once you hear it, you never forget it. The round came from a tree line about 300 meters on the far side of a plowed field to our left.

"All right, form a skirmish line in the ditch and lay down a base of fire on that tree line," shouted a gunnery sergeant who had checked into the company the previous day. He had not seen any combat, but knew exactly what to do. The company jumped into the trench filled ankle-deep with water. A fusillade of M16 rounds returned fire.

I had given Carson my .45-caliber pistol so he wouldn't have to carry a rifle as well as a forty-pound radio. Also, I wanted to look like the lowliest private in the ranks, so I carried his M16.

Plink, plink … craack, craack clattered the sounds of battle. It was show time for the FAC team. The rounds struck close to us, we assumed they were after our radio man—Carson. The three of us huddled together in the safety of the ditch. We needed to call in an air strike on the enemy infiltrated tree line—that's what a FAC does. The nagging fear I had all morning was gone. It was like being nervous before a football game. Once the ball is kicked off, instincts take over. *I am their leader,* I thought. I took action. I took out the kit they had given me at FAC School. *I can't go wrong doing it by the book.*

"Dixon, take this fluorescent square and put it on the top of your helmet and stand on the edge of the road so the jets can identify us," I ordered.

"With all due respect, sir, if that's what they showed you at FAC School, then why don't you stand out there?" He smiled as he said it.

Plink, plink … craack, craack.

"Stupid idea huh?" I said, half scolding myself.

"I didn't say that, sir, but we don't want to make nobody a target."

"Lieutenant, the birds'll be over the top of us in a few minutes," Carson, the eating machine said.

"Okay, let's pop some smoke so they'll know where we are," I said as I checked my small survival compass. "Tell 'em we want rockets and 500-pounders."

Dixon didn't try to hide his laugh. "Lieutenant, we're going to get snakes and napes, that's what they sit on the hot pad with. They know what they're doing, and they can see our tanks. If we pop smoke, it will attract those AK rounds like a nest of wasps hitting us. Just hide and watch us on this one, lieutenant. It's not that complicated. You'll know what you're doing after you see a real air strike in the bush," Dixon's sarcasm was gone.

"Okay, it's your ball game," I said.

The radio crackled to life. "Black Knight's my name, and killin's my game. Where are they?" The thunder from Black Knight's F-4 jet roared over head.

"Roger, Black Knight. They are in the tree line just east of the road. You tally-ho our position?"

"That's affirmative. I've got some tree pruning to do." The F-4 climbed to about 3,000 feet, then inverted right over the target and dove straight down releasing the Snake Eyes (high drag, very accurate) bombs so they could only hit the target, then he pulled out at tree top level.

"Now for a weenie roast," Black Knight said.

"Roger roast," Carson chuckled.

It was a rush watching the plane come in low and release two napalm bombs. They tumbled in the air and engulfed the entire length of the tree line in a huge orange and black fireball. It was surreal. The earsplitting roar of the jet jarred my eyeteeth. The slight warmth I felt from the intense heat at 300 meters away made me wince at the burning death the VC were suffering. The sweltering tropical air was permeated with the smell and taste of the napalm gel that clung to its victims and inflicted a torturous end. The putrid air gagged you by coating the inside of your mouth with the flavor of diesel. It was the real taste of war. Even if the VC ducked into one of their tunnels, they would suffocate from breathing the seared air. It was a death befitting no creature, but to us—napalm was our friend.

"Nice weenie roast, Black Knight. I think that's got 'em," Carson said.

"Roger, you fellas can continue your little stroll in the park now. Black Knight out."

Communications were brief with few wasted words, but pilots and radio men injected a lot of humor into their work.

Putting aside his usual sarcasm, Dixon gave me the Vietnam version of FAC School. "He was sittin' on the hot pad ready to go. You have to take what they've got on board, and I've never seen anything but snakes and napes. Just tell him where the VC are and they'll do the rest. You'll confuse 'em with all that FAC School stuff. Besides, it takes too long and makes us a target."

"Aye, aye, sir," I said.

We chuckled as I tore up the bright square of fabric with my bayonet, and ripped up the instructional cards I had received from FAC School. The ambush was brief, and we had only one minor casualty, a flesh wound from a ricocheting bullet. The Navy corpsman treated him, we put him up on one of the tanks, and the column moved out. The entire engagement took less than fifteen minutes.

The next day, we were on another re-supply mission to a hill that was a little closer. *Whump*! We ducked. I saw a large piece of something green hurtled thirty feet into the air. Bits of flesh began to fall around us like a rain shower of tiny red droplets. Mud puddles turned a brownish red; ants pounced on the scattered tissue. We ran to the front of the column.

He was a black kid who had just checked into the company a few days earlier. He was an engineer who swept the road for mines. His metal detector found one, and he had been digging it up with his bayonet, but it had been booby-trapped. It was his upper body I had seen cart-wheeling through the air.

"Skipper, don't look at it. It'll make you sick," Carson warned.

The skipper didn't listen. A rain poncho had been spread on the side of the road. It held a decapitated torso with one arm attached to it. A new Seiko watch still ticked on its wrist, showing the day, Sunday, in red. I hurled immediately at the sight of piled body parts. It was a violent, instantaneous wrenching that emptied my guts in one gigantic projectile spewing.

"Sorry, Skipper. I tried to warn you. It happens to everyone. Your system kinda gets used to it, but that first time makes you sick all day." That was a gross understatement.

Right after that first air strike, when they saw I was going to pack my own weight and not do anything stupid to get any of us killed, the FAC team started calling me "Skipper," like the captain of a ship. I liked it. In the squadron I was a nobody, but in the bush I was the "Skipper." It was a casual title of respect that meant that I had been accepted into their profession, a line of work so dangerous that in the Marine Corps, FACs are called the "Chosen Few."

Kyle Browdski was a skinny, puny-looking kid with the remnants of acne pocking his undistinguished face. He was the type of kid you would have teased in junior high. The hundred-degree heat caused sweat to run in rivulets from his head into the olive drab towel draped around his pencil-thin neck, which didn't look strong enough to support his steel helmet.

"Lieutenant Ski, there's some beer in the O Club. If the fridge worked at all today, it might even be a little cold. You were good luck for us today—it's the first day we haven't lost anybody."

"Lieutenant Fergy, we may owe some of that to you. I'd be pleased to toast to your good fortune with an adult beverage, because in about fifteen hours, this Marine will be in the rear with the gear and the beer, as the POGs say." (Rhymes with rogues and means People Other than Grunts.)

Ski had already been in the bush for seven months and had received orders to a supply company in Da Nang. He had been with us on the operation that day because the hill commander had delayed his reporting date to the rear echelon for two days so he could replace a wounded lieutenant who would be out of action for a few days.

The back half of the hootch, where the officers were supposed to sleep when not in the field, was laughingly called the O Club, though there were only a few officers left on Hill 37. The VC had been lobbing in mortars on a regular basis at night, so it was only used as a place to stow our gear. We all slept in the well sand-bagged command post bunker.

Somebody, even in the middle of Vietnam, had scrounged an overstuffed chair and couch, making the O Club look comfortable. Unfortunately, the foam padding in them turned out to be better than dirt for the little sugar ants that seemed to dominate every square inch of Vietnam. The first time I sat in the chair, I got a severe case of ants in my pants. They were too little to bite hard, the tiniest ants I had ever seen. But any bites in your crotch are maddening. As I danced around in the hootch that first day, the CO came by to meet me and said, "Well, Lieutenant Ferguson, I see you've met the furniture."

The beer was usually warm, but if you drank enough of it, The Nam would disappear for a few hours. The club was more ramshackle than humble, but after a mission we liked to have some brews and jaw a little bit about the day. We sat bone-tired on the uncomfortable—but ant-less bar stools as the lowering sun gave up on some of its smothering heat.

"What happened when that tank round went off? That baby scared the horse pucky out of me, exploding right out of the barrel like that," I said.

"It was a white phosphorous round. Those Willie Peters are sensitive. A feather can set one off. It's armed once it leaves the barrel, so that little tree twig was enough to explode it." Ski spoke with an Eastern accent that sounded gangsterish, but he didn't murder the English language by using words like "quatas" and "idears."

"We're lucky nobody got sprayed with that stuff," Ski said.

I had been standing just behind the tank that fired it. I was watching the target at the end of its barrel. The explosion was enormous. I hit the deck as thousands of bits of burning white phosphorus scattered all around us. We looked at each other to see who was hit. Finding nobody hurt, we nervously laughed about what could have been a disaster.

"Why were you using Willy Peter instead of a regular round?" I asked.

"Because I wanted those gooks to suffer." He took a swig from his can for emphasis. "That stuff sticks to your skin and burns deep. Not even water will put it out. You gotta pack it with mud."

War has a way of reducing even the finest of breeding down to Darwin's lowest common denominator—survival of the fittest. Kill or be killed and inflict your enemy with maximum suffering.

"It was just a black flag. How do you know they were VC?" I asked.

"I don't for sure, but that's the way Charlie signals each other. A low-flying black flag is hard to see, during the day. We're lucky you spotted it," Ski said, pointing his beer at me. "They were probably setting up an ambush somewhere near there. Our road passed right by that ville. We just got the dinks first," he said with a certain satisfaction in his voice.

I had checked my map, and the ville was in a free-fire zone assumed to be controlled by the VC. Free-fire zones were unrestricted territory for planes to drop bombs left over from a mission or operations like ours, with a secondary mission to destroy any targets of opportunity. That's exactly what we did, but I was still uneasy. Our three tanks trained their guns on the village and wasted it. I had only been in the bush three weeks, and I was still getting my "on the job training." The quick death that rained down on everyone in that little hamlet staggered me. This had been a preemptive strike with no apologies, no twinge of conscience, and no worry about any women and children in the ville. There was no checking with the command post for permission to fire. It was point, shoot, and obliterate. The huge binoculars carried by tank commanders for damage assessment told the story. Any huts that were not destroyed were on fire, and there was no sign of life. We saddled up and moved on.

I'm not sure what I felt, but it wasn't remorse. We were taking casualties every day from ambushes, and a little payback seemed fair. I didn't give the order to fire, but my chance sighting of a black flag being waved on a pole probably led directly to some deaths, which made me queasy. I'm glad we didn't stop to get the body count. I didn't want to see the blood, guts, and gore. I wanted my war to be nice and clean, devoid of the reality that, in war, people get blown up and spew their bowels, brains, and body parts across the luscious, green landscape.

As we each finished off our third warm beer, a messenger came to the hootch to tell us that a medal ceremony was to be held at 1900, and we were to form up in clean utilities. Not even combat stopped medal ceremonies.

"Lieutenant Fergy, today was going good so far. We only had those heatstroke casualties; that tank round didn't burn anybody, I know we got some score in that ville, and this beer was letting me enjoy my last night here in the bush." Ski's words came slowly and slurred. "By this time tomorrow, Lieutenant Fergy, I'll be in a supply company on China Beach, then in a few days, I'm off to R and R. I can tolerate this last little bit of garbage from the CO, 'cuz once I leave, I'm never gonna think of him or this hill again."

The CO began to read from an official document. "On June fifteenth, in the Thuong Duc Province in the Republic of South Vietnam, the leader of the third platoon in B Company in the Third Marine Division was ordered to lead his platoon to rescue the remaining 110 Marines surrounded by a full company of North Vietnamese Regular Army." The CO droned on in a monotone worse than a preacher's. "He distinguished himself by setting an example for his platoon. Having no ammunition, he ordered his troops to fix bayonets and gave the command to attack. He leaped into the trench by himself, and with a grenade launcher, killed two NVA. Using their weapons, he killed three more NVA. His actions so inspired his men, they jumped into the trench and engaged in hand-to-hand combat, killing sixty-four NVA. The fierceness of their actions caused the remaining enemy to retreat, thereby liberating the Marine Company."

The CO paused to give us a moment to comprehend the magnitude of the exploit. "For his conspicuous heroism above and beyond the call of duty, the Silver Star is hereby awarded to First Lieutenant Kyle C. Browdski. This is the second award for Lieutenant Browdski."

You could have knocked me over with a feather as the skinny kid standing next to me stepped out to receive the second-highest medal our country gives. After the ceremony, we drank more beer to celebrate his second Silver Star. I had to ask him. "What was that all about?"

"Some dumb captain got himself surrounded, and we happened to be a few clicks away. By the time we got to them, we were out of ammunition, and all I could say was fix bayonets and then yelled attack." He laughed easily as he told a story about extraordinary bravery as though it were a busy day at the office. "I jumped in the trench and picked up a grenade launcher off of a dead Marine. A gook came around the corner, and I hit him with it. He was too close for the grenade to explode, but it put a big hole in him, and for an instant I saw daylight through him." He laughed at what must have been a macabre sight. "I got lucky— the grenade landed next to another dink about fifty feet away and exploded. That's how I got the first two. Then I picked up their AK-47s and surprised three more gooks and wasted them. My troops were still in a state of shock, so I yelled at them to get their butts in the trenches or I'd shoot them myself."

He took a swig of beer and wiped his mouth with the back of his hand. He was unimpressed with his own valor.

"Those kids came charging, yelling and screaming, and it scared the bejeebers out of the NVA, which gave us the upper hand. If they had waited another second or two, I probably would have bought the farm. I was out of ammo again." After a deep breath he sighed. "They're good boys. I put all of them in for Bronze Stars. I hate to leave 'em, but I've been lucky to survive the bush; especially when you've got captains getting themselves in a hum then giving orders to a small platoon to bail them out."

There was no embellishment to his story. There didn't need to be; it was a documented account of phenomenal courage, and I heard it first hand. It was a petrifying realization that no matter what happened, I would have to show this same kind of courage. The men would count on it. He had set the example. I hoped my opportunity would never come.

I knew as I talked with him that I was privileged to be in the company of a person of such rarity that if I lived a thousand lifetimes, I would never meet another of his magnitude.

Ski hopped into the Jeep of the daily courier. His boots were shined and his M16 cleaned. The only thing non-regulation about him was the paraphased 23d Psalm on his helmet. "Yea, though

I walk through the shadow of death, I shall fear no evil because I'm the toughest Mother in the A Shau Valley." Ski backed it up.

I envied him. I watched the Jeep disappear in a cloud of red dust. He didn't look back. He had survived, but my day would come. I knew he was already thinking of the ladies that would occupy his time on the beaches of Hawaii for an entire week of R and R. He didn't look like much, but I made a vow to watch his career when we got home. He held a degree in economics from an Ivy League school, had been awarded two Silver Stars, a Bronze Star, and two Purple Hearts. He would be a stellar performer at whatever occupation he chose. Extraordinary success could not pass him by.

It was a command-detonated mine that ripped through the Jeep carrying dispatches, a corporal, and a bright star headed for greater things than a jungle war. The two bodies were so grossly shredded they could only be identified by their dog tags. A truck filled with Marines had been following; they collected the mangled body parts and placed them in ponchos tied at the top with anything handy. We knew what the radioman meant when, calling for a chopper, he added, "And be advised, we've got a couple of baggies here."

The CO, maybe from the remorse of extending Ski an extra two days in such a hot sector, asked for two squads to go to the village next to where he died. Their mission would be to find and punish the gooks that killed him. There was no shortage of volunteers. I was one of them.

Up to that point, I had wondered if I could really kill someone, or would a slight pause from a twinge of conscience make me a casualty? That question was answered. I didn't know how to use an M16, but I sure knew how to work a sawed-off shotgun loaded with six shells. I checked one out from the armory, along with two bandoleers of ammo that crisscrossed over my chest. I looked like Poncho Villa wearing a helmet instead of a sombrero.

We set out before noon chow. I had killing in my heart. Lieutenant Ski was loved by his men. He was loved by me. I had no conscience. We all wanted to "get some" for him. We wanted to "kill them all, and let God sort them out." If women and children were killed, so be it. It would keep the nits from becoming lice. Killing was the right thing to do. It was our only thought. We were about to enjoy slaughtering the slant-eyed dinks who had murdered one of our best. Our safeties were off; our fingers gingerly touched triggers. Heat and vengeance blurred logic and ignited an unquenchable flame for revenge. *If we kill them, we'll feel better,* we thought. I would finally get my first confirmed kill. I would not pause.

The old women and men of the village clamored in a loud din, "We no VC! We no VC! No, no VC here." They knew we had come to smother them with death. We knew the VC were there. The mine had been exploded by a hidden executioner. We wanted him dead, and each of us wanted to fire the first shot that would splatter him into his next Buddhist life.

We prayed for a furtive move so we could release our stored rage in a hail of bullets that would tear into flesh like the land mine tore into Ski. I kept my shotgun aimed waist high—waiting, wanting to see my high-load shells cut someone in half. I would rejoice at the sight and laugh about it with the troops.

A young mother, holding a crying, hungry, and dirty-faced baby, stepped into my line of fire. "No VC here," she said. The men looked at me. I looked at her—I raised my shotgun in the air and clicked on the safety. The killing switch had been turned off. She was the face behind our reason for being there—to defend the defenseless. Reason returned. More safeties clicked.

The villagers were caught in a sucking vortex of violent death. If they worked with us, the VC would kill them. They were often conscripted to help the VC, and then were killed by us.

"Get the interpreter working to find out if the bad guys are still here," I said.

After an hour of searching, we found a thirteen-year-old boy wearing a clean, white, sailor's gob-hat. There were no Navy operations nearby, and the villagers said he was just passing through their hamlet. We were miles from any ships; where did he get such a new cap? As our interpreter grilled him, he cried like a baby. He was young, but old enough to be a VC spy. We called HQ, which sent a black helicopter with no insignia to pick him up, along with our interpreter. Before we left the village, our interpreter radioed from the chopper and said the kid had jumped out of the helicopter—from two hundred feet.

Nobody can say for sure if he was pushed or if he jumped. Maybe they had another spy on board, and they used the teen as an example of what happens when they don't cooperate. I only know that the Vietnamese had been numbed by decades of atrocities. For a Vietnamese interpreter to toss a VC spy out of an aircraft would be considered a sick form of sport. I was not yet calloused enough by the war to see the humor in it. I didn't laugh with the others at hearing the report, but I was getting there.

As we hiked back up the hill, we each held our own memory of Lieutenant Ski, but we knew we had to move on. There was no time for grief. Maybe that's a good thing, because my urge to kill had been sapped after hearing about the boy-spy. In the U.S., he would have been playing baseball. If he lived in Eugene, maybe he'd be picking beans and thinking about buying a bicycle.

I climbed the stairs of the bedraggled O Club, took out a warm beer, and tried to forget that a hero would be going home as a baggie. I said a prayer something like, "Lord, let me be half the Marine as the guy I drank beer with last night." Not a very religious supplication, but at that particular moment—I wasn't sure there was a God.

They carried grass mats, blankets, small pigs in baskets and their most valuable possessions with them as they nestled in right against our razor sharp wire. It was a dramatic sight to watch. Hundreds of Vietnamese from the little village below our hill were gathering at the very edge of our perimeter wire. Our intelligence said their village might be attacked by VC that night. Their presence proved it.

As we looked at the swarm of humanity seeking our protection, every Marine on the hill knew that on that day he was in the right place doing the right thing. We were there to save these lives for no other reason than they were helpless against a powerful, cruel, and murderous enemy. The notion of this being an illegal war was ludicrous. How can it be illegal to protect the lives of innocent people?

John 15:13 reads, "Greater love hath no man than this, that a man lay down his life for his brother." It's become passé in today's society, but on that night, a few of our perimeter guards died living it.

"They're in our wire! They're in our wire!" crackled the voice over the radio in the command bunker.

I was moving before the panicked words stopped. I had been sleeping nearby with all of my gear on and my helmet at the ready. Claymore mines exploded in the wire that encircled the listening post about 300 yards away. Tracers were going in every direction as I dashed outside the bunker. The civilians hunkered down with their sleeping mats over the top of them.

"I've got the fifty!" yelled a Marine climbing the tower to a .50-caliber machine gun. "I'll need your help," he said to me as I followed him up the ladder. He didn't know he was giving an order to an officer, but now was no time to argue about who was in charge. I had no idea how to fire a machine gun.

"Just feed the ammo in nice and level so it don't jam," he said.

The gun was restricted in its shooting direction and height, so it shot barely over the heads of the men in the outpost. Every seventh bullet was a tracer that made a swerving, red snake as it fired out in a blinking stream of light. They ricocheted in all directions. It was exhilarating to be in the thick of the fight. The adrenalin flowed like never before. Our weapon was helping to win the battle. It never occurred to me that tracers work both ways. We could see that we were taking the fight to the enemy, but we had a red line pointing right back to us.

Flares hung from small parachutes that had been shot a few hundred feet into the air. They lit up the jungle with a pale orange glow. I saw only fleeting glimpses of the VC. Our field of fire covered the retreat of our men who were scrambling back into the compound.

Artillery shells from surrounding fire bases roared like small jets as they passed over our heads and crashed into the jungle. The coordinates of the most likely avenues of attack were programmed into the guns of nearby fire bases. One call and we were surrounded by explosions that were chewing up the jungle.

In a battle, you don't know if you're going to be overrun and going at it hand to hand. All you can hope for is that you have fire superiority to outlast them. So far in Vietnam, I felt like I was always on the perimeter of the war and never in the thick of it. But in this skirmish, I was in the exact middle; it was ecstasy. I screamed inside myself, *By heaven, I'm a real Marine, and nobody can ever take that from me.* Once a Marine, always a Marine. I could now stand tall like Mike Riley and countless others who had faced the challenge of battle, and God help me if I didn't want it to rage on.

Lieutenant Sharpe would be in charge of a platoon the next day to see if they could make contact with the element that had attacked us the previous night. He had gone on all of the same operations I had been on. He was not a greenhorn, but neither was he experienced in taking a single platoon into an area to be dropped off by helicopters. He would be joined by another group led by Captain Grant.

Our FAC team had been going nonstop. That day, I didn't go into the field; the CO had me standing a twenty-four-hour radio watch inside the bunker. Sergeant Dixon was the only FAC member fresh enough to go out. I sent him by himself; he would have to hump his own radio. Cross gave him my .45 pistol, which now seemed to be community property for our team. Dixon was two days short of going home, but I had no choice. The others on our team were spent, and I felt better about Sharpe leading his platoon knowing Dixon would be with him to call in close air support if it was needed.

The morning was interrupted by slaughter. "Skipper, we need arty right away." Dixon had skipped the usual radio protocol because he knew I was standing the watch. "They're trying to flank us, so I'm going to give you two sets of coordinates. Fire on them both at once. I'll give you the corrections, then fire for effect. It's the only chance we've got."

I forwarded his coordinates to the artillery fire bases. Air support would take too long. I was filled with dread. Two days before he goes home and I had sent him into the jaws of a massacre.

"The captain has been hit twice," Dixon continued. "I'm talking on his radio because mine saved my fanny, but it's shot up. On that first coordinate, correct forty meters north and fire for effect. On that second coordinate, fire for effect and don't stop until I get back to you."

Time crawled by at an agonizing pace. He was in a jam, but he was a cool customer. I knew if anyone could survive, it would be him.

"Cease fire, Skipper."

"Roger," I said into the radio and then passed the message on to the artillery bases.

"We need help now, Skipper! We've got bodies all over the place, along with wounded, but the gooks have dee-deed."

The CO was standing nearby and took command of the radio.

"Who's in charge?" he asked.

"Right now, I guess I am. Lieutenant Sharpe was leading on point and took five rounds in the face. Sergeant Wilhelm went out to get him, but he was killed trying to carry him back, and the captain is all shot up with a sucking chest wound."

"All right Sergeant Dixon, you are now in command," said the CO. "Set up a perimeter and tend to the wounded. We're scrambling right now. Stay near that radio."

We climbed into the choppers as fast as we could and were over the site in a few minutes. The door gunner raked the tree lines to make sure we wouldn't be ambushed. Carnage accosted us as we jumped to the ground. About twenty-five bodies were stacked up like cord wood near the landing zone; I couldn't help but check. The dog tag woven into the boot lace read Lieutenant Carlton B. Sharpe. He knew he should not have been on point. We learned that in OCS, but he never asked his men to do anything he wouldn't do himself.

A poncho covered his torso, and the flies were thick on the dried blood that clung to his hands that must have grabbed at his face when the first round hit him. They were flies being flies—oblivious to the brave soul they were desecrating. I hate flies with a passion.

The twenty or so wounded cared for each other in the tender way that warriors have done, even before the three hundred

Spartans defeated a hundred thousand Persians at Thermopylae. They can be enraged killers one moment, but as soft as a nursing mother the next.

"Saddle up," shouted the CO as he relit his cigar. "You men get ammo and water and march back to the hill," he said to the survivors of the battle.

I couldn't believe what I had just heard.

"What the heck is this, a John Wayne movie?" demanded a corporal.

The CO looked around to see who made the sardonic remark. After all, the CO was not to be mocked.

"Sir, let me divert the working birds for these men," I said.

"Those birds have already got their work to do, lieutenant."

I wanted to slap that cigar right out of his mouth.

"Sir, some of these men will get heatstroke. It will only make our situation worse," I argued.

"All right, lieutenant. Do it if you can," He said, giving into the growing chorus of uncharitable remarks.

The working birds were glad to divert and landed near us within minutes. The rest of us climbed aboard the amtracs for the ten-mile ride back to the hill. There was no chatter among the troops, but I was sure of one thing: Sergeant Dixon would be on a chopper a day early for his trip back to the world. I did not have the authority to send him home a day ahead of schedule, but I saw no reason to mention it to the CO.

After a night of sleeping on the edge of the Da Nang tarmac, Dixon would take his place in that line of soldiers with the glazed-over looks that had greeted me over seven months earlier. I had discovered what made them look like zombies. They had faced hell itself and survived.

With the high number of casualties we were taking, it now seemed unlikely that I would get out without some sort of injury. Nearly everyone on the hill had at least one Purple Heart. I thought, *If I'm going to get it anyway, I'm going to go down fighting.* That acceptance released me from the continuous grip of fear I had been in. It wasn't courage. It was the certainty that the Ol' Ferguson bumbling luck would kick in and I'd get the "golden wound" that would send me home with minimal damage. It was a relief. I could now get some sleep before another re-supply mission to Thuong Duc at 0530.

"A coward dies a thousand deaths, a soldier dies but once." That line contains the genius of Shakespeare. He used the word soldier—not hero, brave, or any other superlative. Shakespeare knew the soldier would rise to the level of duty required. I had used up my nine hundred and ninety-nine deaths as a coward. I was going to check out of this life as a soldier.

It was stronger than a bad feeling; it was a premonition about this mission. It began by running into Lieutenant Kelly at breakfast. His platoon had been ordered to our hill to accompany us on the assignment.

"What happened to your head?" I asked him while gulping down some reconstituted milk. He had a fresh, three-inch-by-one-inch nasty abrasion that started just above his left eyebrow and ran up at an angle to his scalp.

"A round creased my forehead two days ago," he said. "It was the weirdest thing. After it grazed me, it ringed around inside of my helmet and fell out." He pulled a damaged bullet out of his pocket. All wars are filled with strange stories. His is one of many.

"That's a fair-sized wound. Did you get Doc to look at it? He'll put you down for a Purple Heart. Get three of those puppies, and you go home. The other FAC officer that's supposed to be on this hill got his third from some shrapnel the day I got here, and he was out of here the next day," I said.

"Man, I don't have time to see the doctor for this little scratch." He minimized the wound. It wasn't a scratch. "We had to hump it yesterday just to get here before dark." He looked tired. "I guess we're here because you guys have been taking some casualties. What's the mission like today?" he asked.

"I've been on it four times. It's an eight-mile hike one way that takes ten hours because we have to sweep the road." There was no way to make it sound easy. "So far, we've only taken a casualty or two each time. One pretty ugly—a black kid was digging up a booby-trapped mine and got it full force."

"So he was a baggie, huh?" Kelley surmised correctly. "These troops have seen a lot. I've got one kid in my platoon who took a picture of himself in his squad. Everybody in the picture but him is dead. The troops won't let him be in any of their pictures now." He laughed at the macabre humor of it all.

"Heat strokes will be our biggest problem today." I gulped down bites of powdered eggs while talking. "Tell your troops to take as many canteens as they can carry. Last time, the water buffalo truck didn't make it out to the line. I know some of our troops have been filling their canteens with rice paddy water."

"Mine too. I'm surprised we haven't had a lot of dysentery, but I guess the green apple quick step is better than a heatstroke," Kelley said.

With the landmine casualties, the night attack on the hill, and seeing those twenty-five bodies all within a period of a few weeks, I knew the NVA was in the immediate vicinity. I couldn't shake the bad feeling about this road sweep.

I walked the entire eight miles in the tank treads. The water buffalo showed up, we dropped off the supplies, and the gooks were giving us a needed day off with no casualties. Maybe they needed a day off, too. We hopped up on the amtracs for an easy ride home.

"Hey, Skipper," Carson shouted. "Come up and sit up front on the sandbags. You don't want to sit back by that engine housing; it's dangerous. You're a lieutenant and can make any of these guys trade places with you." Once again, the eating machine was looking out for me.

The amtrac lurched forward as I said, "Nah, I'll be okay." It wasn't like taking the point like Sharpe had done, so it seemed unnecessary.

"Well, don't put your feet down in that hatch. If we hit a mine, that cover will slam down on you, and you'll be trapped."

"Aye, aye, sir," I said as I took my feet out of the hatch and sat with my knees up to my chin. I rested my head on my arms, which crossed my knees. I dozed off thinking how well the day had gone and how I only had sixty more days in the bush before I would go back to a cushy job in the squadron. If they were all like today, it would be a piece of cake.

The kid who sat down next to me put his feet down inside the hatch for a more comfortable ride. I didn't tell him about Carson's warning. It wasn't needed; I had been worrying all day for nothing. I felt stupid.

CHAPTER 8

Should Have Listened

Kuu-whuumph! The explosion threw the twenty–eight-ton amtrac two feet into the air like it had hit a giant speed bump. *Whuush!* A ball of flames with blast-furnace heat engulfed me. I knew I was in trouble. Two options: get off the eight-foot-high beast or die.

Quick as a cat, before any of the troops reacted, I was moving. I put my hands on the shoulders of two Marines sitting on the outboard edge of the amtrac and swung my feet between them like a gymnast vaulting from parallel bars. I hit the ground hard. My momentum pitched me forward onto a barbed-wire fence ten feet from the steel monster that was now an exploding fireball. Rusted barbs gripped my clothes like talons. It was bad.

Things got worse. The intense heat from the burning fuel cooked off the ammo for the .30-caliber machine gun. The two-inch bullets burst into deadly missiles. The tracers made the amtrac look like an exploding fireworks stand, and at close range, I was snared like a rabbit.

Lunging backward over the fence, I trusted the flack jacket to protect me from the barbs. It worked—no gashes. I had only one thought: find my FAC team and get the air strikes inbound.

I was the Skipper; the entire company was counting on me. I couldn't be a Fitchner.

"Skipper, you're still on fire!" Carson screamed. From a few yards away, he jumped up from his prone position on the firing line and began yanking off my flack jacket. He stopped in disbelief. Looping like black ribbons of crepe paper draped from a ceiling, the skin on my arms came off with it. The smell of burning flesh accosted my nostrils, and I was still on fire. Wildly I began to slap at my flaming pants with burned hands. Carson and a medic tackled me to the ground and doused the flames with dirt.

"I'll be okay. Get the air support and medevacs moving," I ordered with as much command voice as I could muster.

"It's been done, Skip. As soon as we got hit, I keyed the mike and had them rolling." Carson sounded as though he had just ordered a burger at a drive-in. "I warned ya Skip—you shoulda been up front on the sand bags. It's the safest place to be. That melted hulk we passed this morning blew up a few months ago. The guys up front skated while everybody else got fried."

His scolding was tinged with regret that, once again, I had not heeded his warning.

"I'm sorry, sir, but I'm out of morphine," the medic said.

"That's okay. I don't hurt," I replied.

"That's because your nerve endings have been seared. You'll need it soon enough," he said

"Did we get any of them?" I asked Carson as I lay in the field while the medic poured some water on the wounds to wash away the dirt.

"I doubt it. They hit the plunger on a command-detonated mine, and dee-deed out of there. We fired into the tree line, but who knows if we got some. They knew they hurt us bad with that mine."

"How'd we miss a mine that big on our road sweep?" I asked.

"It wasn't big. It was a C-4 plastic charge. It was our own danged stuff. It's perfect for them. We can't detect it, and the VC know they can hurt us bad because these rigs have their fuel tanks in their belly. They're designed for water landings." I might have moved up to the front if he had told me this earlier. "The fuel is the same stuff used in napalm bombs before it gels. When it gets on fire, it burns as hot as the sun itself."

"What about ..."

"Don't talk, Skipper. We've got it under control. The fast-movers are rolling in to nape the tree line and the medevacs will be here in twenty minutes. You're burned pretty good." He gave me a drink of water. "It looks like you'll be goin' back to the world, Skip. Think how good that's gonna be."

Carson had good bedside manners. He moved on with the medic to other wounded men.

"Who are you?" A big Marine asked, staring down at me.

"I'm Lieutenant Ferguson. Don't you recognize me?"

"No, your face is burned too bad. I'm looking for Corporal Clark," the Marine said.

I didn't know my face was burned at all. It felt hot, but didn't hurt. I was still shocked by the noxious smell of burned flesh. The moaning and screaming of injured Marines added to my fear. I thought I had made it safely off of the amtrac. How could I be burned beyond recognition? If my hands and arms had skin hanging from them, what must my face look like? I had no pain. I didn't think I could be badly hurt. A glance at my nylon jungle boots slightly melted to my skin, told me differently.

"Lieutenant, that guy's an idiot. He wouldn't recognize you anyway; he just got attached to our unit this morning. Your face is burned, but you've only got flash burns. It's just like a real bad sunburn. It'll heal up without any scarring," the medic said.

"Thanks, Doc. I didn't even think about him not knowing me. He had me scared there a little bit. So the face isn't too bad?"

"Nah. It's real bad when you lose your ears and nose. You've only got a layer or two burned."

I hope to God you're right, I thought.

The *giddy-giddy-whop-whop* of rotor blades slicing through the air never sounded so good. I was helped into a sitting position on the medevac chopper. My arms were a ghastly white with looping black skin. The doc was right; it looked like only a layer of skin was gone.

The Da Nang field hospital was a crowded Quonset hut triage unit. Soldiers lying on stretchers with head wounds were so still I wondered if they were already dead. *Thank you, God, for letting my head be okay,* I prayed.

The hospital was so full I was taken to a makeshift overflow area in a breezeway where I straddled a pillow that had been placed over a carpenter's saw-horse. I was fully conscious, and the pain was minimal. I could answer all of their questions and didn't need any other assistance. Lying down was out of the question until the medics removed all of the burned skin. It was simply snip with scissors and pluck with tweezers until the sagging skin was removed from my arms, hands, back, stomach, and legs. It was ugly. I'm surprised I didn't faint.

"It looks like about seventy-five percent body coverage," a doctor said to a nurse who was taking notes while an orderly cut off my wedding ring.

After the snipping and tweezing, I was given a shot of morphine in my outer left thigh, one of the few places not burned. I was placed on my back on large, nonstick bandages that covered the bed. My arms and hands were swaddled in three-inch gauze rolls that looked like they had been soaked in yellow cooking oil. Those were followed by sterile gauze rolls held in place by flesh-toned Ace bandages. A half-circle tent kept the sheet off of my body. The vein on the inside of my right foot next to the ankle bone was used for intravenous fluids—another of the few spots with some good skin.

"You'll heal up as good as new, including your face, and you'll be going home," said the doctor.

A prisoner with his neck in a noose who suddenly gets pardoned could not have felt more relief. I plunged into a relaxation so deep it was a back-in-the-womb experience. It was part drugs and part knowing I was safe. Any pain could be tolerated because the outcome was going to be good. The question of surviving the war had been answered. I could look forward to a life with Ardi.

The drugs couldn't block out all of the pain, but I didn't feel too bad. The ten-inch-thick, shoulder length, mummy-type bandages seemed to put the injuries out of sight and somewhat out of mind. I thought that a couple of weeks of this wouldn't be too bad. In fact, I cheered up when two visitors stopped by.

"Fergy, the doctor says you're going to be okay," Dan Richards, my old hootch mate said. "You'll have a little scarring on your arms, but he says you'll be okay. I can't believe your Ferguson bumbling luck crossed you up. We thought you had it made, protecting Captain Robb and all."

"It's like my Ol' buddy Ben used to say, 'Some days chicken, some days feathers.' But this gets me back to the world, so maybe that's lucky in the long run."

"You could be right, Fergy," Colonel Parker, our CO said. "The doc say's you've got what he called flash burns. It's like a severe sunburn." He had repeated what the medic said, so it must be true. "He says you'll probably be back on flight status in a few weeks after getting back home."

"That's good to know," I lied. I could have cared less about getting back on flight status. I wanted to get on with "life" status.

"I'm personally going to notify your wife and let her know I've seen you," the CO said. "Those telegrams the Marines send can sound rather brutal, and I know you don't want her worried. Corporal Magnus is getting your gear together to send home."

He was letting me know some friends in the squadron were giving me some special treatment, and I appreciated it.

"Say, Rooftop, how about taking a look at my little soldier for me? I think he got burned pretty good."

We called Dan Richards Rooftop because he and his pilot had been shot down on the edge of the South China Sea a few weeks before I was sent out to be a FAC. The VC were closing in on him, but Marine Corps planes and choppers were on site providing cover shortly after his parachute hit the beach. When he got back to the squadron, the shock of the event hit him. He got drunk and climbed on the roof of our hootch and serenaded us all night. Nobody complained. We were glad to have him back, but the nickname Rooftop stuck with him.

"Well, Fergy, the little sergeant has seen better days. Let me get the doctor's opinion." When he returned, Rooftop had a grin on his face. "The good news is that he'll be able to report for duty. The bad news is, he's still going to be short."

It now hurt to laugh, but the three of us had a good one.

"The doc is making us leave—they've got some more work to do on you," the CO said.

We looked at each other uncomfortably. I would be going home, and they would stay behind in harm's way. Marines don't hug, and we couldn't shake hands, but the clearing of throats and hands fidgiting with hats said more than their simple words of departure.

"Take care. We'll see you back in the world."

I nodded slightly to return their salutes as they left.

Curiosity had me. "Can I get a mirror, Doc? I'd like to see how my face looks."

"Marine, it's not a pretty sight, but you're going to be fine. There's no need to see what you look like now. What's important is how good you're going to look when you heal up. Besides, there are guys off of your own amtrac that need my help right now."

He didn't have time for the whining of someone with only a severe sunburn. I felt an inch tall and meekly said, "Aye, aye, sir."

The field hospital sorted the living from the dead and dying. Some went into body bags; others would be patched up and returned to the field. Others were shipped to the nearest military hospital that could best treat their type of injury. This sometimes meant a flight to Thailand or elsewhere for spinal cord injuries, Japan for burns, and Europe for amputees. The wounded were kept at Da Nang until they could survive the long trip to their next hospital. Our little group of twenty, with varying degrees of burns, would be shipped to U.S. Naval Hospital, Yokuska, Japan. It was a burn center where we would get the best immediate care.

We were scheduled to be airlifted out the next day. Our beds were needed by an endless line of wounded soldiers who would die without the next level of care.

The VC shelled the runway that night, preventing the big Air Force, C-130 air-vac transports from landing. Our departure was delayed for three days. No bandages were changed, and any waking period now meant pain—and lots of it. I'd never had a sunburn like this. Drugs and the body's own pain defenses caused me to slip in and out of consciousness. I didn't cry out or moan; doing so did nothing to ease the pain, and I was going to be okay. The doctor had tactfully reminded me of being a Marine Corps Officer. I would try to keep a "stiff upper lip," as the British say.

Runway repairs were made, and we were loaded into the huge airplanes. The C-130s ferry in choppers, trucks, and tanks, then get reconfigured to carry litters back out of the country. We were stacked three high on the curved bulkheads of the plane. Each litter was fastened like a bookshelf hung on slotted tracks, with an assortment of IV paraphernalia hung above the litters. I lay naked except for the bandages covering my arms and a nonstick bandage across my hips. The term "nonstick bandage" is definitely a misnomer.

"Lieutenant, if you get dehydrated, you'll get a dangerously high fever, and we never have enough help on these flights," the nurse said. She was the first Caucasian female I had seen for months. "I won't be able give you or the other wounded the attention you need, so I've rigged up an IV pouch with water in it and a tube you can drink from. You need to drink as much as you possibly can. You're burned over so much of your body that the wounds will weep more fluid than your body can replace from the IV in your foot, so you must drink from this tube."

She was right. The ten-inch diameter bandages had been changed just before we boarded, but they soaked the bedding like a bucket of water had just been spilled. Nothing could be done about it until we reached the hospital in Japan. The water from the IV bag tasted like plastic and made me throw up; I could tell the fever had started. The nurse gave me some fresh water from a cup and straw. Once I got a belly full, the nausea ebbed, the fever subsided, and for a while I listened to the droning of the engines and the sounds of the wounded.

One Marine was continually moaning and crying for his mother. He became a major irritant, like the whining child that sits behind you on an airplane. The young Marine across the aisle from me shouted, "Massy, shut your fat mouth. You're driving us all crazy. You're not burned nearly as bad as the lieutenant, and he hasn't said anything." I was shocked at his reference to me. "If you think you're in pain now, wait until I get my good hand on you. I'll give you something to cry about." The whining stopped.

I learned two things on that flight: my stiff upper lip had worked and when kids are badly hurt, they never cry out for their fathers. God Bless Mothers.

Taking care of casualties is an afterthought in every war. It takes years to build hospitals or become an MD, but it only takes the flash of a few explosions for thousands of young men to need both—now. The number of wounded troops overtaxed the limits of Naval Hospital Yokuska. An emergency ward had been set up in the gymnasium of a nearby Japanese grade school. The lights were always on; night and day blurred together. During a conscious moment, I recognized the Marine in the bed across the aisle facing me. He was the one who had yelled at the screamer. His right arm and hand were bandaged, and a head bandage covered his right eye. Some of his body had already begun to heal. His good eye caught mine.

"How many of us?" I asked, barely moving my lips.

"Five dead and twenty four wounded—all burns" he said.

"How bad are they?" I asked.

"You're one of the worst that survived, but the guy that was sitting next to you on the amtrac died in the field. His feet were down inside the hatch, and that big steel lid slammed down on his legs."

Carson's words flashed through my mind: "Don't ever put your feet in that hatch, Skipper." His warning had saved my life.

"Sergeant Cole jumped back up on that rig, pulled up the hatch cover, and threw him off, but it was too late. He was charred bad and died before the choppers came. I reckon some of the others who died seared their lungs by gulping in that blue flame, but that's just what I heard the doctors say."

"How's the Sarge?" I asked.

"He's here with us. He burned his hands, but he's in good shape. He's one brave son-of-a-buck to get back up on that rig with those thirties cooking off."

The nurse gave me a shot of morphine. I got an incredibly euphoric feeling that all was well just before passing out.

That was the last time I saw the Marine. I've always wondered if he lost his eye and if the sergeant received a commendation for his extraordinary heroism. I wasn't a Fitchner, but I could never have done what the sarge did. Where do we get such kids? How can they not be exceptionally rewarded for such extraordinary action that guarantees severe wounds, if not death? We should be in awe and reminded daily of such magnificent valor. But as a country, we reserve our deepest adulation for celebrities who entertain us, not the valiant who protect us.

I love the morning sun, but today it was my enemy. We lay on gurneys outside the hospital waiting for the paperwork to be completed. The sun was hot, my IV was empty, and I needed water. After several requests for a drink, my leadership example deteriorated into overly dramatic begging. The stiff upper lip was literally going to be the death of me.

"If I don't get something to drink, I'm going to die right here," I said to the orderly standing next to me.

"You're going to be just fine. We'll get you all you want to drink once you've been checked in, but I can't give you anything without the doctor's orders."

"No, no, you don't understand. I can feel the fever coming on. It's getting too high because the sun is so hot."

"There are lots of other Marines here and they seem to be okay. Aren't you an officer?"

"I can't help it. The sun hurts. I need water or the fever will get worse—please help me."

"Lay back and try to relax. We'll get you all fixed up when we get inside. There's nothing I can do right now."

"But my brain is starting to cook. I'm going to be sick—please, please help me ..."

"Sir, I'm sorry, but ..."

I spewed a Technicolor sunrise in all directions, decorating everyone within three feet. I couldn't stop the contractions. I knew I was convulsing, but could do nothing about it. A flurry of activity surrounded me, and I was quickly moved into the hospital.

"We can't put him on the burn ward. He's an officer," said the head nurse.

"But the officer's rooms aren't set up for burn patients," said someone else.

"Put him in the first available room," said Dr. Vasquez. "While you are worrying about protocol, we might lose him. He needs help now!"

"There's too many DBs in this room. I can't take the DBs," I said. Ice bags were placed over me as I was ranting.

"What are DBs?" asked the nurse

"DBs make my ears hurt," I moaned, trying to describe the warning sound of a surface-to-air missile that seemed to be pounding in my ears.

Dr. Vasquez said, "He means decibels! Turn off the air-conditioner, it's too loud. He must have some problems with his ears from the concussion of the explosion. For God's sake, hold him down without hurting him so we can give him a shot and get him stabilized."

"You gave us a bit of a scare this morning, Lieutenant Ferguson. You had a temperature of 105 degrees, and that's when we were finally able to take it. It was probably higher, which made you delirious," the nurse said. "Dr. Vasquez wants to examine you right away so I'll call him, even though it's eight thirty at night."

Dr. Vasquez had thick, black hair that was graying at the temples. His mustache matched his hair and made him look like a Spanish don. His impeccably starched and pressed Navy whites gleamed next to his dark complexion.

After our hellos, I said, "I'm sorry I was out of control. I hope I didn't embarrass myself too much."

"Not at all, during your fever you kept asking us not to send you back. Lots of Marines say the same thing or they cry out for their mother; it's normal, nothing to be ashamed of." But I was ashamed. "Going back is one worry you can forget about—your skin will need lots of healing time, so you won't be going back to Vietnam. I know you are worried about your face; it's going to be fine. The skin on the face is the toughest part of your body, because it's always exposed to the elements. I'm going to let you look in a mirror just this once, and then don't ask again. Don't be scared of what you see. I am telling you as honestly as I can, your face will heal up with little or no scarring at all."

The image in the mirror was unrecognizable. My head was charred as black as a marshmallow left too long over a camp fire and as round and hairless as a basketball.

He ran his finger across my forehead and gave me the low-down on what he knew my concerns were. "This charring will flake off in a few weeks. As the skin underneath heals, the swelling of your head will go down. If we've learned anything from this war, it's how to treat burns. Just a year ago, we wouldn't be able to save someone burned over as much of their body as you are. The burns are only superficial, not complicated like an internal injury, but people with such a large affected area would die from either infection or dehydration. This morning you experienced how easily that can happen, but now we've got good treatments. So let's put this behind us and focus on getting you home." He took the mirror away. "Tomorrow you'll start therapy. It's painful, but you'll be loaded up with Demerol. It's a nonaddicting synthetic pain killer. You've had all the morphine you're going to get."

Dr. Vasquez removed the arm bandages to reveal what looked like two raw masses of bloody meat. They washed my arms with sterile water poured from jugs and applied a white salve that burned intensely. "This stuff really kills the bugs," he said. Then the big bandages were reapplied.

A ritual began that would last for nearly a month. First came breakfast: solid foods fed to me by an orderly. Next came a shot of Demerol, then removal of the nonstick bandages that were stuck to my entire backside, then I was loaded into a wheelchair covered with more nonstick, sticking pads. We took the elevator down to the therapy room where, finally, I climbed into a large whirlpool bath to soak off the bug-killing salve.

A corpsman began pouring water over my head as he said, "Well, we've got ourselves an officer Crispy Critter here. We don't get too many 'ociffers' down here. I want you to know, sir, that what I have to do is going to hurt, but it's what all Crispy Critters have to go through. That Marine in the tub across the way," he pointed some large tweezers at him. "He was burned by a white phosphorous grenade that went off as soon as he released the pin. That stuff sticks to you. They had to pack him in mud to put it out. He's been here two months and gets this every day. The mud gave him some infection, so he's had it pretty rough. He'll need lots of skin grafts, but the doc says they'll patch him up and even give him some new ears, so you are already way ahead of him." The orderly talked like the poor wretch wasn't even in the same room.

This Marine robbed me of my self pity. He just stared into space, accepting what needed to be done without a whimper. His face was charred and only partially there. His ears were gone, and he had nubbins for fingers on his right hand. His entire upper torso looked like charred meat left on the grill too long. I could stand the pain because I knew I would fully recover. I thought he tolerated the pain because all hope was lost, or maybe he was just one tough hombre.

"Yeeoow! What the hey are you doing?" I yelled.

"We have to scrape the salve and scabs off or else you'll get infections. Besides, I like doing this to 'ociffers.' You can't order me to stop. My orders come from the admiral of the base," the orderly said asserting his authority. "My job is to get you back to the best condition I can. Your job is to do what you can to get well. I will be hurting you, but we are on the same team. It hurts me to hurt you, so we laugh and call you Crispy Critters to get through the day."

With that, he began removing scabs from my scalp with tweezers, then scraped the salve off my arms with a squeegee.

"You can swear and yell at us, but we know we've helped you get better. We get to see you heal, up and that's what makes this job tolerable," he said.

It was torture, but the Marine facing me was getting the same procedure and didn't wince. *Lord, help me be as strong as him,* I prayed silently. It then occurred to me that I never prayed unless I was asking for something. Why should God treat me any differently than the engineer who was blown to bits? Those thoughts were too deep, so I kept asking for help.

"All right, you got me, doc. I'll do my best, but I can't be as quiet as he is," I said.

"Don't let that scrawny frame fool you. He's a tough Jose. He can hardly talk, but he wants to stay in the Corps."

I had been ouching and grouching from the start. I thought to myself, *he probably thinks I'm a whining wimp like that kid on the airplane.* Where had my stiff upper lip gone? It had escaped me.

After hydrotherapy and a shot of Demerol, the burning salve was reapplied. I would sleep until lunch, get fed by an orderly, sleep until dinner, and so on. The pain shots came every four hours, but lasted only three. There was lots of gritting the teeth time.

A welcome visitor said, "So you *are* the Lieutenant Ferguson I checked into the battalion with. The first couple of days, all I could see was your face. Your face was so charred I thought you were a black man," said Lieutenant Robb.

"Well I'll be a son-of-a-buck. How in the world did you get in here?" I asked.

He held up his right hand. It was missing the tip of the index finger down to the second knuckle. "I got the absolute golden wound. The Marine Corps counts you 4F if you're missing any part of your trigger finger." He shoved the finger tip up his nose making it look like he was scratching the inside of his skull. It was good to laugh again.

"I got hit with shrapnel in a hot landing zone. Every place we went, we got attacked because they thought I was Captain Robb. I can't believe they've left him in the field."

"They took him out of country the same day I got hit. He was on the amtrac right behind me. It could just as easily have been him," I said.

"He was getting too many of my guys killed and wounded just because I had the same last name, so I'm glad he's gone. Have you heard anything about the other two guys we checked in with?" he said.

"Yeah, Sharpe was on point on his first lone mission and took five rounds in the face. His sergeant was killed trying to save him, and twenty-three other guys bought the farm. They didn't prep a tree line with any artillery or look it over with a scout. They walked right into an ambush," I said, relating the details of that day, starting with Dixon's radio call.

"Why was he on the point instead of in the middle where he belonged?" Robb asked.

"He was gung-ho and going to prove himself to his troops, but instead he got wasted by an NVA unit that was set up in a tree line. We found tunnels and a small infirmary, but only one cartridge from an AK-47. They even cleaned up their brass before they left."

"How about Kelley?" Robb asked.

"He was on the same mission with me when I got hit. He was a couple of amtracs behind the real Robb, but I'll tell ya, he's one lucky Marine." I recounted the tale of the grazing bullet. "You know, that little fool wouldn't even stop to go see a doctor and get a Purple Heart."

I admired Kelley for his dedication to his men, but not collecting a Purple Heart for such an injury just might get him killed.

"He might need it. I can't believe how many guys we've had go home with their third Purple, and he's still got an entire year to go," I said.

"So we've got one left in the field, two wounded, and one dead." He counted on his good hand.

"That's right," I said. "The intel says that area is a major point of attack for the Tet Offensive, so I don't know if we were gettin' hammered because of Captain Robb or if we are the point of their attack."

"We killed a few gooks in those hot landing zones. One of them had orders to assassinate Robb, but they got the two of us mixed up. I betcha he's the reason for the major offensive." He was guessing, but it added logic to his story. He could be right.

"When do you go back to the world?" I asked.

"I leave first thing in the morning, so I've been shopping. I bought a new Seiko watch and some stereo gear at the PX. Now I'm just killin' hours," he said

He held up his wrist showing me his huge Seiko watch with the day and date with Sunday in red.

"I'm glad I got to see you before I leave. It's a tough deal about Sharpe. I've gotta believe that the odds now favor Kelley making it through," he said.

It was good to know what Lieutenant Robb's fate had been. We said our goodbyes as the pain shot kicked in. "I'm getting me a new watch with the red Sunday before going home," I vowed.

The Silent Marine kept my bleating to a minimum. Every day, I was thankful I was not him. My burns were healing fast, but he showed no improvement.

"He wanted to know how you were hurt, you bein' an ociffer and all," the orderly said.

"Did you tell him?" I asked.

"Yeah. He wanted you to know that he wishes you a full recovery and that somewhere God has a plan for you," he said.

I nodded and mouthed the words "thank you" to the Marine. He nodded back.

That's how he endured. The intensity of his pain was matched by the strength of his faith that God had a plan for him, no matter how his burns turned out. He knew he was part of God's scheme.

It gave me a strange feeling to think that God had a plan for me, like I was a puppet playing out a rehearsed script. I believed in God. I thought about all of my "gimme and help me" prayers: "God don't let me die before I've lived," or "God, please don't let my face be scarred." My prayers were like Post-It-Notes for

His bulletin board. I expected Him to put the earth's rotation on hold, forget the other planets, and get down here and heal me of every little hangnail. That was my plan for God. But the Silent Marine saw that it was the other way around. We each endured because we knew, in our own way, things would work out. He had faith in God; I had faith in the doctor.

By the end of the fourth week, healing came rapidly. A chunk of charred skin flaked off of my face like the skin on a charred hot dog. I could see that the pink skin underneath was perfect. I was ecstatic. My face would heal just like the doctor said. My arms had started to scab over, so I would soon go home.

As I left the therapy room after my last treatment, I wished the Marine good luck. He still faced a mountain of pain. His injuries were so severe, I couldn't begin to empathize with what he would have to endure in the hospital and in life. He raised his nubbin of a hand, looked with his left eye slightly bulging because the eyelid had been burned off, and with what remained of his lips twisted into a partial smile. He nodded and waved goodbye.

Years later I saw a preacher on TV holding a group of middle school kids in rapt awe. He had nubbins for fingers on his right hand, the plastic surgery on his face was marvelous and his tour in Vietnam was the same time frame as my own. The cause of his injuries was from a white phosperous grenade. It was him.

He told the story of how his wife accepted his new "face." She said "It made me a stronger person." He said, "It was all part of "God's plan in building our ministry together."

The normally antsy, talkative kids sat in stone silence and teared up. So did I. The Silent Marine is now an inspiration to hundreds of thousands of kids. The proverbial "Mustard Seed"is not even close to the size of his faith.

CHAPTER 9

Homecoming

A roaring cheer from a couple hundred thankful Marines filled
the huge aircraft the second it touched down at Travis Air Force
Base. Home at last, home at last, thank God Almighty, I am
home at last.

The sun was shining its welcome only for us. Some kissed
the tarmac; most of us stood, breathing in the cool morning
air thinking about the loved ones we would see in the next few
hours. We could now make plans beyond the next ambush or
surgery. Our mission was simple: get well as best we could and
live happily ever after.

We took a bus to the brand-new Oakland Naval Hospital.
It was not quite finished yet, so we would be housed for a few
days in the WWII hospital, which consisted of several intercon-
nected one story barracks. There was a short briefing, where
they checked us in and gave us some advance money for travel.
We were told that those of us far enough along in the healing
process would be given two weeks recuperation leave right away.
We would then report back for the various medical procedures
and therapies that would be required in the months ahead.

The nurse I checked in with at the barracks gave me a single room. She told me that my wife would be at the hospital in a few hours. I couldn't wait. It had been nine months since we had clung together at the airport, not knowing what the future held. Now we had opportunities and each other to explore.

She was tan, wearing a green, sleeveless dress and a gold and jade brooch I had sent her from Okinawa during FAC School. She was more beautiful than that day at the park.

"It's okay to kiss a little harder than that. My lips have pretty well healed," I told her as we embraced without letting go for a long time.

I thanked the nurse for putting an extra bed in my room, but I checked out of the hospital and we caught a cab to the nearest cheap motel.

With the exception of thick scars on my arms and hands, huge scabs on my ears, and blotchy red skin on my face and scalp, I didn't think I looked too bad. At the motel A blonde floozy was checking in at the same time. Apparently she thought I was Frankenstein. She took one look at my ears and said, "Oh my gawd, I can't look at you. That is horrible. Oh my gawd, I can't stay here." Having loudly made her disgust known, she ran out of the office.

The innkeeper was flabbergasted. Ardi and I looked at each other and laughed. The large scabs on my ears were the result of having been covered with placenta. The healing properties of the tissue that gives life to a fetus was also used for burns. The scabs would eventually peel off, leaving the ears without any noticeable scarring. The apologetic motel manager gave us a big discount.

The room had a small trail of sugar ants running up and down a wall near the bed. I had been living with ants and other bugs for months, so it didn't matter to me, but Ardi was upset.

"We're moving rooms," she said.

"Well, he did practically give us the room for free after that lady's episode. I'll take care of the ants. Besides, at night they just go into their little nest, and we'll be gone tomorrow."

"There is no way I'm taking my clothes off with ants in the room."

Within five minutes we were in a new room—with no ants.

She slipped into the black negligee that I had given her as a Christmas present three days before we were married. It was a gift meant to be opened in private. Over my embarrassed insistence that she wait until we were alone, her parents encouraged her to open it at the family gathering on Christmas Eve. After a slow-motion unwrapping that increased the beads of sweat on my forehead, she held up the sheer negligee with three appropriately placed maple leaves for all to see. A chorus of restrained "Ooooohs, and Aaaaahs" was emitted through several pursed lips. Who cares now? She looked ravishing in it.

"I hope that telegram didn't scare you about my face being burned and all. I was afraid you might think the scarring could be hard to live with."

She then said the most loving words I've ever heard. "Colonel Parker's letter said you still had your sense of humor, so I knew you would still be the same person inside. The scars didn't matter." Romance ensued.

"Do you mind if I join you?" he asked with his good-looking grin.

"Please do, and judging from your face, I'd say you're attached to Oak Knoll." I said.

I was letting him know I knew where his scars and stitches had come from—shrapnel covered with gunpowder had left grayish blue dots the color of a tattoo on his handsome face.

"You don't win any beauty contests yourself," he said laughing as we shook hands and introduced ourselves.

The red splotches on my face, a scalp covered in peach fuzz, scabs on my ears, and a uniform that draped like rags on a scarecrow told him I was also attached to the Oakland Naval Hospital. He was one of those people in life that you are willing to trust with your deepest secrets over your first cup of coffee.

"You got wheels?" he asked as we finished our dinners.

"No, the wife's got the car up in Oregon, where she's going to school. She just left a few days ago after my recuperation leave," I said.

"I just bought a Volkswagen convertible today. Let's go for a ride."

I knew that a bachelor with a new car meant trolling for girls. His VW convertible was not a babe-mobile, but it was fun, cheap, baby blue with a white top, and had lot of personality—like Phil.

"You're excused from the bar activities, but you don't mind if I chase a few ladies, do ya?" he said.

"Hey, even a blind pig finds an acorn once in a while," I said, using one of Ben's one-liners.

"You got that right. You did, so there's hope for me," he said with a twinkle in an eye that was bright red around the pupil from his injuries.

The large pink scar along his right cheekbone and over his eye seemed to be a part of him. The speckling of small blue dots that ran from his jaw bone down into his shirt added to his mystery. He lit a cigarette in the corner of his mouth. He looked cooler than James Dean and tougher than Superman.

Phil was pretty much all talk when it came to the ladies. I'm sure I cramped his style, but we enjoyed each other's company.

"Ya know, it's getting tough to find a good woman. Who wants to marry somebody you meet in a bar?" He paused to flick ashes out the little window wing of his VW. "The college chicks are all too young, and it's tough to carry on a decent conversation with someone who hasn't been to college. You got lucky," he said flicking his thumb toward me.

He was verbalizing for the first time something we both knew: at age twenty–five, it was time to get down to the business of life.

Phil had been out on a night ambush when the VC had mortared his position. The blast from a mortar shell tends to go up and out at a forty-five-degree angle, so most of the shrapnel hit him from the waist up. The right side of his body was peppered with hundreds of small, blue-gray marks. His face would have some scarring, but it added to his rugged good looks and increased his intrigue ten-fold. Some of the shrapnel entered body organs and needed to be removed, which is why he had been at the hospital for almost six months before I met him. He lived at the BOQ between hospital stays and would be discharged in about five weeks.

We had a few beers in a couple different places, but I couldn't spend too much money. My pay record had been lost when I was evacuated from Vietnam. Ardi and I were living on an allotment of $200 per month. This included paying ninety-eight dollars a month for the apartment in McMinnville, where she still had to finish her education degree at Linfield. My job was to let my skin heal to a point where it would accept skin grafting.

Phil and I established a routine: wake up, go check in at the hospital, spend the rest of the day seeing the sights of San Francisco, and return to the BOQ to drink cheap wine and talk about life. We exchanged our stories about Vietnam, and we arrived at the same conclusion. We had served in the right place at the right time, and we had made a difference by helping the helpless. History proved us right. When the U.S. pulled out, hundreds of thousands of Vietnamese cast themselves adrift on boats to escape the looming slaughter.

Ardi called one day when I was shaving, so Phil answered my

phone. He introduced himself to her, and by the time I could get rinsed off, I could tell they were already friends. He had a knack for meeting people.

"She says she'll marry me if you fool around with those bar flies," he teased, handing me the phone.

"What do you mean he sounds handsome," I said to Ardi. "He looks like a turkey. I guess he talks better than he looks," I laughed. Phil was plain fun to be around. He was a great kidder and liked to be kidded.

The upshot of that telephone conversation was that Linfield had worked it out so Ardi would be able to come and live in the Bay Area in two weeks. I would fly up on a Friday, and we would drive our '60 Chevy back down in a straight shot.

"Where are you going to stay?" Phil asked.

"I've got no idea. I don't have enough money to rent a place down here until I get my pay record squared away." Money always seemed to be an issue. "The captain at payroll said it could be months before they get it straightened out, so somehow I have to figure out how to live on only two hundred bucks a month." Phil had no answers. "What do you think would happen if we just stayed in the BOQ? There's no rule against having women in the room," I said.

"That Navy lieutenant a couple doors down has a different gal just about every night," Phil said, confirming the plan of action I was thinking of. "What are they going to do to you, send you back to Vietnam if they catch you? As long as you're attached to the hospital, it's free. All you'll have to pay for are her meals. You'd be nuts not to do it," Phil encouraged.

I liked the way Phil was thinking. The next few days were spent trying to get my pay record corrected. The payroll sergeant finally asked his CO, a sarcastic, and by the ribbons on his uniform, a POG of a captain to ask me to leave the building. That was it. I had no options. We would set up house in the BOQ.

Ardi arrived, and according to the rules of the BOQ, we lived in sin for about a week. She came with us as Phil and I checked in at the hospital each morning. Sometimes the visits were lengthy because they were always finding small pieces of shrapnel working their way out of Phil's body. After that, we would become tourists or play three-handed pinochle in the small, dorm-like, BOQ room. The three of us ate together at night, but I felt a little sorry for Phil. It cut out a lot of our old fun now that Ardi and I had our own plans.

One afternoon, Phil showed up with a gallon of Gallo Brothers wine and announced we were going on a picnic. I had gone for a very slow jog that morning so I jumped in the shower. I was trying to get some tone back into my muscles. Ardi was sitting on the single bed and Phil was sitting in the lone, dormitory-type chair. That's where the BOQ manager found them when he knocked, but before they could get up, he opened the door with his master key and burst in.

"Lieutenant Ferguson," I heard him say to Phil in a loud gruff voice. "And, I presume this is Mrs. Ferguson," he said, leaning over her.

He wore an old fashioned black tuxedo with long tails with food stains on the sleeves that came from years of working at the BOQ. It was an odd scene. The "sand crab," as civilian base workers were called, flaunted his authority in this 1920s formal tuxedo that made him look like a skinny, six-foot-five Emperor Penguin. His schnoz even had beak-like qualities.

Glowering at Phil, he said, "Why are you laughing, Lieutenant Ferguson? I am here on a very serious matter. You and your wife cannot stay in the BOQ and must move out immediately. I see nothing funny about that!"

Phil had already taken a few pulls of wine before I took a shower, and he had a buzz on. "I'm laughing because *that's* Lieutenant Ferguson," he said pointing at me as I stepped out of the bathroom completely naked except for a small towel.

Ardi was terrified. I decided to follow Phil's irreverent lead. I started to casually dry my hair with the towel. The sand crab was flummoxed. His beady eyes flashed at each of us as he tried to process all the possible relationships through his gutter-trap of a mind.

"Sorry, Mr. Manager, perhaps you should have called first. I could have come down to the desk in my uniform for a more formal meeting," I said.

"She has to move out at once." He pointed his long, bony finger at Ardi. "It ... it's ... well, it's simply not allowed," he finally managed to say. He sounded like an irate parent talking to an errant daughter.

"There's no rule against women in the rooms. I checked with your chief," I said.

"This is the Bachelor Officer's Quarters. Spouses may not stay here." His squeaky voice came from somewhere under his imposing beak.

"I've seen the Navy lieutenant have the same woman in his quarters for three nights in a row—" He cut me off in mid-sentence.

"But *they* are not *married*." He emphasized married as though the Holy Union was a cardinal sin.

"I think that's *my* point. I only need a few more days to get some money together, my pay record—" Without sympathy, he cut me off again.

"I will not argue with you. I will be calling your commanding officer." He brushed his sleeves off like we had contaminated him with germs and straightened his tuxedo like a penguin preening its feathers.

Phil was laughing uncontrollably at the absurdity of the situation. A man old enough to be our grandfather was bashing marriage and shouting, "It's not a laughing matter!" As he spun around, the tails of his tux flared out like Fred Astaire's in the old black and white dance movies. His heels even clicked on the floor like Fred's tap shoes as he stomped out.

Within five minutes, the sergeant major of the base called.

"Lieutenant Ferguson," he said in a firm but polite voice.

The sergeant major was the top enlisted Marine on Treasure Island. He was a veteran of two different wars. He deserved and would get my respect.

"Yes sergeant, I'm listening."

"Colonel Jepson would like to speak with you in his office right now, lieutenant."

"I will be there in a few minutes," I said.

Maybe the penguin was right; this wasn't a laughing matter. He had made trouble for me. I didn't know what to think as I wheeled the big Chevy into the slot marked "visitors." The Marine Corps did everything by the book. I knew I had crossed the line. I had never seen anyone cut any slack. Break the rules, suffer the consequences. I was apprehensive.

"Lieutenant Ferguson reporting as ordered sir." I stood ramrod stiff and looked straight ahead just like I was back in OCS.

The colonel finished signing some papers then angrily said, "Why on God's green earth are you living at the BOQ with your wife?"

"I'm broke, sir, and can't afford an apartment," I said feeling foolish about the whole situation.

"You are a lieutenant in the United States Marine Corps. What have you done with all of your money, young man?"

"My pay record was lost when I was medevaced from Vietnam. My wife and I have been living on her allotment of $200 dollars a month." I told him my sad tale. "The cheapest apartments we've seen are almost twice that. The captain at payroll told me not to come back anymore because I've been going there twice a day."

My eyes were locked on the back wall, so there had been no eye contact.

"Listen, lieutenant, go to a bank and get a loan," he growled. He was fulminating.

"With respect sir, if I did, will the Marine Corps pay the high interest rate on a short-term loan, sir?"

"Well borrow the doggone money from your parents then!"

"Again, with respect sir, I won't do that. My parents aren't in a position to help." I mustered all of my confidence for an offensive play. "Sir, I think it would embarrass the Marine Corps. We pride ourselves on taking care of our own. Now a combat veteran is being asked to borrow money from his parents so he can rent a place to stay while recovering from war injuries." He relit the stub of his cigar. "I would add, sir that we didn't leave anybody in the field no matter what the circumstances." He looked out the window like there was something to see besides the parking lot. "I would ask the colonel to remember that the cash situation is not my fault. I have plenty of money, but I'm not getting paid."

He took a large drag on his cigar. I knew he was using the stalling tactic to mull things over. He blew a cloud of smoke and shuffled a few papers. I knew I had hit him where he lived. The duty of Marines to one another is a sacred trust. The pause was too long. It became awkward. I had miscalculated. I had broken the rules. There must be a penalty. I began to sweat.

"Stand easy, lieutenant." His voice softened. He paced the floor with smoke curling around his head. "I've been behind this desk too blamed long, and maybe I've lost touch with the troops. That sand crab at the BOQ is always complaining about something. He has more clout around here than the admiral because he's outside our chain of command. I understand the money part, but what's this he told me about another lieutenant being in your room with your wife while you're running around buck-naked?"

I snapped back to attention.

"Sir, Lieutenant Cotterman is a good Marine, the kind you trust with your life and your wife. We're both attached to Oak Knoll, and we have become good friends. The manager barged in with his own key while I was in the shower and caused a bit of a commotion."

I stated all of that in a monotone and in one single breath.

"I apologize, sir, for not being an officer and a gentleman; we did have a little fun with the sand crab. But if he has something on his dirty little mind to damage our careers, ask him to put it in writing. I *will* borrow the money to hire a civilian attorney and—"

"Simmer down, lieutenant, simmer down. I get the picture. Now get your tail end down to payroll. Tell the captain how much money you'll need, and he will personally get it for you. He will also personally reconstruct your pay record this weekend, I will see to that. Then you check out of the BOQ, ASAP. You got that, lieutenant?"

"Yes sir, thank you sir. But I'm a little concerned about what the manager might—"

"Lieutenant, no sand crab is going to tarnish the reputation of good Marines, which *is* something I can and will take care of. You are dismissed."

He lifted the phone to his ear. When he started speaking, his voice sounded like he was chewing out a private.

"Now listen, Mr. Barnacle, about those two Marines and the wife of Lieutenant Ferguson. I want you to apologize to them for creating an awkward situation by barging in on them and if you ever, ever ..."

The San Francisco air never smelled so good. I could hardly wait to get back to my wife, my entertaining friend, and the Brothers Gallo. The back pay the little POG captain personally handed to me felt good in my hand. My wallet was stuffed. I had finally won an argument with a colonel. I stopped and bought some cigars. Phil and I were definitely CO material.

CHAPTER 10

Hospital Stories

He made a high-pitched noise that sounded like a fire truck.

"I'm a siren, but I can be lots of other things," the patient said.

Underneath the Oakland A's batting helmet, I could see that a large part of his skull was missing. His siren changed to the sound of British police cars, and by the time the elevator reached the floor where I was scheduled to report, Ardi and I had also heard his air-raid siren. Catastrophic injuries were everywhere. I was thankful not to be one of them.

Burns are superficial, but they take time to heal. I would need three operations for skin grafts to get the right hand back into working order. Each surgery would take two weeks in the hospital, followed by weeks of recuperation. During those hospital stays, I was in the company of some special people. One of my great regrets in life is that I didn't write a book about the courage of those men. It would be a greater lament if did not include a few of their stories here.

"We were going in on an extraction mission of a recon team," Captain Barnes said as he used his recovering hands to show the flight of his helicopter. "All of a sudden, the entire front of the chopper fell off in one big explosion." Along with other burn patients in the room, I listened in awe. "We were low enough to the ground that I tumbled out and fell into some thick briars. I saw my copilot and crew go up in a fireball with the rest of the chopper. I knew I was on my own."

"Man, how'd you keep quiet with all that pain?" I asked.

"It was be quiet or be dead. I could hear Charlie all around me. They ate lunch and dinner right in front of me for three days. I was afraid I would moan if I passed out, so I fought to stay awake. Most of my burns were second and third degree, so there were no nerve endings left, but I drifted in and out of consciousness."

We all knew what he was talking about; it seemed impossible.

"The third day I woke up to the sound of choppers," he continued. "The gooks had left in the middle of the night, and I knew the Marines would be back for me. One of the recon grunts that made it out on the other chopper saw me fall out the front. He got his colonel to come back and get me. I knew they would, so I just prayed and held on."

Thank God for colonels listening to their lowliest privates. If he hadn't, we would have been deprived of witnessing the wedding of Captain Barnes and Nurse Wilson. Every war has stories of soldiers marrying their nurse. Why not these two? They were exceptional people brought together by historic circumstances in an environment filled with caring. In the last analysis, isn't that what love is all about?

When young soldiers get married just before shipping off to war, they take a risk. Separation by time and distance can make pledges made in good health disappear with a disfiguring injury.

Sergeant Landis was sucked into that nightmare when the entire lower half of his face was shot off by a sniper.

"How ya doing, Sergeant Landis," I said as I joined him in leaning on the counter of the nurse's station for a late-night conversation.

"Not so good, captain," he said using my new rank and as best he could with a partially reconstructed jaw.

He kept his wounds hidden behind a large gauze bandage that ran from his neck up to just under his nose and all around his face. The round mercifully left him with the ability to be understood.

"My wife has filed for divorce."

"When was the last time you saw her?" I asked.

"The day I left for Nam. I was in country for ten months, and I've been here for fourteen."

"You mean you haven't seen her for two years?"

"Yup. Because I'm in the hospital, the Marine Corps won't help move her out here from Mississippi. They say it's not a duty station, so we can't get help with a dependent move, even though I'm going to be here another year or more. I wanted her to come out so we could celebrate her twenty-first birthday, but no dice."

This government policy robbed vets of family support during their long-term care. In every sense of the word, it was criminal. I was incensed. By heaven, I would use my new captain's rank to help Landis. The next day, I called whoever could correct this injustice and get Landis' wife moved out west to possibly avoid an emotional catastrophe. No joy.

On another night, when my medication wore off long before the next pain shot was due, I was pacing around the ward when I found Landis slumped in a chair in the solarium. A legal decree dangled from his hand. Government apathy and a restless young wife conspired to do what a sniper's bullet could not: they crushed his spirit. Tears streamed from his closed eyes.

Human misery is guaranteed by war. I knew he would do well with his physical reconstruction; I could only hope he could rebuild his young life.

He was a Vietnam vet who had survived the war without injury. He had been mustered out of the Corps for about a year. He was bailing hay by himself on a remote section of his parents' farm east of Oakland. The bailer was jammed, so, like he had done a thousand times before, he climbed into it and tried to free it by stomping on the bunched hay. The bailer lurched and pulled his leg into its mechanism up to the knee. He was stuck while an artery was spurting blood. There was no one to yell to for help. If he was unable to free himself, he would bleed to death—quickly. He took off his belt and cinched it above his knee. He opened up his pocket knife and amputated his own leg. He dragged himself to his pickup truck and drove himself thirty miles to the hospital.

He was able to use his veteran's benefits at the hospital and was assigned to our room. He had a great sense of humor and talked about how he could still feel his toes. He actually believed that anybody else would have done the same thing. He didn't know that I faint easily at the sight of my own blood, and so would most people in that situation. I had the feeling a missing leg would only be a minor inconvenience to this hard charger.

"Captain Ferguson, would you like to be in an officer's room?"

"No, I prefer to be in with some of the troops, it's worked out well before," I told the admissions nurse.

She put me into a room with Corporal Dan Belderain and Sergeant Charles Gunther. Both were stellar young Marines. Sergeant Gunther had spent sixteen months in Vietnam. I spied the Silver Star on his nightstand. "Nice piece of metal there. How'd you come by it?" I asked, knowing they were not easily acquired.

"We were on a night patrol and got bushwhacked. We beat feet out of there, but I saw one of our guys get hit and fall down in a ravine. We laid down a base of fire, but they started hittin' us with mortars. I told my guys to get up the trail as fast as they could and form a perimeter." I later learned Guenther had been on many dangerous missions. "I went back for him. When I lugged him up out of the creek, I didn't know who he was. My squad had just been attached to a new unit. He turned out to be a captain, and he put me in for the medal."

Going back alone to an area where you had just been attacked sounded insane—but Audi Murphy brave.

"He must have asked the other guys who I was, because I never saw him after that," Sergeant Gunther told us.

"So your paw wasn't part of your medal story?" I gestured to his left hand.

"Ya know, that's the dumbest thing of all. After being in the bush for sixteen months without gettin' a scratch, I'm in my hootch with a beer in one hand and leaning against the wall with my other," he said while showing us his position. "My hootch mate is cleaning his pistol and he's got the clip out, but forgot about the round in the chamber. The .45 goes off, just misses my head, and goes right through the middle of my hand. I felt like shootin' him for being so dumb."

Dan and I laughed. It wasn't funny, but he made it comical with his reenactment of the round whizzing by his head and piercing his hand.

"To make it even dumber—since it was not due to an enemy action, I don't even get a Purple Heart."

Dan Belderain barely missed stepping on a land mine, but the Marine behind him wasn't so lucky. He set it off and was killed and it took off most of the calf muscles of Dan's legs. He joined up at eighteen, became an ace marksman, and went to sniper school. Only a select few become snipers. He was in the bush three weeks, and by age nineteen, he was in our room taking Demerol shots every four hours as he awaited a slew of skin grafts to cover the backs of his legs.

We played chess and listened to music on his new tape machine. He talked about The Doors, The Who, and other bands I had never heard of. We were six years apart in age, but an entire generation separated us in music and philosophy. He was a sharp kid and we were pretty even in our chess matches.

"Okay, white moves first," I said, moving my queen-pawn two spaces forward. "You know, Dan, I know you think Modesto JC is a good school, and it probably is, but man, you are going to get tuition, books, and fees to any school of your choice. That's about twenty thousand dollars right in your lap."

I had hoped the sound of all that money would have some impact on him. He countered with the same move with his pawn.

"You'll even get more than you need to pay for room and board," I went on. "It's like you've got this chessboard all set up for a checkmate on life. All you have to do is make your move."

I moved the king-pawn one square, building my usual defensive position. He made the same move. Now we could get down to playing chess.

"Naaah, I've been away from my girl too long as it is. They'll still pay me to go to Modesto JC," he said.

"You know, I worked my tail off to get through college and you're going to get it for free," I said

"You mean free if I don't count walking with a limp," he said.

"All right, you're getting it the hard way. Even more reason to get the maximum benefit," I said.

I moved my knight to take up an offensive position.

"My grades weren't that good, but I know I can get into Modesto," he said.

"You graduated, so you must have had a C average."

I had to move my queen after he put it in danger with one of his knights. He played a strong offensive game. I had to make another defensive move with my bishop. I knew he was where he liked to be on the board.

"I didn't work too hard on the grades, but I worked pretty hard on my art projects. Guard your queen," he warned.

"You're not getting my queen that easy." I was on the defense. "Your grades couldn't have been any worse than mine, and I got accepted at Linfield. You might be able to get in. It's worth a shot."

"Yeah, but my girlfriend could never afford to go there, so that's not a possibility. Checkmate," he bragged.

His young love was in full bloom, and my sage wisdom must have sounded like his dad nagging him to clean up his room—the very stuff that drove him to join the Marine Corps.

Impetuous puppy love can indeed overcome all things, but that's not the way to bet. When the talk turned serious, she confessed to him that she had been keeping company with her date to the senior prom while he was in Vietnam. He was inconsolable. I was happy. We gave him his space for a few days. We knew he would work through it.

"Checkmate. You're not focusing on your game today," I said, taking his queen. "Your girlfriend may have done you a favor. She proves that old adage, 'Distance makes the heart grow fonder—of the one you're with.'"

It was good to see him laugh again. The old Dan was back.

"Do you really think I could get into Linfield?" he asked.

Every once in a while you get an opportunity to lend a hand. I knew Dan would flourish at Linfield. He might do the same at other schools, but I knew for certain the two would be a good match.

> *Dear Registrar,*
>
> *Over the past several months, I have gotten to know a young man by the name of Dan Belderain. He has everything it takes to be a good Linfield student. He resides in the same room with me at Oakland Naval Hospital, and I have given him the brochures you were kind enough to send.*
>
> *Dan's high school grades are not the measure of his academic capabilities. He is an artist of some talent, an engaging personality, and I believe his Marine Corps training will make him a good student and a strong leader at Linfield College.*
>
> *Sincerely,*
>
> *Bob Ferguson*
> *Captain USMC*
> *Class of 1965*

We have kept in touch off and on over the years, but I didn't know exactly what transpired after I left the hospital until he called me recently.

Dan's laughing voice sounded like he was still sitting on the edge of a hospital bed playing chess when he said, "I don't know what you wrote in that letter you sent to Linfield, but it must have been a doozy."

"I'm sure I bragged about you a little more than I should

have, but I thought you might be able to start a chess club at the school," I said.

"I had lunch with Ad Rutschman the other day, and I told him that Linfield didn't even send me an admissions application. They sent me an acceptance letter, a housing assignment, and the freshman stuff about when to show up for school and I hadn't even applied yet. Ad was shocked to learn that after all these years, I ended up at Linfield because you and I had been in the hospital together."

Having won national championships in two sports, football and baseball, Ad is the biggest celebrity in McMinnville. He and Dan have been good friends since Dan was a student photographer snapping pictures of his championship teams. He was also the photographer for the weddings of Ad's sons. I was connected with Ad through Linfield football, but I had no idea the two knew each other. Now here we are—a group of old guys still having fun.

Dan became the president of Pi Kappa Alpha fraternity, received an education degree, married his college sweetheart, and retired as an art teacher from McMinnville Middle School. That's a lot of success for the price of a six cent stamp.

Before Phil went home to Worcester, Massachusetts he gave us one last little giggle with a gift for us to remember him by.

"I couldn't get you anything better than a Phil-adendron," he chortled.

We were happy for him to begin his new life, but hated to see him leave. He had been a good friend at a time when I needed one.

Ardi's mom had sent the phone number of Carolee, Ardi's best friend in high school. She was living in Berkeley with her husband, Ken Strom and Ardi thought it would be fun to get together with them. I had met Ken once when he was a freshman in college. He drove a souped-up '55 Chevy, wore his hair in a ducktail like I did when I was in junior high, and spoke with a slight stutter. I didn't think the young hoodlum would graduate from college, so when he announced his plan to get a PhD in chemistry; I had to bite my tongue to keep from laughing. He was having the last laugh. He was doing just that at UC Berkeley.

I really didn't want to get to know Ken and Carolee. Besides eating crow, I thought he might have turned into one of those egotistical types who would continually remind me that he was working on his PhD.

Over my objections, Ardi accepted their dinner invitation. The evening began with Ken and me drinking his homemade beer a couple weeks before it was ready. It tasted like swill but made the mood festive. Carolee baked a terrific meatloaf, and while I was obligated to say that the beer tasted great, it served the purpose of making us both giddy.

"There's nothing like getting a degree in chemistry and then putting it to use making homemade spirits," I said.

He liked to play chess. I found that he could only think one move ahead, so he was easy pickings. Maybe it was beating him at chess with the tricks I had learned from a nineteen-year-old kid, or possibly it was the beer, but we became good friends.

I had only one responsibility: get well. Due to the back pay and my promotion to captain, we had a little bit of extra money for the first time in our lives. We knew we wouldn't settle in the Bay Area, so we did everything possible there was to do. We soaked up the ambience of Fisherman's Wharf, rode the trolley cars, and had a riotous camping trip with the Stroms at Pogies Point. That Pogies outing rivals anything Chevy Chase' could dream up for the Griswolds, but that's another story.

On the anniversary of the great 1906 San Francisco earthquake, Mayor Alioto organized an Earthquake Party. Along with thousands of others, we gathered in front of city hall at five in the morning to party. This could only happen in the free-spirited city of San Francisco.

While I healed from the surgeries, the Stroms regularly visited our room and snuck in meatloaf and beer for all the troops. Ardi and I snuck off the base and had picnics as often as possible. I would hide in the back seat under a blanket. She would drive through the gate in that beautiful, '60 Chevy Impala, the guard would give her a snappy salute, and off we would go for a glorious day. I had to be careful of the sun, so I would make a paper hat out of a newspaper that provided plenty of shade.

It was a story book time of life. We had great food, always chose a romantic setting overlooking the bay for picnics, and the touch of someone I was passionately in love with was healthier than any doctor's orders.

The operations I needed were not invasive, but required hundreds of little stitches. The procedures were long and required lots of anesthesia.

The first surgery was to restore flexibility to the right wrist, where the scarring was too thick for it to bend. The plastic surgeon took a four–inch-square patch of skin from my hip, put it right across the back of my wrist, and wrapped it in a gigantic bandage the shape of a goose's neck. After a few days, pain wasn't an issue. Those became picnic days.

After a week or so, the doctor wanted to see his handiwork.

"What's all that stuffing? It looks like wood shavings," I said to the doctor as he changed the dressing.

"That's exactly what it is—wood shavings. It's used as furniture stuffing. It's been kiln dried and that makes it absolutely sterile."

"Wow, it kind of looks like an arts and crafts project," I said

"A lot of medicine is like arts and crafts. We needed a medium that would put enough pressure on the donor skin without crushing it. This stuff is light and springy and does the job better than anything else we've found." He examined his handiwork like a painter viewing his masterpiece.

"This is just excellent. We're going to get over a ninety percent take to the injured area. This stuffing presses into every nook and cranny of the injury and gives us incredible results," he said.

The second surgery was very similar to the first, except it restored the back of the right hand. The donor portion came from a four-by-eight rectangle on the right side of my back. I knew the drill, and it was fairly easy, but the healing time stayed the same. And there is no getting used to being drugged and waking up in a freezing recovery room.

The last operation was to reduce the webbing that had grown between the fingers of my right hand. The scarring was so thick the webs went clear out to the first knuckle and made the hand as useless as a duck's foot.

After I healed up, the doctor took me to a luncheon in down town San Francisco where I was examined as a case study. I was up on a platform and large images of my hand flashed up on a huge screen, showing the stages of recovery. His explanation was in medical terms and the furniture stuffing was called "the medium." Some of the slides were taken while I was sedated and showed the hand with all of the rough scarring removed. They were gory, but interesting. Then he showed something that seemed to excite the crowd. In bloody detail, he explained the slide that depicted how he took a flap of good skin that still remained partly attached to the finger and moved it over the top of the knuckle, giving the joint maximum flexibility by staying covered with original skin. The technique was repeated on four fingers. The donor skin from my back was then used to fill in those parts of the fingers where the good skin had just been moved. It worked marvelously and probably became a standard procedure for hand repair at that time.

I felt like a lab rat. Doctors examined my hand at close range, but never said so much as hello. I halfway expected one of them to pat me on the head and give me a piece of cheese.

I'm not sure when Ken worked on his PhD. It seemed like we were doing something every night. Ardi joined their bowling team, and I kept score. Their apartment complex had several graduate students living there, and we were adopted into their culture. We shared a lot of food, wine, and arguments about the war in Vietnam. We had many spirited debates, and I held my own. Once we understood we couldn't sway each others' opinions, we moved on to the more important topics: life, sports, Herb Caen's daily column, and where to get cheap, but good Chinese food.

Ardi and I had our first Thanksgiving turkey in a little apartment we had rented in Alameda after we were unceremoniously kicked out of the BOQ. We invited over a few Marines from the hospital and a Navy officer who had been at Pensacola with me.

I met him by mere chance. I was having lunch at the BOQ on Treasure Island while I was getting some paper work completed. I just happened to spot him in the chow line. He was mustering out of the service after flying as a navigator in P-3s, a prop-driven submarine chaser, off the coast of San Diego.

Over the turkey dinner we discovered he was truly guilt-ridden that he hadn't been sent to Vietnam to do his part. He knew Ben, Paul Gee, and a few others that had bought the farm from our class. I'm not sure I would have felt guilty if I had been left behind to storm the beaches of Southern California.

When spring arrived, riots came to the Berkeley campus. It is written somewhere in the rioting by-laws that they can only be held in the very best of weather. Ken and I were picking up the wives at the fashionable Gump's Department store, in the middle of the Haight-Ashbury district, when the traffic was stopped by demonstrators. They were protesting about the war, turning the "People's Park" into a parking lot, cruelty to animals at one of the labs, and anything else they thought to be protest-worthy.

Ahead of us in the traffic jam were two girls driving a nice convertible. They were probably high school seniors. Two hippies who looked like they hadn't showered in months jumped over the sides of their car and into the back seat. The girls freaked out. Ken and I double freaked out and jumped out of his VW. We each grabbed one of the skinny wimps by a convenient hand-hold—their long hair. We jerked them out of the car and sent them back to their own crowd.

That night, we watched the news. The talk was all about police brutality. We hadn't seen any, and we had been caught in the middle of it. One of the interviewed protestors said he was twenty-three and a victim of the "generation gap." Being twenty-five, I wondered which generation he was talking about.

I found it disgusting that people with such vulgar behavior, poor hygiene, and high drug use had self-anointed themselves as the paragons of virtue who would save Mother Earth.

It was 1969, and the hippie movement on the Berkeley campus was in full swing. I was headed to the gym in my Marine Corps uniform to play a game of raquetball with Ken.

"Pigs off campus," ordered a bold young lady.

"Are you speaking to me?" I asked incredulously.

"We don't want pigs on the Berkeley campus," she snarled.

She was another member of what I called the, Great Unwashed Culture, which displayed their nonconformance to society by wearing long, stringy hair, grubby clothes, and a need to show their utmost disdain for anyone in authority. Her body odor, the pungent smell of pot, and her dirty, bare feet were better than a picture ID card for establishing her hippie membership.

"Well, looking at your dirty clothes and filthy hair, I have to ask you: are you announcing your departure from campus? If so, take that sty stench you probably call your boyfriend with you." I was pleased with myself for keeping her pig thread going. "You both look like escapees from a pig farm." Sometimes I can conjure up quality insults, and this was one of those times.

"I think you got the wrong uniform, babe. He's not a cop, he's a soldier," her scruffy boyfriend said. As she was preparing more insults to hurl at me, he pulled her away in another direction. He knew I would not let her brazenly degrade me and get away with it.

"See you pigs later!" I yelled at them as they sauntered off.

As I sat on the locker room bench, I said to Ken, "Some of the campus denizens took exception to my uniform and called me a pig."

"Well, technically a pig is a cop. These love children say they love everybody, but they hate anybody in a uniform. I get that sometimes when I wear my R-R-ROTC uniform on campus." His slight stutter told me he was embarrassed that I had been insulted by fellow students.

Being in the ROTC program, Ken had a great respect for Vietnam vets. He invited us to attend his ROTC graduation ball. I looked forward to wearing my dress white uniform with all of my medals. I was as proud as a peacock in that uniform and I would be wearing it for the last time. I was rapidly healing up, and one way or another, I would shortly be leaving the Marine Corps.

"I'm afraid I must tell you that your Marine Corps uniform

makes you look like an ice cream vendor," said a brash young man sitting at our table during the ball.

Thinking he had had a little too much to drink, I said, "You must be thinking of the Navy. I like our whites."

"No, it's that collar thing around your neck, like priests and ice cream salesmen wear. You know, the Good Humor man."

He was pressing his luck.

"I don't think you ought to be saying anything to a Vietnam vet wearing a Purple Heart," Ken said. "He's a captain a-a-and you're not even an o-o-officer yet."

"That's okay, Ken. I'll assume he's drunk and in his youthfulness, he doesn't know any better," I said

"Hey, captain, I'm just talking about the uniform, not the man in it," he said.

"Personally, I love the uniform and what it stands for. Insult it and you insult me, so I think you should be quiet before you bite off more than you can chew," I said.

"You're in the Marine Corps. You aren't senior to me; I'm in the Army," the insolent ROTC cadet said.

"You're n-n-not in the Army yet," Ken said, as we all got up to dance and then moved to an empty table.

The next week was my birthday. Ken bought me the *International Book of Paper Airplanes* and a jug of Gallo wine. That night we made every airplane in the book. It was the perfect gift, along with the satisfaction of hearing Ken say, "You remember that loudmouth at the ball the other night?"

I slurred out a "yes" as I launched a paper airplane that sailed across the room. I had gently shaped the ailerons, giving it the ability to bank. It executed a perfect left turn into the kitchen.

"I told our commanding officer about his wisecracks, and after what you told me about your OCS, I didn't think he'd be a very good officer. The CO kicked him out of the ROTC program. He lost his scholarship and the whole works."

"Wow, I didn't expect that. I've got a new respect for Army discipline."

Ken would have made a good Marine. He did his hitch in the Army Reserve and went on to found several start up companies. He is a multimillionaire these days, and his hobby is day-trading on the NYSE from his mansion in Elk Grove, California.

The Stroms split the sheets many years ago. We've lost contact except to exchange Christmas cards and attend the weddings of our kids. Everyone has friends that happens to, but the few times we have seen them, we laugh about those days. We relive that best year of any of our lives, and we've never forgotten that you can call a Marine a jarhead or leatherneck, but you can never call him an ice cream salesman.

I wanted to end my career strong by going back to a squadron as an air crewman. Being a FAC and Vietnam vet I could probably pick my collateral duty, which would be; teaching tap-dancing on tables as the Special Services Officer. I got the news. The Marine Corps did plan to send me back—but without flight status. In a squadron filled with aviators, I would be a lame duck officer and get stuck with every paper-shuffling job that came down the pike. I was in a quandary. I had only six months left on my four-year hitch, and it would be a good time to apply for jobs. But I also wanted to get on with the next phase of life instead of marking time in a squadron.

I tried to get billets as a recruiter or an instructor back in Pensacola, but my job as an RO was considered a critical billet to the Marine Corps. The giant computer at HQMC could not give me any other job without some reprogramming. It made no sense, but that's how it shook out.

Given no options, I would try to get an early out by asking

for a physical evaluation board. My plastic surgeon signed my request under protest, saying, "You're not going to get any disability. Look at all these other men that are much worse."

He was right, but I didn't care about disability pay. I just wanted an early-out. When the computer over ruled common sense, I submitted the paperwork. My case was reviewed by reserve officers who had never seen any casualties. The pictures sent from my medical file were taken when the wounds were fresh and garish. It was a best-case scenario for an early-out.

My fondest expectations were exceeded. I would be medically retired with a thirty percent disability and out of the military within thirty days, with a three hundred dollar monthly disability payment for life. It was exhilarating. All of my obligations had been met. I could now chase chickens 'til the cows came home. If I came up with only feathers; that would be my fault.

Ardi and I both knew I was compelled to chase my teenage dream of being the camp director of Camp Easter Seal. I was pleasantly gripped by one of life's riptides that left me no options.

The Ferguson luck was back in high gear. I bought a new fountain pen and blank stationary paper that came with a dark-lined sheet. I placed the lined paper under the slightly textured sheet and began to write.

May 1, 1970

Dear Mr. Torson,

As I prepare to leave the Marine Corps my thoughts return to Camp Easter Seal, so I am writing to inquire about the position of Camp Director. You may be assured that my physical injuries incurred in Vietnam are minor and will not interfere with the job requirements.

If the position is open at this time, please consider this as an application for Camp Director of Camp Easter Seal.

Mr. Torson, even when I was a young counselor at the camp, I knew I wanted to pursue the job as the Camp Director; and my desires remain unchanged.

Sincerely,

Bob Ferguson,
Captain, USMC

Photos

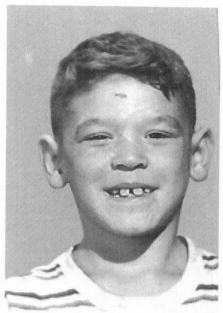

Second grade class picture

"I can hardly wait to
play the Nail!"

Earl and I before we
go do some ropin'.

Third Grade Cub Scouts.

Undefeated Fifth-Grade Hot Shots

Going to a Sea
Scout Dance with
Bonnie. Larry drove
us in his bathtub-
shaped '48 Dodge.

9th grade Spring
Dance: Bob and
Bonnie with
Pat Hallin, Ron
Brown, Sue
Landrum and
Moe. In what
had to be a close
vote, I humbly
accepted the
King's Crown.

The Green Pea after Danny and I just washed it.
The sling was from the Medford game.

John Dirlam
and I just
before putting
on our robes
for graduation
at SEHS.

Babe Edman and I are fooling around
before a church basketball game.

Right: In a pouring rain,
wearing my tanker jacket,
I head out to train for
the state track meet.

Senior High Football Picture; All-Nothing in 1961.

© Associated Press
Little-All American,
Linfield College
1965-weighing in
at 227 pounds.

Conferring how to beat Willamette with QB Terry Durham.

Newly dubbed as second lieutenants Bob Ferguson and Jerry Bennett fool around with a football in the warm Pensacola, Florida sun.

Years later on the back of this picture I find that my future wife had this to say about a couple of hard-charging Marines.

Jerry Bennett and Bob. They just got a new football — like a couple of kids.

This is what she looked like when I picked her up at the bus
station after her three day trip from Seattle to Pensacola.

She had a sense of history and humor with her
comments on the back of this pic. (That is the tail
end of Jerry's Aztec Red Chevy Super Sport.)

This is for a laugh.
Don't we look like "World
War II" romance.
How do you like the wind
blown look for 1966?

We all cleaned up pretty good for a Change of Command Ball on the base. (A partial glimpse of the Batmobile can be seen to the left as the cars look good at the Snake Ranch.)

Jess Haggerman, a Pacific Lutheran footballer dropped by the Ranch to see the ladies.

LUCKY MARINE from Eugene, Ore. drew the assignment of escorting Miss Universe to the Coronation Charity Ball in Miami, where she was crowned. Here Lt. Robert Ferguson chatted with Margareta Arvidson, former Miss Sweden.—(AP Photo.)

When the girls left, life went back to normal for aspiring Radar Officer, 2nd Lieutenant Ferguson except for one thing; I landed some good duty escorting Miss Universe.

Ardi and I married that Christmas and she came back to Glencoe, Georgia for the remainder of my radar training. I am wearing the new navigator's wings and holding orders to El Toro, CA.

Ron Robson, far left became a FAC and was wounded and reported KIA. I was shocked to see him standing at the Da Nang O Club bar. I said "It's nice to see you're not dead." We were not too sentimental in Vietnam. Jim Parker (middle) flew his tour of duty unscathed.

We bought a '60 Chevy in Seattle and headed to MCAS El Toro, CA.

I'm headed to one of my first flights in the RF-4B Phantom jet.

We attend our first Marine Corps Birthday Ball
while at El Toro, November 10, 1967.

January 30, 1968
I put out the bills
to be mailed,
lock the door and
leave unit 8 in a
small apartment
complex in
McMinnville,
Oregon for Da
Nang, Vietnam.

Leaving for
Vietnam, but
my luck has
never failed!

Welcome to the headquarters of VMCJ-1, Da Nang, Vietnam.

Flight Crew Hootches. Ours was just around the corner on the left.

Living conditions were crowded, but the
morale of the men was terrific.

Better sleeping conditions, but not as much fun as the old hootch.

Life in the bush was much harder. This is a web picture
of bombs that were frequently brought in by civilians for
a reward. It made for one less booby trap. The bunker in
the back is the command bunker on hill 37. We slept in
the bunker due to frequent shelling from mortars.

This is the tower on Hill 37 where I fed the ammo into a
.50 caliber machine gun to help repel a night attack.

This is a scene in "Dogpatch" below Hill 37. Young
Marines regularly visited with the villagers.

While I was "across the pond," Ardi returned to
Linfield to complete her education degree.

WESTERN UNION TELEGRAM

UNION RAM

```
                    R BC5 730P PDT TKS
MO19591CO- WU2214 SYA220 SY WA359 XV GOVT PDB 2 EXTRA
WASHINGTON DC 10 846P EDT
MRS ARIDS K FERGUSON, DONT PHONE
   307 EAST 17 ST APT 8 MCMINNVILLE ORG
THIS IS TO CINFORM THAT YOUR HUSBAND FIRST LIEUTENANT
ROBERT E FERGUSON USMC WAS INJURED  5 AUGUST 1968
IN QUANG NAM PROVINCE REPUBLIC OF VIETNAM. HE SUSTAINED
BURNS TO BOTH ARMS AND BOTH LEGS AND FACE WHEN A COMMAND
DETONATED MINE WAS SET OFF.HE IS PRESENTLY RECEIVING
TREATMENT AT THE USS NAVAL HOSPITAL YOKOSUKA JAPAN.
HIS CONDITION AND PROGNOSIS WERE GOOD. YOUR ANXIETY
IS REALIZED AND YOU ARE ASSURED THATHE IS RECEIVING THE
BEST OF CARE. IT IS HOPED THAT HE WILL COMMINICATE
WITH YOU SOON INFORMING YOU OF HIS WELFARE. HIS PARENTS
HAVE BEEN INFORMED. MAIL MAY BE ADDRESSED TO HIM
AT THE U S NAVAL HOSPITAL YOKOSUKA, JAPAN, FPO SEATTLE,
96765
   L W WALT LTGEN USMC ACTING COMMANDANT OF THE MARINE
CORPS
(915).
622P PDT AUG 10 68
```

Two Marines delivered this telegram to Ardi
at our McMinnville apartment.

After nearly a month in Japan I was sent home
for a few weeks of convalescent leave.

We snuck off the base
several times and got
re-acquainted in the
surrounding parks .

This article recounts an ambush of our convoy. It sounds like Robb saved the trucks all by himself! He could have given a little credit to the air strikes called in by our FAC team which really saved the day!

Robb Asking No Favors, Viet Buddy Says

KANSAS CITY (AP)—President Johnson's son-in-law was reported Wednesday to be taking the same chances as any Marine in Vietnam — ducking enemy mortar fire, trying to avoid ambushes and grabbing sleep when he can get it.

"He's a good leader trying to do his job like the rest of us, and he's not looking for any special treatment," Marine Capt.

Richard Cavagnol said of Capt. Charles S. Robb.

Cavagnol, a chunky 24-year-old officer who played fullback for the University of Rochester (N.Y.) football team, just returned from Vietnam where he spent four months on a hill outpost with the husband of the President's older daughter, Lynda Bird.

"Of course everybody had

heard about Robb coming over to Vietnam," Cavagnol said, "but he's just a regular Marine captain— polite and congenial, professionally competent and well thought of by his troops."

Robb arrived in April on Hill 65, situated some 18 kilometers southwest of Da Nang, Cavagnol related.

Within a week after Robb came to the outpost, Cavagnol

said, an enemy 82-millimeter mortar round landed about 15 feet from the bunker where Lynda Bird's husband was sitting. Robb, however, was not hurt.

Cavagnol said during a recent sweep toward the Cambodian border, the truck convoy Robb's troops were guarding was ambushed. Although the Marines suffered some casualties, Robb got the trucks through.

6   Pacific Stars & Stripes
Friday, August 2, 1968

SMOKE rises from explosion of a 500-pound bomb in forested area a few hundred yards from Thuong Duc, a village 50 miles southwest of Da Nang in South Vietnam.   LOS ANGELES GI Gerald House

Thuong Duc was riddled with tunnels and trenches that surrounded the village and the hill. This was a re-supply mission we did regularly. This looks like a picture of one of our air strikes.

A cartoonist at Oakland Naval Hospital drew funny caricatures of everyone. This is the only serious one he did. I think he thought I was pondering how to catch my share of chickens.

Made in the USA
Charleston, SC
09 June 2010